# SENECA
## SUASORIAE

*BCP Classic Latin and Greek Texts in Paperback*

Current and forthcoming titles in this new series are listed below:

*Calpurnius Siculus: The Eclogues*, C. Keene
*Cicero: The Poems*, W. Eubank
*Empedocles: The Extant Fragments*, M. Wright
*Euripides: Helen*, A. Dale
*Euripides: Troades*, K. Lee
*Nikander: Poems & Fragments*, A. Gow & A. Schofield
*Seneca the Elder: Suasoriae*, W. Edward
*Tacitus: Dialogus*, W. Peterson
*Tacitus: Germania*, J. Anderson

# SENECA
## THE ELDER

# SUASORIAE

Edited with Introduction,
Translation and Notes by

William A. Edward

Bristol Classical Press

This impression 2006
This edition published in 1996 by
Bristol Classical Press
an imprint of
Gerald Duckworth & Co. Ltd.
90-93 Cowcross Street, London EC1M 6BF
Tel: 020 7490 7300
Fax: 020 7490 0080
inquiries@duckworth-publishers.co.uk
www.ducknet.co.uk

First published by Cambridge University Press in 1928
© 1928 by W.A. Edward

A catalogue record for this book is available
from the British Library

ISBN 1 85399 504 5

# PREFACE

THIS work came into being on the suggestion of the late Professor Phillimore of Glasgow University. He watched its growth and at every stage gave me advice and assistance without which it could never have been brought to completion. No one was more pleased than he when the Senate of the University of Glasgow accepted it for the degree of D.Litt. But for the generous encouragement and support of Mr J. D. Duff of Trinity College, Cambridge, I doubt if it would ever have been printed. Sir George Douglas, Bt, of Springwood Park, employed his fine sense of English style in criticising and emending the original draft of the translation: his copious notes bear fruit on almost every page. I cannot refrain from acknowledging also the kindly interest of Professor Alexander Souter of Aberdeen University in my attempt, and the many useful hints he gave for the proper organisation of the work. I am also indebted to Mr R. G. Nisbet of Glasgow University for several useful criticisms and suggestions.

The Librarians of the Universities of St Andrews and Glasgow must also be thanked for much assistance and for permitting me during several vacations to pursue my researches in their libraries. Of all my authorities I have to make particular reference to the works of M. Henri Bornecque of Lille University. Had his books on Seneca not existed my labour would have been increased tenfold.

While the book was passing through the press Mr George A. Lawrence, Headmaster of our Demonstration School, read the proofs with the patience and precision of a true scholar, and I am grateful to him for many suggestions and corrections.

WILLIAM A. EDWARD

ABERDEEN
*November* 1927

# CONTENTS

# THE SUASORIAE
## of SENECA
### the *Elder*

❧

## INTRODUCTORY ESSAY

### CURRENT VIEWS OF SENECA AND HIS BOOK—ERRORS AND APPRECIATIONS, §§ 1, 2

1. The full title of Seneca's book, which might be described as "Reminiscences of the Roman Orators and Declaimers," is *Oratorum et Rhetorum Sententiae, Divisiones, Colores*. It consisted of ten books of Controversiae and one of Suasoriae, but only the latter are here reproduced. No apology seems necessary for the attempt, as the book has never before been annotated in whole or in part in English, nor till 1902 in any European language since the Elzevir edition of 1672. Indeed it is quite remarkable that this work has received so little attention from English scholars. Its author has been almost entirely ignored, or, worse still, completely misrepresented. He is usually referred to as Seneca the rhetorician, to distinguish him from his son, Seneca the philosopher, Nero's minister. He is frequently stated to have kept a school of rhetoric in Rome. Professor Simcox in his *History of Roman Literature* gives an account of him and of his book which is unsympathetic, inaccurate, superficial and perverse. Smith's *Classical Dictionary* speaks as if he were the author of the extracts from the Declaimers which he merely records. His style is criticised as if it were a jumble of all the qualities of the men from whose declamations he quotes. Mr J. D. Duff,[1] in his edition of three of the son's dialogues, is the only English scholar who, so far as is known to me, gives an account which, though brief, is both true and accurate. In English the only really satisfactory account of the book and its author is found in the translation of Teuffel and Schwabe's *History of Roman Literature*.[2] It has been exhaustively studied,

---

[1] *L. Ann. Senecae Dialogorum Libri X, XI, XII*, J. D. Duff. Cambridge Univ. Press, pp. xxxvii–xl.

[2] Vol. I, pp. 567–570.

on the textual side mainly, in Germany; for its subject matter in all its aspects, in France. It was very popular in the Middle Ages, as is proved by the number of MSS. of the Excerpta or Extracts from it, as well as by the traces of its themes in the *Gesta Romanorum* and later European literature.[1] Professor Mayor[2] in his edition of Juvenal tells us that the book is well worth reading. Schott, Faber, Gronovius and other Renascence scholars thought worlds of it. In Schott for example we find the following among many other equally flattering notes: "De cuius scriptoris stylo ita iudicare non dubitem, nihil esse in lingua Latina cum a Cicerone Fabioque discesseris scriptum purius aut elegantius"; and Schott is right.

2. First then, to eliminate error—Seneca was not a rhetorician, that is, he was not a professional teacher of rhetoric. There is not a single indication that he ever declaimed or taught declamation, there is not a particle of evidence that he ever kept school in Rome, or anywhere else. His own style as opposed to the style of the quotations is not of the silver age, but much nearer to that of the classical period. A study of the preface to each book of the work at once reveals this; it is to these especially that Schott refers. The decadence of style is seen in the extracts, not to anything like the same extent in Seneca's own writing. It is quite wrong to state that his book is perfect in form and worthless in ideas.[3] Such a statement reveals an entire misconception of its form and purpose.

ORIGIN, AIM AND GENERAL FORM OF THE WORK, §§ 3–6

3. It is attractive to assume with M. Boissier[4] that when Seneca's children were approaching man's estate, being according to the fashion of the time deeply enthusiastic in the pursuit of eloquence, their father and they had many discussions on the great orators of the day and on those of former times. They took him to hear their favourite rhetoricians.[5] They

---

[1] See note to pp. vii and viii of text by H. J. Müller, Praef., and Bornecque, *Les Déclamations et les Déclamateurs d'après Sénèque le père*, p. 32.
[2] Mayor's ed. of Juvenal, vol. I, note on *Sat.* I, 16.
[3] See Smith's *Classical Dictionary*, article on Seneca.
[4] See M. Boissier's brilliant article in *Revue des deux Mondes*, vol. II, 1902, pp. 480–508, on 'Les écoles de déclamation à Rome'.
[5] C. x, Praef. 2 and 9, "cum vos me illo perduxissetis".

must have debated whether the newer, sparkling, pointed, anti-thetic style or the older, rounded periods were the better. According to Seneca they continually urged their father to set down for them what he remembered of the older orators and rhetores of whom they had no personal knowledge.[1] This is what the old man undertakes to do. He will, in his wistful, humorous phrase, go back to school,[2] and recall what he regards as the better part of his life.[3] At the same time he will show how eloquence has declined.[4] He will record the great sayings of these old rhetores, and publish them so that the world may not entirely forget them:[5] for no true records of the greatest declaimers are extant,[6] and in these days people are so slothful or so dishonest[7] that they produce the ideas of these declaimers as their own, and their plagiarism passes quite undetected.

4. While he is really writing a serious work for the public[8] he adopts and maintains the artistic illusion that he is writing merely to gratify the curiosity of his children.[9] This enables him to employ a personal and conversational style which is very charming. In each preface he gives a vivid picture of one or more of these older rhetoricians,[10] with some analysis and criticism of the main qualities of their style. In the subsequent Controversiae or Suasoriae he first states the theme, and then quotes with the name of the rhetor prefixed the most striking passages that he remembers. He does not confine himself to quotations from those rhetors only whose characters he has sketched but adds quotations from others for comparison or contrast. Then he analyses and criticises the plan (*divisio*) they pursued in their treatment of the topic, and concludes with the *colores* they employed. These will be explained later. He does not confine himself to passages or sentences to be admired: he

---

[1] C. I, Praef. 1 and 4; C. VII, Praef. 1; C. IX, Praef. 1; C. X, Praef. 1.
[2] C. I, Praef. 4, "mittatur senex in scholas".
[3] C. I, Praef. 1, "meliores ad annos respicere".
[4] C. I, Praef. 6 *et seq.*              [5] C. I, Praef. 10 and 11.
[6] C. I, Praef. 11, "fere enim aut nulli commentarii maximorum declama-torum exstant, aut, quod peius est, falsi".
[7] C. I, Praef. 10.              [8] C. I, Praef. 10, "populo dedicabo".
[9] See beginning of C. I, VII, IX, X, Praef.
[10] C. I, Praef., Porcius Latro; C. II, Praef., Fabianus, style of Fuscus; C. VII, Praef., Albucius; C. IX, Praef., Votienus Montanus; C. X, Praef., Scaurus, Labienus and others; C. III, Praef., sidelights thrown by C. Severus on Cestius, Passienus and Silo Pompeius.

quotes expressions also that he condemns. The book is in a way an anthology of the oratory of the rhetoricians, but it is an anthology, if one may so use the term, both of what is good and of what is bad.[1] It is a collection of the remarkable, not of the excellent. He relieves the book with sound and shrewd literary criticism, with witticisms, with anecdotes.[2] He for his part never forgets that this declamation is not a serious thing.[3] It is only a school exercise to develop the art of expression. It is play, not earnest. The serious, solid things are history and oratory.

5. When he feels that the work is now long enough, and that he has accomplished his purpose, he still keeps up the illusion. He implores the young men to let him be, he pretends that he is tired of the task, that he has sported with trifles too long.[4] He does so to point the criticism, which his age needs, that declamation is a thing which is not to be carried too far, that it is not an end in itself, but merely a preliminary stage in the progress to genuine oratory. And then the superficial reader asserts that Seneca himself felt at last that the subject was silly and that he was sorry he had undertaken it. Could misconception go farther astray?

6. Such readers criticise without really doing the author the justice of trying to understand his aim and of judging how nearly he has attained it. Seneca desired to make the great rhetores of his day known to the public; to record their most famous sayings; to give examples of what sound taste would follow and what avoid; to expose the dangers that declamation brought in its train; to show its weaknesses as well as its uses and to set it in right relation to true culture. To lighten the subject, which might become arid and uninteresting, he introduces those jests, stories, anecdotes and quotations, and the whole he combines in this beautiful setting of a series of talks to his sons, entered upon with joy, and finally abandoned with a pretended weariness, when the task is done. There is a singular charm about these prefaces to the controversiae.

---

[1] C. II, 4, 12, "aeque vitandarum rerum exempla ponenda sunt quam sequendarum".

[2] For examples, cf. S. I, 5, 6, 7, 12; II, 12, 17, 19, 23; III, 6; IV 4, 5; VII, 13, 14

[3] S. v, 8; S. vi, 16; C. x, Praef. 1; C. i, 8, 16; still from S. II, 10, we see declamation had its serious side ("non esse suadere sed ludere").

[4] C. x, Praef. 1.

Before going more fully into what is known of Seneca's life and character it would seem desirable to give a short *résumé* of the origin of declamation, and to show how it arrived at the peculiar development of Seneca's day.

## THEORY OF RHETORIC IN ROME. ORIGIN AND DEVELOPMENT OF DECLAMATION, §§ 7-11

7. Oratory in Rome was in its origin thoroughly practical. The Romans for a long time were not so much interested in its theory as the Greeks were. Still practical speakers must soon have discovered that while the truth was the truth there were methods of presenting it that made it more persuasive. Cato the Elder wrote a manual of the art, of which only two quotations survive, his definition of the orator "vir bonus dicendi peritus", and the well-known adage "rem tene verba sequentur". The *Ad Herennium* is in Latin the first complete Art of Rhetoric that we possess. Cicero's works, the *De Oratore* and the *Orator* with his *Partitiones Oratoriae, De Inventione* and *Topica*, contain the fruits of his experience as a successful orator, and in spite of the popular form constitute his τέχνη. Quintilian's work is the most scientific and profound in Latin, and at the same time the most elegant and charming. Later, as can be seen from the *Rhetores Latini Minores* (edited by Halm) there was no lack of manuals, as the theory became more and more technical, and through over-refinement lost most of its interest and usefulness.

8. But it is not relevant to this work to go into detail regarding the development of the theory of rhetoric in Latin. About the same time as Cato produced his manual Greek teachers of rhetoric began to appear in Rome. They were at first attached to the houses of the nobles: and as long as they remained there they must have been safe. The Scipionic circle and the Gracchi must have come into contact with Greek professors of the art. When however the latter tried to open schools and teach in public they became the objects of persecution. We know that Pomponius[1] the praetor secured a decree of the senate against them. The censors,[2] Crassus and Domitius, had them expelled: but as often as they were driven out they returned. It was,

---

[1] Suet. *De Rhetoribus*, 1.
[2] Suet. *ib.*; Aulus Gellius, XV, 11; Cicero, *De Oratore*, III, 24.

however, the Latin rhetores against whom Crassus directed his attack, on the ground that they were sciolists, that they taught the youth to idle, and that their schools were schools of impudence, and on the grand old conservative plea that what they taught was "praeter morem maiorum". It may be that the party of reaction was hostile to the spread of popular education, and did not desire the teaching of rhetoric to become common and open to all, as it would be if its doctrines were enunciated in Latin. However that may be, after L. Plotius Gallus[1] first opened a school in which rhetoric was taught in Latin, the success of the new method was not long in becoming so pronounced that it was impossible to withstand it; and when the Roman knight Blandus[2] took up the profession it became of course respectable and it was no longer "turpe docere quod honestum erat discere". The Latin schools went on flourishing more and more. Cicero,[3] himself, was eager in his young days to go to these newer and more attractive teachers, but was persuaded to confine himself to the Greek professors, and to practise in Greek, as otherwise he could not have had his errors corrected so well. By Seneca's day there were numberless schools and a host of teachers flourishing in Rome.[4]

9. [5]It would appear that before Cicero's time the school exercise was what is called *thesis*, a discussion of a general question such as "Ought one to marry?" "Is town life better than country life?" In Cicero's day the theme was called *causa*: and was generally framed on some historical incident or modelled on a cause that had been actually pleaded in the forum. At the same time Cicero undoubtedly did declaim, or at any rate knew topics[6] quite like those that form the subject of Seneca's Controversiae. After Cicero's time the exercise received the name *controversia*; the newer term in Seneca's day was *scholastica*. The change of name indicates in each case a change either of subject matter or of method of treating it.

---

[1] Suet. *De Rhet.* 2; Seneca, C. II, Praef. 5; Quin. *Inst. Or.* II, 4, 42.
[2] Seneca, *loc. cit.*
[3] Suet. *De Rhet.* 2; Cic. *Brutus*, 90 (310).
[4] Seneca mentions more than 100 rhetores in his work.
[5] For this paragraph see Seneca, C. I, Praef. 12.
[6] Cic. *De Oratore*, II, 100; Seneca, C. I, 4, 7; Cic. *Tusc.* I, 4, 7; *Ep. Ad Att.* XIV, 2; *Ad Fam.* IX, 18, 1; IX, 16, 7; Seneca, C. I, Praef. 11; Quin. *Inst. Or.* XII, 11, 6; Suet. *De Rhet.* 1.

10. *Declamatio* is always, in actual fact, at the beginning and till Cicero's day a speech for practice, and in theory at any rate the same till Seneca's time. Aeschines, the rival of Demosthenes, seems to have started the practice at Rhodes;[1] Demetrius of Phalerum[2] is also credited with its initiation. Quintilian employs the term in this sense, but from Seneca's time onwards the emphasis is laid on its meaning as 'a speech for display'.

The verb *declamare* up to Cicero's time denotes something derogatory,[3] and is often a term of reproach, but to Cicero in the technical sense it merely means to exercise[4] oneself in private in the art of speaking. This is the sense it has when we hear of Antony declaiming for several days in Scipio's villa[5] at Tibur, of Pompey declaiming in order to meet Curio, and of Octavian[6] doing the same before Mutina. It is the sense also in which Cicero declaimed with Hirtius and Pansa. To Cicero the public delivery of a speech was *dictio*.[7] So far there is nothing startling in the idea of delivering speeches in private on purely fictitious themes, or on subjects taken from the law courts or from history, in order to develop one's mastery of the art: but this is not the declamation that Seneca says he has known from its earliest beginnings.[8] This statement of Seneca's has caused difficulty, but to me it seems perfectly clear. It is the peculiar subject matter that is new, and the fashion of delivering speeches of this nature in public. Here and there in the Controversiae we note the conservative characters refusing to declaim in public, Pollio,[9] Labienus,[10] Cassius Severus,[11] Montanus.[12] They regard the practice as trivial and ostentatious.[13] They dislike its lack of reality, and count it for many reasons a bad preparation for the forum.[14]

11. What was originally a school exercise, or one for private practice, by a curious development has become, in the early life of Seneca, a formal, elaborate, and, in the hands of masters,

[1] Philostratus, *Vitae Sophistarum*, I, 5 (Kayser).

[2] Quin. *Inst. Or.* II, 4, 41; IV, 2, 29; II, 10, 12.

[3] Cic. *In Verr.* IV, 66; the noun similarly, Cic. *Orator*, III, 138; *Pro Plancio*, 83.     [4] Cic. *De Fin.* V, 2; *Brutus*, 90 (310).

[5] Cic. *Phil.* II, 17, 42.   [6] Suet. *De Rhet.* 1.   [7] Seneca, C. I, Praef. 12.

[8] *Ib.*   [9] C. IV, Praef. 2.   [10] C. X, Praef. 4.   [11] C. III, Praef. 7.

[12] C. IX, Praef. 1.          [13] C. X, Praef 4.

[14] See the views of Cassius Severus in C. III, Praef., and of Montanus in C. IX, Praef.

an almost perfect work of art—a speech not aiming at victory in a court, but at giving pleasure to the spectators or rather auditors. A controversia or suasoria aims at being a work of the highest art, aims at beauty, and is constructed in accordance with the strictest and most elaborate rules. It is a speech on a fictitious topic, it is true, but the topic is only the framework on which the orator is to weave a fabric as beautiful, as intricate, as fine-spun, as glittering, as dazzling as he can make it. It is a speech that gives him an opportunity of showing all the cleverness, wit and eloquence of which he is capable. It gives him, too, an opportunity of showing how far he can suit his delivery, tone, voice, look, gesture to the subject of his speech. For the declamation, like the oration, is to the Roman the expression of the whole man. It is not a mere matter of words. Words, tone and gesture must all be in harmony. That, if anything, as regards oratory is perfectly clear from Cicero's rhetorical works, and just as clear in Quintilian. If the precepts regarding the management of the voice, regarding the use of action in delivery, later on become extravagant, theatrical and ridiculous, this decline is in keeping with the decline in style, in subject matter, and in national taste in everything else.

## CAUSES OF THE DEVELOPMENT AND POPULARITY OF DECLAMATION, §§ 12–18

12. How is it that what was at first merely an exercise of the schools of rhetoric, or the term applied to the private practice of a distinguished orator, has become in the early years of Augustus's reign a fashionable and public performance, a thing practised for itself, and to such an extent that all classes of society are enthusiastic about it? The cause must be found in the changed political conditions. The republic was extinct at Philippi; the power of Augustus finally established at Actium. The prince had concentrated all power in his own hands: the assemblies of the people were now infrequent or of no political importance, the deliberations of the senate had lost significance and reality; their decisions might be forestalled at any moment by the Emperor's personal intervention. Free oratory on great themes, such as had inspired the eloquence of Cicero, was no

longer heard. Genuine pleading, where the decision could be affected by the advocate, was confined to the centumviral courts and to causes that did not lend themselves to oratory. The "winged word" no longer might lead to the highest prizes in the state; it was better to practise the art of gaining the Emperor's favour than that of swaying the passions and winning the suffrage of the once sovereign people.

13. One may say, though with some qualification, that there was no really significant stage, no tragedies, no comedies, only *mimi* and *pantomimi*, vulgar farces or ballets with dumb show. At the same time one must remember that Roman society had neither reviews, magazines nor daily papers. Books were few, but no doubt accessible. There were literary coteries centring round prominent nobles like Maecenas and Messala. The luxurious banquets must often have given opportunity for literary, philosophical or historical discussions.[1] The energetic must still have had their daily exercises in the gymnasia, in the baths, or in the *campus*: but all this was not enough to satisfy the intellects and emotions that had lived and struggled in the free, passionate life of the old republic.

14. Barred from its natural and most attractive arena the Roman aptitude for oratory had to find another field for its display.

If there are no great causes to set the forum on fire, still there are great teachers declaiming daily in the schools. The public in increasing numbers flock to these. There they may hear eloquence comparable in style to the best of old days and speakers like Porcius Latro, who, if born under a happier star, might have commanded the applause of senates. The subjects of the declamations are no doubt fictitious, unreal, bizarre in the extreme, but they afford endless opportunity for the display of wit and ingenuity. There the Romans may hear to their heart's content "keen, arrowy rhetoric".[2] There, as they have no romances to read, they may be rapt into worlds of fancy, and see pirates with chains standing on the shore, disinherited heroes

---

[1] C. x, Praef. 15, "Latro numquam solebat disputare in convivio aut alio quam quo declamare poterat tempore". Seneca would not say this if Latro were not an exception.

[2] De Quincey, *Essay on Rhetoric.*

launched on stormy seas in crafts with neither sails nor oars, tyrants throned in their impregnable citadels issuing cruel decrees, or, as the licence for digression is unrestrained, they may hear eloquent denunciations of the vices of the age,[1] of the inordinate love of money, of the unnatural craving for unnatural things, of the insensate and extravagant luxury in building, in dress, in eating and drinking; or, if it is a suasoria that is afoot, they may launch on perilous seas with Alexander,[2] stand with the Spartans at Thermopylae,[3] anguish with Agamemnon over the sacrifice of Iphigenia,[4] or hear a last echo of the old republic in the eloquent advice given to Cicero[5] to die rather than bend the knee to Antony.

There is hardly a topic debated in the world of the day that may not find its expression in these declamations.

15. Throughout the whole time of the republic, and especially after the barriers of birth were broken down and the highest offices were open to all, it is quite easy to understand the great value put upon the art of public speaking. The highest honours in the state were the prizes of successful oratory. What is rather harder to understand is how, when oratory no longer led to power and influence, the passionate pursuit of it grew and expanded. One would not have been surprised if, as the power of Augustus was consolidated and was more openly displayed, the interest in oratory and in the schools had flagged. A decline in the number of successful teachers, a falling-off in interest and in the number of students, a closing down of the schools would have caused no surprise: but it took some time, and Augustus's crafty dissimulation helped this, for the changed conditions to be appreciated. Parents and pupils did not realise all at once that the old prizes were no longer open to success, or that, if open in name, they were empty in substance, and gave only the pomp and not the reality of power. By the time the facts of the case were too patent to be ignored the schools were firmly established and had created an interest of their own. The

---

[1] For examples see C. II, 1, 4 *et seq.* (Fuscus) where wealth, luxury, foppery, effeminacy, gluttony, lust and drink are condemned, while poverty is extolled; and C. II, 1, 10, 11, where Fabianus condemns great wealth, wars to secure it, proscriptions, extravagance in buildings and furnishings, all reminding us of Juvenal; see also C. II, 6, 2.
[2] S. I.       [3] S. II.       [4] S. III.       [5] S. VI and VII.

young people of the day had to have their natural and national liking for the beauty of the spoken word satisfied. The declamation as a work of literary art had become an end in itself. The whole art of expression was taught in the schools, and the subject matter embraced every topic of interest to the intellects of the time—philosophy, social and political history, literary criticism and poetry.

16. The subjects of the declamations, whether those of the school or of the public displays, were of little importance. It was the manner of treating them that counted, and this as we can see gave endless opportunity for displays of wit, ingenuity, analytic power, for digressions, even for expression that rises often to the height of genuine eloquence. The comparatively small number of themes and the frequency with which the same one was treated compelled originality in thought and expression and made eloquent digressions inevitable. The wide range of topics that might be introduced, all studied with a view to finding the most effective expression, made the schools an excellent preliminary education for all purposes. They aimed at perfecting the instruments of expression, and that being achieved the transition was easy to any other of the liberal arts. So says Seneca[1] himself with perfect truth.

17. By the time then that oratory might have declined as no longer leading to distinction in the state, the study of the art of expression as crystallised in the schools had become the higher education of the day. Such careers as were still open to the young and ambitious necessitated this preliminary training, as the whole of society had it and there was no other. Whether we approve of this training or not, for four or five centuries it remained the system of Roman education, embodying in it the elements of all the culture of the time. It spreads to Gaul, to Spain and to Africa. Its rhetorical quality colours all subsequent literature; no writer afterwards seems to be able quite to get away from the idea that he is speaking and trying to impress an audience, and the idea is reflected in his methods and in his style.[2]

[1] C. II, Praef. 3, "facilis ab hac in omnes artes discursus est".
[2] For the influence of the schools of rhetoric on Ovid, see two very interesting chapters (III and IV) in *La Jeunesse D'Ovide* by La Ville de Mirmont.

18. After the civil wars then declamation as an end in itself rapidly became fashionable. The schools of rhetoric quickly increased in numbers, and individually flourished. The number of famous teachers, both Latin and Greek, was very great. We find praetors, senators and even consuls among the pupils;[1] we find a class growing up, the *scholastici*, who spend their whole time in the schools; we hear of the Emperor Augustus, with Maecenas and Agrippa, being present at declamations.[2] Pollio,[3] if he does not do so in public, nevertheless declaims at home, and joins in the discussions upon the declaimers. Messala[4] is obviously interested in them too. In fact the older orators who had seen the free republic, like Pollio, Messala, Cassius Severus and Labienus, are jealous of the schools and of their popularity.[5] They may object to the new fashion as frivolous and ostentatious, but they are impelled to give displays in private if not in public, and later the orators are always declaimers as well.

## WORK OF THE SCHOOLS IN DETAIL—CLASS PROCEDURE—PUBLIC DISPLAYS AND PUPILS, §§ 19–22

19. When we try to investigate more closely and find out particulars of the work of the schools in detail the task is not very easy. It appears that after the pupil had completed his course with the *grammaticus* (whom we might call the teacher of grammar and literature), could read, write and spell correctly, had perfected himself in the simplest kinds of composition, such as short narratives, paraphrases of the poets, *ethopoiiae*, descriptions, and had read and studied the chief historians and poets, he went to the *rhetor* (the teacher of the art of public speaking). The transition appears to have taken place at 12–15 years of age, or even later. With the rhetorician the pupil begins with suasoriae, an exercise akin to the *genus deliberativum* of oratory. These were supposed to be easier than the other exercise—the controversiae—allied to the *genus iudiciale*.

---

[1] C. I, 2, 22 (a praetor); C. I, 3, 11 (a senator); C. IX, 4, 18 (a consul).
[2] C. II, 4, 12 and 13; C. VI, 8 (end); C. IV, Praef. 7; C. X, 5, 21.
[3] C. IV, Praef. 2; criticisms by Pollio of the declaimers are scattered throughout the Controversiae.
[4] S. III, 6; C. II, 4, 8.
[5] See especially prefaces to C. III and IX.

20. Apparently the procedure on a class day was this. The rhetor entered and took his seat at his desk, which was set on a kind of platform. He propounded the theme, gave some hints as to how to treat it, and outlined the main divisions of the argument. The pupil then composed and wrote out his version, after which he brought and read it to the master. The latter corrected it phrase by phrase, and when these corrections had been incorporated in the version the pupil then learned it by heart and delivered it standing up in his place with appropriate tone and gesture. After hearing the pupils the rhetor made some preliminary remarks upon the theme and the manner in which it had been handled. Then in most cases he delivered a version of his own, as an example of how he considered the subject should be treated. We construct this outline from various indications in Seneca and Quintilian and scattered references in poets and other writers.[1] We cannot be sure that the practice was the same throughout the whole period of the writers mentioned; it must have varied both in procedure and in detail. We may be certain that the rhetor also delivered lectures either formally or incidentally on the theory and principles of the art. Probably it was in these that he criticised the methods and the actual speeches of other declaimers.[2] From what Juvenal says we may infer that the continued hearing and correction of the same exercise must have been just as great a bore to the rhetor as the correction of school exercises is to the teacher of to-day. Curiously enough two of the greatest professors of the art, Latro[3] and Nicetes (the latter a Greek), seem to have refused to listen to their pupils. They merely lectured and declaimed: and in consequence their pupils were called in derision *auditores*, a term which subsequently became the name for any student: but it was only the most distinguished that could behave thus, and in general the pupils insisted that their efforts should be heard, and the parents judged the efficiency of the school from the number of declamations that their sons delivered.[4]

[1] See Quin. *Inst. Or.* I and II; Persius, III, 45; Juvenal, I, 16; Quin. x, 5, 21; Statius, *Silvae*, v, 3, 216; Juvenal, VII, 154 *et seq.* See also *La Jeunesse d'Ovide* by Mirmont and 'Les écoles de déclamation à Rome', by Boissier.

[2] As an example take Cestius on Albucius, C. VII, Praef. 8, 9.

[3] C. IX, 2, 23.            [4] Quin. Inst. *Or.* II, 7, 1; x, 5, 21.

21. It is not likely that the school was always open to the public,[1] although probably it was always open to parents and relatives of the pupils. It is certain that there were definite occasions on which the general public could enter.[2] These would probably be occasions of display either by the pupils or by the master. No doubt the rhetorician also would on occasion hire a hall, and give a display of his art in order to make himself known to the public. It was probably on a great occasion like this that Latro delivered his declamation in the presence of Augustus, Agrippa and Maecenas.[3]

22. The rhetorician's class was by no means homogeneous: we might divide it roughly into three groups. There were the ordinary pupils, their pedagogues[4] or attendants, and the occasional visitors. Among the pupils there were both *pueri* and *iuvenes*; and we even hear of senators, praetors and consuls attending the schools of rhetoric, and submitting themselves to the criticism of the rhetorician. This criticism could be sarcastic and harsh:[5] and the atmosphere of the schools seems to have been distinctly lively at times. The rhetorician could be interrupted by bursts of applause[6] or disapproval, and even by interjected remarks.[7] The pupils applauded or hissed one another, although they were more inclined to show approbation in the expectation of having the compliment returned. Such were the subjects, such the schools, and such the public displays that had grown up and become fashionable during the life of Seneca, till at last Declamation as distinct from an actual speech on a real theme had come to be pursued as an end in itself, as a thing to give pleasure, as an artistic work like poetry or drama, aiming at a beauty and an effect all its own.

## LIFE OF SENECA, §§ 23–27

23. Let us now see what is known of the life of Seneca, and what we can gather of his character, before concluding with an explanation of the scope and character of his work, and of its peculiar title.

[1] C. VII, Praef. 1.   [2] Note Cassius Severus and Cestius, C. III, Praef. 16.
[3] C. II, 4, 12–13.     [4] Suet. *De Gram.* 23.
[5] For example, Cestius to Quintilius Varus, C. I, 3, 10, and S. IV, 5.
[6] C. I, 1, 21; I, 7, 14; II, 1, 36, and many others.
[7] C. III, Praef. 16.

We do not know much about the life of Seneca.[1] We can make a few safe inferences from his book, but it does not contain many direct statements as it was addressed[2] to his sons who did not require such information. The ancient writers preserve a profound silence about him. This is easily explained in the case of Tacitus, for that part of his work in which naturally he would have mentioned Seneca is lost; but the silence of Quintilian is remarkable. Is it that Seneca was merely an amateur, who wrote only a book of reminiscences? Was he regarded not as a serious writer, but merely as a writer of a book for pastime? We do not know. At any rate we can draw a few conclusions about him from statements here and there in his son's works, from what Tacitus says about his children, from Suetonius and from Martial. Apart from detail, however, his own book sheds a very vivid light on his character, and contains by implication the portrait of one of the most charming and lovable characters in Roman history.

24. He appears to have been born in Cordova, a Spanish colony,[3] to have been of equestrian rank,[4] and to have been very wealthy.[5] He tells us himself that he might have heard Cicero declaim to his *consules designati* (Hirtius and Pansa) but for the fact that he was detained by his parents in Spain because of the civil wars then raging throughout the whole world.[6] This gives us good ground for inferring that in 43 B.C. Seneca was old enough to have heard Cicero declaim. Most editors have inferred from this that in that year he was of an age to leave

---

[1] Seneca's full name is L. Annaeus Seneca (according to the best MSS.). At the Renascence he and his son were confused, and their works also. Raphael Volaterranus first saw that there were two different persons. Justus Lipsius proved it. Raphael, however, called the father Marcus not Lucius, possibly thinking of the custom by which grandchildren received the *praenomen* of the grandfather. The two grandsons of the elder Seneca were called Marcus: but this custom was not invariable. All editors followed Raphael for three centuries. Identity of praenomen would be another reason for the confusion between the two Senecas and their works.

[2] The prefaces to the Controversiae always begin: "Seneca Novato, Senecae, Melae, filiis salutem". (1) Novatus, the eldest, adopted by Junius Gallio, taking his name; he was proconsul of Achaia when Paul came to preach at Athens. (2) Seneca, the second son, the philosopher, Nero's minister. (3) Mela, father of the poet, Lucan.

[3] Martial, *Ep.* I, 61, 8; Seneca, S. VI, 27.

[4] Tac. *Ann.* XIV, 53; Seneca, C. II, Praef. 3 (end).

[5] Seneca, phil., *Ad Helviam*, XIV, 3.          [6] C. I, Praef. 11.

the grammaticus and go to the rhetor. We have seen that this transition took place as a rule between the ages of 12 and 15 years. This would place Seneca's birth in 58–55 B.C.: but it is not really necessary to put his birth so early. We know that his son Seneca the philosopher was brought to Rome when quite young,[1] probably when two or three years old. The fact that, as the younger himself states, he remembered Pollio,[2] who died in A.D. 5, has caused his birth to be set as early as 5 B.C., and as late as 3 B.C. It is not necessary to put it any earlier than 3 B.C. If Seneca the younger could be brought to Rome at the age of two or three, why should it be unlikely for the father to be brought to Rome at a comparatively early age? When he said that he might have heard Cicero why should he be considered to be referring to an age of more than six or seven? Had he been referring to a time when he was 12 to 15 would he not rather have made some reference to the fact that he might have heard the divine *Philippic*? He surely means that he was too young to go to the forum, but old enough to have heard the great orator at home. It does not appear necessary then to put Seneca's birth at an earlier date than 50 B.C. The son of a wealthy family, who was precocious or promising, might quite well be brought to Rome at a younger age than usual to enjoy the superior educational facilities of the capital, even to attend the school of a more competent or more distinguished grammaticus than could be found in his native town. We know that he and Latro attended in Rome the school of Marullus,[3] a rhetorician sprung from their town, and that the class probably contained 200 pupils![4]

25. In the fragment that remains of the life of Seneca written by his son we read that the elder wrote a History of Rome and brought it down almost to the day of his death.[5] As apparently Suetonius[6] quotes this history for one version of the death of Tiberius, Seneca must have lived beyond A.D. 37. How far

---

[1] Seneca, phil., *Ad Helviam*, XIX, 2. (See J. D. Duff's note, *op. cit.*)
[2] Seneca, phil., *De Tranq.* XV, 13.
[3] C. I, Praef. 22; C. II, 2, 7; C. VII, 2, 11.
[4] C. I, Praef. 2 (end).
[5] L. Seneca, *De Vita Patris* (vol. III, 436, Haase).
[6] Suet. *Tiberius*, 73 (see *Life of Suetonius*, by A. Macé, p. 264, Bibliothèque des écoles françaises d'Athènes et de Rome, 1900, No. 82).

beyond we cannot say. Seneca the younger was exiled to Corsica in A.D. 41,[1] and we know from the *Consolatio ad Helviam* (written about 43) that the elder was then dead.[1] Indeed the death of the father is there alluded to as an event the sorrow for which has had time to cool. We must then place Seneca's death in A.D. 38 or 39.

26. He heard Pollio probably in Rome "et viridem et postea iam senem".[2] He heard Ovid declaiming to Arellius Fuscus.[3] He heard Latro declaiming in the presence of Agrippa, Maecenas and Augustus,[4] and from internal evidence we can date the declamation as taking place in 17 B.C. He may have been present in Spain when Latro broke down in the lawsuit which was being heard in the open air, and could not proceed till the court was removed to one of the covered rooms.[5] As his children apparently were born shortly before the dawn of our era it is inferred that he had gone back to Spain shortly before that to find a wife. We know that he married Helvia,[6] a Spanish lady. He might have done so in Rome, and he might have done so many years before his children were born. Such inferences are interesting and not improbable, but by no means certain. All that can with certainty be gathered from these facts is that Seneca was in Rome about 29–24 B.C.,[7] also about 3 B.C.,[8] certainly in 17 B.C.,[9] and again before 5 A.D.[10] His movements in the intervals are unknown.

27. He was a wealthy man, a man of culture, not a professional rhetorician, not so far as we know an imperial official, but the first would certainly necessitate his frequent presence in Spain to look after his estates, and the second certainly necessitated long periods in Rome. He has an intimate knowledge of the schools and of the rhetoricians, a knowledge which must have taken a long time to acquire; he was familiar with many of the nobility of the day, with Messala and Pollio for

[1] Seneca, phil., *Ad Helviam*, 11, 4 and 5.
[2] C. IV, Praef. 3.
[3] C. II, 2, 8. The elder was probably a pupil of Fuscus, S. II, 10.
[4] C. II, 4, 12.   [5] C. IX, Praef. 3.
[6] For her character see *Ad Helviam*, XVI, 3; XVII, 3 and 4.
[7] Ovid declaiming.
[8] Seneca, the younger, brought to Rome after Latro's death.
[9] Latro declaiming before Augustus.
[10] Before Pollio's death.

example: he has a copious fund of social and literary anecdote, and his reminiscences require a long period of intimate relation with the varied life of the capital.[1]

## THE BOOK—DATE OF WRITING AND PUBLICATION, §§ 28, 29

28. When did he write his book? From one passage[2]—that in which he affectionately praises Mela for his leaning to rhetoric and a private life, and expresses the desire to keep him in the harbour while his brothers embark on the perilous sea of politics—we infer that that part was written when the elder sons were about 25 years of age. This would mean about A.D. 20: but the book contains references to the fall of Sejanus in A.D. 31,[3] and to the death of Scaurus in A.D. 34[4] and to some events even later.[5] Mr J. D. Duff thinks that Seneca kept the book by him and made additions to it.[6] It does not give one the impression of being a hasty or ill-considered work, and Seneca may have kept it by him for quite a long time. It shows no evidence of senility, although one might find in it here and there, especially in the Suasoriae (the last part to be written), a tendency to garrulousness.[7] Still Seneca's own style is well-formed, lucid, strong and balanced, and singularly pure. The form of the work, artistic in the extreme, indicates long and careful consideration. Everywhere he speaks to his sons as to young men just entering on the serious business of life, and the general impression left on the reader, from the main parts of the work, is that it refers to the time when they were comparatively young men. Their tastes still show the eagerness, the bias and the immaturity of youth. They love striking thoughts, they care neither for jests[8] nor for anecdotes, they prefer rhetoric

---

[1] Seneca's claim to an almost miraculous memory may be noted here. He says (C. I, Praef. 2) that he could repeat 2000 names in the order in which they were uttered to him; and when each of his fellow-pupils had repeated a line of poetry so that there were 200 lines altogether, starting from the last he could repeat them all in order.

[2] S. II, Praef. 3 and 4.          [3] C. IX, 4, 21.          [4] S. II, 22.

[5] S. III, 7; possibly S. II, 22; the statement on the burning of books, C. X, Praef. 5, was probably not written till Tiberius was dead, and the work of Cremutius Cordus, burnt under Tiberius, was probably not available till after the same date (S. VI, 19 and 23).

[6] Seneca, *Dialogues*, Introd. XXXIX.

[7] Especially, S. I, 5 and 6.          [8] C. VII, Praef. 9.

to history.[1] One fails to convince oneself that the book as a whole was written after A.D. 34, that is, when his sons were 40, and he himself was at least 84 years of age. There are too many evidences against that.

29. We do not know when the book was published. Apparently it was not published before its author's death. With the exception of the short period of toleration under Caligula there were few periods when it would not have been dangerous to be related to the author of this book. The sentiments have often too much of the candour of the old republic.[2] It does not appear to have been published when Seneca the younger began to write the biography of his father.[3] It probably saw the light when Nero, as well as his victims, the whole house of Seneca, was no more. There was then a brighter time, and no one of the blood of the author left to expiate his frankness. Seneca the son would certainly not have liked this book to be on sale in Rome during the days of Claudius and Nero.

## CHARACTER OF SENECA, §§ 30–34

30. If we do not know many details of the life of Seneca, his book leaves a very vivid and detailed impression of his character, of his likes and dislikes and of the quality of his judgment and taste. If we cannot rank him among "Rome's least mortal minds", if he is neither a great original writer, nor a brilliant stylist, he is yet a person of real culture, and one who does credit to his age and country. While his contemporaries and the younger generation are tending towards what is meretricious, ingenious, and startling in style and thought, descending to luxury and effeminacy, and to every form of extravagance, exalting to the rank of the supreme literary type a preliminary exercise, which however highly developed can be no more than a charming or beautiful pastime at the best, forgetting that it can never rival poetry, history or philosophy through the lack of reality in its subject matter, Seneca preserves his own balance, and shows few, if any, traces of the prevailing vices of his age.

[1] S. vi, 16.

[2] The attitude, and many of the references, to Cicero, S. vi and vii, and the burst of eloquent indignation at the burning of books, C. x, Praef. 6.

[3] Fragment of the Life already mentioned, "si quaecunque composuit pater meus et edi voluit iam in manus populi emisissem...".

He dislikes, nay hates, the luxury, effeminacy and slothfulness of the youth of the day. He pours out his contempt upon them, exposes their licence and their ignorance, and concludes that it is hopeless to look for orators among *them*.[1]

31. For what is an orator? In the words of Cato the elder, Seneca's ideal, whom he regards almost as an oracle, "Orator est, Marce fili, vir bonus dicendi peritus".[2] The emphasis on the moral quality is significant of the Roman and in particular of Seneca. He has no regard for the misplaced ingenuity that would attempt "to make the worse appear the better cause". The high moral tone of this passage in Seneca's work illuminates the lofty sincerity of his character, just as a famous passage later rises to real eloquence,[3] as the writer expresses his belief in gods who are just avengers of human sin, and sure if slow punishers of cruelty and persecution.

32. Seneca's character has undoubtedly the *gravitas, dignitas* and *constantia* of the old Roman. The son talks of his father's *antiquus rigor*,[4] old-fashioned austerity. In that luxurious and sophisticated age he is indeed a surprising example of Roman simplicity. He appears to have disliked philosophy[5], but this, I think, refers to the new-fangled ideas that were fashionable towards the end of his life, to the faddists and cranks that overflowed Rome, not to the austere study to which Fabianus devoted himself.[6] He hates what is obscene,[7] trivial[8] or bombastic: he dislikes the Greeks for their licence and extravagance.[9] He condemns the judgment that would sacrifice sense to sound, substance to form.[10] He yields to his sons' desire to hear sententiae,[11] to study ingenious colores, to know how the most famous rhetoricians analysed their topics. He probably enjoyed these displays of intellectual acuteness, but he has a greater enthusiasm for history and real oratory, and he tries, although he feels he has little hope of success, to turn his sons to the pursuit of these higher studies.[12]

---

[1] C. I, Praef. 7–10.
[2] Quoted by Seneca, C. I, Praef. 9.
[3] C. x, Praef. 6, "sunt di immortales lenti quidem, sed certi vindices generis humani".
[4] *Ad Helviam*, XVII, 3.
[5] Sen. phil., *Ep.* 108, 22.
[6] C. II, Praef. 1.
[7] C. I, 2, 23; I. 5, 9.
[8] C. VII, Praef. 3–4.
[9] C. x, 4, 18 and 23; S. III, 6; C. x, 5, 23.
[10] C. VII, 4, 10.
[11] C. VII, Praef. 9.
[12] S. VI, 16.

33. He is a provincial; but for Rome and things Roman he has a burning enthusiasm that surpasses that of the true sons of the eternal city. He worships the greatness of the empire, and Cicero for being worthy of its greatness—the one Roman that can be opposed to insolent Greece and its Demosthenes.[1] Sallust is comparable to Thucydides![2] Vergil has so sure a place that Seneca feels he does not need to assert it.[3] He cannot bear that the Greeks should ever surpass the Romans in anything,[4] and in general he quotes them only to decry them. The old free spirit of Rome seems to echo most fondly in his soul.[5] He has acquiesced in the new regime, he appreciates the mildness, toleration, magnanimity of Augustus,[6] he hardly sympathises with Pompeian sentiments when the benefits of the principate are so clearly established.[7] But nevertheless we may be sure that the eloquence of the passages quoted from the rhetoricians in the Suasoriae dealing with Cicero, reflects Seneca's fondness for the independence and courage of the old free state.

34. He is a man of culture, but no pedant. He recognises that genius is above rules: he will have nothing to do with pettifogging criticism.[8] He makes no ostentatious display of erudition. He knows the rules of the game of declamation. He can enjoy its *tours de force*, its rhythmical effects, its luxuriant descriptions, its eloquent invective. It is the human interest however that chiefly attracts him. He has been all his life a shrewd critic of men and things. He loves a jest, an anecdote, an aphorism, a pointed retort. He can paint a vivid picture in a sentence. He has an eye for the essential. He can sum up and decide the point at issue in a few sentences. Can Roman literature show a more vivid portrait than that of his great friend Porcius Latro,[9] a masterly sketch of character, which rescues, as he intended it should, the great declaimer for ever from oblivion? Albucius, Arellius Fuscus, Cestius, Cassius Severus and Labienus are almost as clearly drawn, and many

---

[1] C. I, Praef. 6 and 11.  [2] C. IX. 1, 13.
[3] See general tone of references to Vergil, S. II, 20 and S. III, 5.
[4] C. X, 5, 28, "sed nolo Romanos in ulla re vinci".
[5] S. VI and VII.  [6] C. II, 4, 13; C. VI, 8.
[7] C. X, Praef. 5.  [8] S. II, 13.
[9] C. I, Praef. 13 *et seq.*

others characterised if not fully defined. Think of the vivid sidelights thrown on the character of Messala, of Pollio, of Maecenas, of Augustus. Nearly a hundred rhetoricians or orators are mentioned: it is a crowded stage, and yet there is no confusion. As was said before, if not one of the greatest Roman writers, Seneca must rank high for his sincerity, his moral fervour, his humour, his sanity of judgment, his power of portraiture, qualities in startling contrast to those favoured by the fashion of his day.

### THE BOOK—ITS PRESENT CONDITION, § 35

35. The title of Seneca's work is according to the MSS. *L. Annaei Senecae, Oratorum et Rhetorum, Sententiae, Divisiones, Colores.* It is divided into ten books of Controversiae and one of Suasoriae. There was originally at least one other book of Suasoriae, but it has not been preserved.[1] Even the beginning of the book that remains is not extant. In the codices the book of Suasoriae comes first, but there is no doubt that it was composed last.[2] To each book of Controversiae there was a preface, but the prefaces of books V, VI, VIII are lost, as well as the books themselves. The preface to the book of Suasoriae has also not been preserved. The loss of these prefaces is in the highest degree regrettable, as it is just these in which we are most interested, for the controversiae in themselves are wearisome to modern readers. A writer in the fourth or fifth century of our era made extracts from the Controversiae, and all these Excerpta as they are called are preserved. From them we can gather the themes of the lost Controversiae and many of the Sententiae. It is not remarkable that although Seneca wrote the book of Suasoriae last, this book appears first in our MSS., as some subsequent scribe would quite naturally invert the order; for suasoriae were always practised by the pupil of the rhetorician first, before he proceeded to the more difficult controversiae.

---

[1] MSS. B, V, D end the book of Suasoriae thus: "liber primus explicit, incipit liber secundus".

[2] See C. II, 4, 8: "quae dixerit, suo loco reddam, cum ad suasorias venero".

## THE CONTROVERSIAE, §§ 36-40

36. Of the three main species into which ancient oratory was usually divided—the *genus deliberativum*, *genus demonstrativum*, and *genus iudiciale*—the suasoria is allied to the first, and the controversia to the third. The suasoria is a fictitious deliberative speech in which the speaker gives advice to a historical or semi-historical character regarding his future conduct; whereas the controversia is a fictitious speech in an assumed civil or criminal suit. At the head of his extracts Seneca states the subject or theme of the controversia. There may be in addition a statement of the law or laws under which the suit falls, and sometimes there is a title. Then follows a brief narrative in outline of the case. As an example let us take the 8th controversia of Book I:

Qui ter fortiter fecerit, militia vacet. Ter fortem pater in aciem quarto volentem exire retinet: nolentem abdicat.

The assumed law is: "He who has thrice distinguished himself in battle is to be free from military service". The narrative is: "One who had distinguished himself thrice desired to go out to battle a fourth time. His father tried to detain him. When he refuses his father disowns him".

37. The 6th of the first book has an interesting and romantic theme, which inspired Scudéry's story *Ibrahim ou l'illustre Bassa*. The theme is as follows:

A man who had been captured by pirates asked his father to ransom him, but was refused. The captain of the pirates had a daughter who induced the captive to swear that if released he would marry her. She abandoned her father and followed the youth on his escape. He went back to his father and married her. An heiress comes on the scene. The father commands the son to divorce the pirate's daughter and marry the heiress. When the son refuses the father disowns him.

One more example may be given to illustrate a theme taken from alleged Roman history: it is of interest as it is referred to in one of the suasoriae:

### De moribus sit actio

Popillium parricidii reum Cicero defendit; absolutus est. proscriptum Ciceronem ab Antonio missus occidit Popillius et caput eius ad Antonium rettulit. accusatur de moribus.

Cicero defended Popillius when accused of parricide. Popillius was acquitted. When Cicero was proscribed Popillius was sent by Antony to slay him. He brought back Cicero's head to Antony. He is now accused *de moribus*.

38. There appears to be little or no foundation for this story nor for the others which are taken from Greek or Roman history. The majority of the topics are indeed purely fictitious, laws and all. The laws sometimes have analogues in Greek law or custom, but seldom have any connection with the Roman system. The characters are stock characters or types, like those in the new comedy. We have pirates, tyrants, tyrannicides, vestals who have broken their vows, adulteresses, poisoners, ravished maidens, and so on. It has been objected that the characters and topics are unsuited to the minds of youth. The objection cannot be met. At the same time it may be noted that there are many precedents for these topics in the historical and criminal records of the time.[1] The schools are merely reflecting the age. Those who would like to pursue this interesting aspect of the subject farther must be referred to the controversiae themselves, or to the exhaustive analysis of M. Bornecque.[2]

39. The declaimer takes whatever side he pleases in the controversia, accusation or defence. He must not alter the facts as stated in the theme. He may plead in defence one day, in accusation the next. He may assume what he pleases as having been advocated against him. He cannot be refuted as there is no one to reply. The facts are admitted, there is no evidence, no witnesses to examine or cross-examine. His whole task s limited to that of construction of the facts. He does not speak in his own person but as one of the persons engaged in the suit. Hence he is partly an actor and he must speak as his assumed character would speak, that is, he is part dramatist as well. His speech is always a serious composition, at least for the great displays. It may be a very long thing, and does not appear ever to be short. Latro declaimed on one topic for three days![3] Albucius declaimed on occasion for at least six hours.[4]

---

[1] See K. V. Morawsky, *Wiener Studien*, 1882, vol. IV, pp. 166–168.

[2] H. Bornecque, *Les Déclamations et les Déclamateurs d'après Sénèque le père.* Lille, 1902.      [3] C. II, 4, 8.

[4] C. VII, Praef. 1, "saepe declamante illo ter bucinavit", sometimes taken as implying nine hours, but the trumpet may have sounded thrice in just over six hours.

The technique of these speeches in the hands of a great rhetor must have been masterly; the performance must have been artistically satisfying. We cannot believe that great statesmen like Augustus, Maecenas, Agrippa, and all the wits and men of genius in Rome throughout the reigns of Augustus and Tiberius would have interested themselves in this literary form had it been quite so trivial and foolish as Mr Simcox would have us believe. The subject matter was of just as much importance as the plots of many of our novels, and surely it will not be denied that many of these are trivial enough. The fact that the same topics remained the stock themes over so many years shows conclusively that they could not have furnished the main interest, but that the manner of treatment was everything.

40. Seneca never quotes a declamation in its entirety. He records only short extracts or quotations. It is extremely dangerous to infer from such the general character of anyone's style. The quotations are only of the striking or abnormal passages. They are never fair samples of the work as a whole. What opinion would be formed of the style of Macaulay from twenty pages of examples of his use of antithesis, and nothing else? A declamation cannot have been all point, all epigram. The declaimer must have used the ordinary language of men some of the time.

## THE SUASORIAE, § 41

41. If, however, the subject matter of the controversiae and the nature of the extracts that Seneca quotes, and especially the qualities that he illustrates, render them not very attractive to most modern readers, the same cannot be said of the suasoriae. Their subject matter has most attraction for us. The characters are either historical or semi-historical, are generally well known to us, and the situations are romantically or dramatically interesting. We have only seven of the common topics left in Seneca's work; but we know from other sources many others. Quintilian quotes quite a number,[1] and many more can be

---

[1] For example, Quin. *Inst. Or.* VII, 1, 24, "deliberat Numa an regnum offerentibus Romanis recipiat"; III, 5, 13, "an sibi uxor ducenda sit deliberabit Cato".

gathered from Philostratus.[1] Juvenal quotes one that has Sulla for its chief character.[2] Persius refers to one on Cato the younger.[3] Of the seven on which Seneca's notes are left, two relate to Alexander the Great, two to the Persian invasions, one to Agamemnon, and two to Cicero. Whatever we might have thought of any one of these declamations, as it was delivered in its entirety by a great master, we cannot deny that Seneca's seven chapters as they stand have a varied and absorbing interest. The actual quotations do not constitute the chief interest. We are fascinated more by the digressions, the anecdotes, the jests, the sidelights thrown on Antony, on Messala, on Augustus, on Tiberius, on Pollio and on Vergil. The two poetical quotations, eloquent or rhetorical as they are, make us wish that more of the poems from which they come had survived: and the quotations from the historians regarding the character and death of Cicero are precious reliques. To mention only two, the passages from Arellius Fuscus, in the second and sixth suasoriae, by their eloquence enable us to conjecture what a complete suasoria was like.

## SENTENTIAE, DIVISIONES, COLORES, §§ 42–44

42. The words *sententiae, divisiones, colores* in the title require a more particular reference. They are not divisions of the speech, but elements in the speech revealed by analysis. *Sententiae* may appear anywhere in the speech. They are merely the remarkable things that the rhetor said. Any striking or clever expression is a sententia. The term in this use is narrower in meaning than sententia as 'a general maxim', 'a sententious remark', 'a moral saying', although Seneca uses it in this sense too. The term involves always something terse, pointed, antithetic, witty or sparkling. It does not merely denote the opinion of the rhetor as to the "application of a law to a particular case".[4]

43. Again, as the subjects were hackneyed, whether in the

---

[1] *Lives of the Sophists*, I, 20 (514), "The Spartans debate whether they shall fortify themselves by building a wall"; I, 24 (528), "A Spartan advises the Lacedaemonians not to receive the men who had returned disarmed from Sphakteria"; II, 5 (572), "Advice to the Scythians to return to their former life as nomads, since their health is declining through their residing in cities".     [2] Juv. *Sat.* I, 16.
[3] Persius, III, 45.     [4] Teuffel, *History of Roman Lit.* par. 269, 6.

Controversiae or in the Suasoriae, it was of great importance to know how the rhetor had marshalled his arguments. In this mainly could one find the distinctive quality of his declamation. The *divisio* is then a brief summary of the plan of the speech. It enumerates the *quaestiones*, the various points at issue, and how the rhetor arranged them, and the degree of importance he attached to them. To discover a fresh point to be debated *pro* and *con.*, a still finer thread in the argument, was of course, the thing to aim at. We may briefly and contemptuously dismiss the subtlety, but there must have been an intellectual pleasure in this display of acuteness. Mental gymnastics seem to me as defensible and useful as any other form. That our taste rejects them does not necessarily condemn them absolutely.

44. Lastly we have the *colores*. These from the nature of the case cannot appear in the Suasoriae, as will be evident at once if we briefly explain what they are. The colores are the pleas alleged by the accused in explanation or extenuation of his act, or by the accuser to make the accused appear guilty or more guilty, to deepen as it were the shade of his guilt.[1] They constitute the colour given to the act by the speaker. In a suasoria as you merely have a speaker pointing out to some historical character the advantage or disadvantage of a future course of action you cannot have colores. The color may be found anywhere in a controversia, implicit or explicit. It will naturally be an important element in the general impression produced by the whole speech. Pollio is really stating this when he maintains that the color should be merely indicated in the *narratio* (narrative of the facts of the case) and developed in the *argumenta* (the reasoning in support of the speaker's view of the facts).[2] From this time on the students of rhetoric were intensely interested in colores.[3] Juvenal is referring to this interest when he writes, "dic, Quintiliane, colorem"[4] and this again is quite natural and inevitable as the declaimer in his colores had another field for the exercise of his ingenuity. To sum up the whole matter, as the subject was given, was hackneyed and had been handled scores of times, the interest of the declamation

---

[1] See Mayor's ed. of Juv., *Sat.* VII, 155 note.    [2] C. IV, 3.
[3] Seneca mentions rather contemptuously four books of *Colores*, edited by Junius Otho, C. II, 1, 33.
[4] Juv. *Sat.* VI, 279.

rested on the originality with which the ideas were expressed, on the novelty of the line of argument and of the colores. These being the three main topics of interest are chosen by Seneca as the three heads under which to give his reminiscences of the orators and declaimers.

### CONCLUSION, §§ 45, 46

45. The works of Seneca's son were, as we are told, probably preserved through the belief that the latter had had some connection with the apostle Paul. The works of the father in turn were preserved because for a long time they were believed to be part of the literary remains of his son. Such are the chances of the tradition. The rhetoricians travelled all over the Roman world, to Gaul, to Spain, to Africa; and whatever we may think of them and their exercises, the latter were the vehicle by which the ideas of Roman philosophy, literature and literary expression, in short all the culture of the time, were spread everywhere. Higher education flowed on in this form for five or six centuries, and we even find suasoriae on biblical subjects, once Christianity had ousted the old religion. When the dark ages begin to lighten we find Seneca's work and its topics very popular. They give themes to many of the tales of the *Gesta Romanorum*. M. Boissier finds in them the source of the Discours of the French colleges.

46. As scholarship becomes ignorant and uncritical, as men of genius become rarer, as the world settles into barbarism, it is little wonder that these exercises become more arid, more wearisome, more sterile, and lose all merit till the very name of rhetoric becomes a term of reproach. But this is no more true of the declamation than of all other literary forms. We no longer regard it as a form of fictitious literature worth cultivating. It may be doubted whether we should not do better to cultivate a little more our sense of beauty and propriety in public speaking. If we have the best of matter for eloquent expression it is to be regretted that we do not devote more pains to finding the best expression for our matter. At any rate we should not disparage so much as we have done and still do, these declamations that in Seneca's time were cultivated by the best intellects of the day with an enthusiasm almost too great for pastime.

# THE TEXT

The text in this edition of the Suasoriae is based on that of H. J. Müller, Vienna, 1887. M. Bornecque in his edition of the Controversiae and Suasoriae (Garnier Frères, Paris, 1902) reviewed the text, and made a large number of alterations in Müller's. The latter, however, remains the standard. I have compared the two, and where they differed chosen that reading which so far as I was able to judge seemed preferable. I have also seen all or almost all of the articles published in the various Classical periodicals since 1902 on this subject.

For the following brief notes on the MSS. and editions I am mainly indebted to Müller's elaborate introduction to his edition of the text.

The MSS. fall into two classes: (i) those which contain the full text of the surviving Controversiae and Suasoriae, (2) those which contain only the Excerpta or Extracts from the Controversiae (apparently made in the fourth or fifth century for school use), with some of the prefaces. As these latter contain no Excerpta from the Suasoriae it is not necessary to say much about them here. I will merely add that they are very numerous, belong to the ninth to the fifteenth centuries, and by their number testify to the great popularity of the book in the Middle Ages.

The MSS. of the first class contain only Books I, II, VII, IX, X, of the Controversiae, and the book of Suasoriae. They omit the Prefaces to the first and second books. The Preface to the book of Suasoriae is totally lost, a loss much to be regretted. I add a short enumeration of the chief of these MSS.:

1. Codex Antverpiensis, denoted by the letter A, in the State Library at Antwerp, written in the tenth century.

2. Codex Bruxellensis, B, in the Royal Library at Brussels, tenth century.

3. Codex Vaticanus, V, in the Vatican Library, end of tenth century.

A, B, V are from the same non-existent archetype, C, according to Müller, a conclusion which he arrives at from their similarity in corrections, in omitting words, and in the writing of the Greek quotations. A, B he also concludes are much more closely related to one another than to V. He infers that A, B derive from one copy of the archetype which he calls X, V from another which he calls X', and that A, B are nearer the archetype.

4. Codex Toletanus, T, in the Royal Library, Brussels, written in the thirteenth century from V.

5. Codex Brugensis, Br, in the Royal Library, Brussels, written in the fifteenth century from T.

6. Codex Bruxellensis, D, in the Royal Library, Brussels, fifteenth century.

Müller also considers the corrector (sixteenth century) of the codex Toletanus as of importance for the text, as he seems to have had a good text from which to correct his MS.

### EDITIONS

1. Editio Veneta. Suasoriarum et Controversiarum Libri, first published at Venice, 1490, and again in 1492. Greek wanting.

2. Editio Frobeniana, edited by Erasmus, printed at Basle, 1515.

3. Edition of J. Hervagius and B. Brandus, Basle, 1557. Greek wanting.

4. Edition of Muretus, Rome, 1585. Muretus was the first editor who tried to decipher the hieroglyphics (as Müller calls them) in which the Greek quotations were written. He died before completing more than those in the Suasoriae.

The editors of these editions all thought that the work was by Seneca the son.

In the following editions the works of the father are separated from those of the son:

5. Edition of Nicholas Faber, Paris, 1587.

6. Edition of Andreas Schott, Douai, 1603.

7. Edition of J. F. Gronovius, Leyden, 1649.

Faber and Gronovius did much for the elucidation of the text, and Schott, considering the corrector of the Codex Toletanus of high value, put his corrections in the text. Thence they got to the Gronovian edition and so to the Vulgate.

8. The Vulgate (so called). Editio Elzeviriana, Amsterdam, 1672. This is the best and most important of the old editions. It contains the complete prefaces of Faber, Schott and Gronovius and their notes, as well as notes of J. Schultingh, unpublished up till that time. With the exception of the brief notes in Bornecque's edition, these are the only notes available to a modern editor. I found them very useful.

Then for nearly two centuries the book was neglected, until in the middle of the nineteenth century the interest rose again:

9. Edition of Conrad Bursian, Leipzig, 1857.
10. Edition of Adolph Kiessling, Leipzig, 1872.
11. Edition of H. J. Müller, Leipzig, 1887.
12. Edition of H. Bornecque, Paris, 1902.

M. Bornecque published the critical notes on his edition of the text (as the nature of the series in which his work was published did not permit of such) in the *Revue de Philologie*, vol. XXVI, 1902. He explains that he introduces corrections in the ends of phrases (when these are not in accordance with the laws of prose rhythm) as often as the most frequent faults in the MSS. of Seneca seem to justify these corrections. For his views on the laws of prose rhythm see his article in the *Revue de Philologie*, 1902, pp. 117 *et seq.* His other corrections return to the MSS. readings or to conjectures already made. He also added many corrections made since 1894, especially those of Emil Thomas of Berlin, published in 1900, *Philologus*, Supp. vol. VIII, pp. 159–298.

# NOTES ON THE DECLAIMERS

Of the 120 orators or declaimers mentioned in the whole work of Seneca only some 50 are represented in the Suasoriae. The majority are by origin from Italy or Rome, but a very large number came from other parts of the empire. Thus Latro, Marullus, Gallio, Statorius Victor are from Spain, probably from Cordova. Cestius was born at Smyrna, Moschus at Pergamum; Arellius Fuscus and Argentarius are Greeks from Asia Minor. Of those who speak only in Greek, Diocles is from Euboea, Lesbocles and Potamon from Mitylene, Damas from Tralles, and Hybreas from Mylasa in Caria.

Hybreas, Marullus, Menestratus and Nicetes are older than Seneca; Albucius, Arellius Fuscus, Cestius, Haterius and Latro, among many others, are his contemporaries; Argentarius, Gallio, Fabianus and others are his juniors.

They vary greatly in capacity, from masters like Latro to botchers like Murredius. Not all keep school. Not all speak Latin. Nicetes declaims only in Greek.

The rhetoricians, generally speaking, range themselves in two camps, the *Attici* and the *Asiani*. There is a further cleavage among them into *Theodorei* and *Apollodorei*; the difference between whom is rather obscure.

Seneca places four of the declaimers in a class by themselves, which he calls the *tetradeum*, the "quartet" or "tetrad" (C. x, Praef. 13). These supreme four are Latro, Fuscus, Albucius and Gallio. He makes the peculiar comment, "hi quotiens conflixissent, penes Latronem gloria fuisset, penes Gallionem palma", which means, I suggest, that, had they competed with one another, Latro would have shown himself more brilliant, Gallio would have carried off the prize, i.e. the latter was the more effective speaker, the former the more brilliant.

A few notes are given on the "tetrad" first, then the notes on the others follow in alphabetical order:

1. C. ALBUCIUS SILUS, born about 60–55 B.C. at Novaria, where he became aedile, then came to Rome, and opened a school. One of the most competent declaimers, he was also advocate, in the latter

rôle not too successful. His love of figures of speech led him into trouble on one occasion (C. VII, Praef. 6–7), his independence on another (Suet. *de Rhet.* 6). He starved himself to death about A.D. 10 to escape from a painful malady. Seneca says he was "homo summae probitatis qui nec facere iniuriam nec pati sciret" (C. VII, Praef. 7). Excellent portrait of him and criticism of his style in C. VII, Praef. He does not figure much in the Suasoriae.

2. ARELLIUS FUSCUS, probably born in Greece, or in one of the Greek cities of Asia Minor, 60–55 B.C. He came to Rome and opened a school where he had as pupils, possibly Seneca himself, certainly Ovid and Fabianus. He was alive after the publication of the *Aeneid*, 17 B.C., but we do not know how long. He was very famous. He figures largely in the Suasoriae, and his style is brilliant and throbbing with passion. He has the faults and the merits of the Asiatic school. See note on S. II (**10**, 20).

3. L. JUNIUS GALLIO, born about 30 B.C., probably came from Spain, a great friend of Seneca and Ovid, adopted Seneca's son, Novatus, after Seneca's death. He was a senator and on intimate terms with Tiberius, with whom, however, he ultimately fell into disfavour. Seneca calls him a master of the familiar style, but probably is too partial to him. He was too continually straining after effect, after originality, and is accused of excessive use of figures of rhetoric, especially antithesis, hence Tacitus, *Dial. de Or.* 26, "tinnitus Gallionis".

4. M. PORCIUS LATRO, born in Spain, probably at Cordova, contemporary of Seneca, and his most intimate friend. He committed suicide in 3 or 4 B.C. to escape from the pain of a quartan fever. He was Seneca's fellow-pupil both with the 'grammaticus' and in the school of Marullus. His reputation was very great as he and Nicetes were the only two rhetoricians of whom we know that they merely lectured and declaimed and refused to listen to their pupils' efforts. In the preface to C. I Seneca gives a brilliant portrait of him, of his character, his restless energy, his extraordinary memory and his methods of work and play. He seems to have been more sober and sound in judgment than his contemporaries, always striving to restrict them to what was natural and probable.

5. ANTONIUS ATTICUS, S. II, 16; mentioned only once, and condemned for puerility.

6. APATURIUS, Greek rhetorician, mentioned twice, S. I, 11; S. II, 21.

7. ARGENTARIUS, born in Greece, pupil of Cestius, mentioned S. I, 2; S. III, 2; S. V, 6; S. VI, 7; S. VII, 7; the last passage qui eloquent.

8. ASILIUS SABINUS. Seneca calls him "disertus", and "urbanissimus homo", in the Suasoriae (II, 12) "venustissimus inter rhetoras scurra".

9. ATTALUS STOICUS (S. II, 12), the well-known Stoic philosopher of the reign of Tiberius, teacher of Seneca the younger, characterised here by Seneca as the most acute and eloquent of the philosophers of the day.

10. BARBARUS, a Greek rhetor (S. I, 13, where unfortunately his quotation is lost).

11. CATIUS CRISPUS, S. II, 16; only this and one or two quotations in the Controversiae known of him.

12. L. CESTIUS PIUS, born at Smyrna, 65–60 B.C., came to Rome and opened a school, died after A.D. 9 (defeat of Quintilius Varus by Arminius); note the anecdote of him and the younger Cicero in S. VII, 13. The main qualities of his character are revealed in the Controversiae or the Suasoriae. He was "homo nasutissimus" (S. VII, 12), "mordacissimus" (C. VII, Praef. 8), "nullius ingenii nisi sui amator". His inordinate conceit made him rank himself above Cicero, which raised the ire of C. Severus and of Cicero the younger. He was highly successful, perhaps just because he was imbued with the fashionable literary vices.

13. M. CLAUDIUS MARCELLUS AESERNINUS, grandson of Pollio, who considered him the heir of his own literary genius.

14. CORNELIUS HISPANUS, a rhetorician known only from Seneca's work; mentioned in the Suasoriae in II. 7; II, 9; III, 2; VI, 7; and several times in the Controversiae.

15. CORVUS, known only through Seneca; see S. II, 21.

16. DAMAS, surnamed Scombrus, Greek declaimer, born at Tralles in Caria. (S. II, 14; S. I, 13.)

17. DIOCLES, of Carystus in Euboea, highly praised by Seneca in the Controversiae.

18. DORION, Greek rhetorician, mentioned in S. I, 12; S. II, 22; and S. II, 11, but the quotation is in each case lost.

19. GARGONIUS, S. II, 16; S. VII, 14; usually mentioned by Seneca only to be condemned.

20. GAVIUS SABINUS, S. II, 5; little known of him except Seneca's quotations.

21. GLYCON, surnamed Spyridion, a Greek. In S. I, 11; S. I, 16; S. II, 14, he is mentioned twice with approval, once with disapproval.

22. Q. HATERIUS, the orator celebrated for his eloquence and adulation of the Emperor under Tiberius; senator, perhaps consul, born about 63 or 62 B.C., died about A.D. 26. He was voluble and impassioned and lacked restraint. Hence Augustus said he needed the curb, and Gallio said "et ille erat plena deo" (S. III, 7, where see note). He seems to have preferred Suasoriae, and the passages in VI and VII are quite eloquent.

23. HYBREAS, famous Greek orator and declaimer, born at Mylasa in Caria about 80 B.C., played a great rôle in his native town.

24. LESBOCLES, Greek orator of Mitylene, where he had a school (S. II, 15), according to Seneca justly famous.

25. LICINIUS NEPOS, S. II, 16; mentioned by Seneca only to be condemned for bad taste.

26. MARULLUS, taught declamation at Rome, probably came from Spain, perhaps from Cordova, teacher of Latro and Seneca, not in the first rank. (S. I, 3; S. II, 5; S. III, 2.)

27. MENESTRATUS, Greek declaimer, of the generation preceding Seneca, a mediocrity.

28. MURREDIUS, mentioned by Seneca invariably with condemnation.

29. MUSA, Latin declaimer, a freedman, favourite of Seneca's son, Mela, but not of Seneca. He was dead when Seneca wrote his book.

30. NICETES. Greek rhetorician of the time of Augustus, flourished about 33 B.C.: came to Rome with a great reputation. Note the story of the visit of Gallio and Seneca to Messala after hearing him (S. III, 6 and note). He, like Latro, refused to hear his pupils' efforts. He obviously belonged to the Asiatic school. He must have been really great as Seneca always praises him, though a Greek, in the highest terms.

31. P. NONIUS ASPRENAS, Latin declaimer, no details of life known.

32. PAPIRIUS FABIANUS, born about 35 B.C., pupil of Arellius Fuscus and afterwards of Blandus, soon abandoned rhetoric for philosophy and opened a school of philosophy where he had the younger Seneca as a pupil. As a declaimer he had great success. (S. I, 4; S. I, 9.)

33. PLUTION, Greek rhetorician (S. I, 11); mentioned by St Jerome as, in 33 B.C., a very famous teacher of rhetoric.

34. POMPEIUS SILO, born about 50 B.C., probably a moderate declaimer and first-rate advocate. (S. I, 2; S. II, 7; S. VI, 4; S. VII, 5.)

35. POTAMON, famous Greek rhetor of Mitylene, son of Lesbonax, contemporary and rival of Lesbocles, born about 65 B.C., died about A.D. 25; sent on embassies to Rome in 45 B.C. and 25 B.C. by his native town; great orator, wrote works on rhetoric and history. (S. II, 15; S. II, 16.)

36. RUBELLIUS BLANDUS, born at Tibur, probably about 45 B.C. Fabianus was his pupil, and Latro probably his teacher, first Roman *eques* to teach rhetoric at Rome. (S. II, 8; S. V, 7.)

37. SENECA (Grandio), Latin rhetorician. See Seneca's portrait of him, S. II, 17.

38. SENIANUS, nothing known except that Seneca quotes him always with disapproval. (S. II, 18.)

39. STATORIUS VICTOR, declaimer and writer of *fabulae*, quoted S. II, 18, in a foolish *sententia*.

40. SURDINUS, declaimer who also translated some Greek *fabulae* into Latin, pupil of Cestius. In S. VII, 12, Seneca calls him "ingeniosus adulescens", 'a talented youth'.

41. TRIARIUS, Latin declaimer, probably a pupil of Cestius, born about 30 B.C. (S. II, 3; S. V, 7; S. VI, 5; S. VII, 6.)

42. TUSCUS, Latin declaimer and historian (S. II, 22), where see note.

43. VARIUS GEMINUS, orator and declaimer, no details of life known, seems to have been a pupil of Cestius; C. Severus heard him, and we know he pleaded a cause before Caesar. (S. VI, 11 and 12.)

44. VOLCACIUS MOSCHUS, born at Pergamum, pupil and fellow-townsman of Apollodorus. Kiessling suggests that he was given the citizenship by the consul L. Volcacius Tullus in 33 B.C., and came to Rome about the beginning of Augustus's principate; was accused of poisoning about 20 B.C., defended by Pollio and Torquatus, but condemned and exiled. He opened a school in Marseilles, and on his death in A.D. 25 left all his wealth to that town. His contemporaries rallied him on his excessive use of the figures of rhetoric. (S. I, 2.)

# BIBLIOGRAPHY

I have given a list of the editions of Seneca's work already, p. xxxvi. The following are the chief works or articles in Classical periodicals that have some bearing on the Suasoriae. The more important are starred.

AULARD, F. A. De Gaii Asinii Pollionis vita et scriptis. Paris, 1877.

BERGK. Monumentum Ancyranum, p. 97, on Pedo's verses (S. I, 15).

BOISSIER, G. (1) L'Opposition sous les Césars. Paris, 1892.

—— (2) La Fin du Paganisme. Paris, 1894.

**—— (3) Article on Declamation in the Dictionary of Daremberg and Saglio.

**—— (4) Les écoles de déclamation à Rome. Revue des deux Mondes, II, 1902, pp. 480–508.

**BORNECQUE, H. (1) Les déclamations et les déclamateurs d'après Sénèque le père. Lille, 1902.

*—— (2) Notes on text of his edition. Revue de Philologie, XXVI, 1902.

—— (3) Rhythm in Prose. Revue de Phil. 1902, pp. 117 et seq.

CERRATI, M. La Grammatica di A. Seneca, il retore. Le libraire Montrucchio, Turin, 1908.

**CUCHEVAL, V. L'Éloquence romaine après Cicéron. Paris, 1893.

DECKER, J. DE. (1) On the text of S. II, 10. Revue de l'Instruction publique en Belgique, LV, 1912.

—— (1) Les rhéteurs spirituels à Rome. Bulletin de la Société pour le progrès des études phil. et hist. 1909, No. 1.

DOSSON, S. Étude sur Quinte Curce. Paris, 1886.

FRANK, T. On the text of S. VI, 22. American Journal of Phil. XXXIV. No. 135, p. 325.

FRIEDLÄNDER. Darstellungen aus der Sittengeschichte Roms. Leipzig, 1890.

HAUPT, M. On the text of S. I, 15, on Pedo's verses, S. I, 4 and S. I, 8. Opuscula, III.

JULLIEN, E. Les Professeurs de littérature dans l'ancienne Rome. Paris, 1885.

KOERBER. Ueber den Rhetor Seneca und die römische Rhetorik seiner Zeit. Cassel, 1864.

LEO, F. On the text of S. I, 5. Hermes, XL, p. 608.

LINDNER. (Dissertations.) De M. Porcio Latrone commentatio. Breslau, 1855.

—— De L. Cestio Pio commentatio. Züllichau, 1858.

—— De Gaio Albucio Silo commentatio. Breslau, 1861.
—— De Arellio Fusco commentatio. Breslau, 1862.
—— De Junio Gallione commentatio. Hirschberg, 1868.

Macé, Alc. Essai sur Suétone. Paris, 1900. (Also in Bibliothèque des Écoles françaises d'Athènes et de Rome, 1900, No. 82, p. 248.)

*Mayor, J. E. B. Various notes in his edition of Juvenal's Satires. Macmillan & Co., 1893.

Morawski, K. V. Article in Wiener Studien, 1882, iv, pp. 166–168.

Sander, Max. Der Sprachgebrauch des Rhetors Annaeus Seneca. I. 1877; II, 1880. Berlin: Weidmann.

Sandys, J. E. Sketch of History of Roman and Greek Oratory, in Introduction to his edition of Cicero's *Orator*. Cambridge University Press, 1885.

Thomas, Aem. Schedae Criticae Novae in Senecam Rhetorem. Philologus, Supp. viii, 1900, pp. 159–298.

Spengel, L. Rhetores Graeci. Teubner.

*Teuffel and Schwabe. History of Roman Literature.

Van der Vliet. On text of S. vi, 5; S. vi, 10; S. vi, 11; S. vi, 24; S. vii, 1; S. vii, 8. Revue de Phil. 1895, xix, p. 38.

Walter, Fr. On the text of S. i, 2; S. iv, 1; S. vi, 12; S. vi, 21. Berliner Philologische Wochenschrift, 1918, No. 10.

*Wernsdorf. Poetae Latini Minores. Lemaire, 1824. iii, 221, Notes on Pedo's verses (S. i, 15). iii, 208, Notes on verses of Cornelius Severus (S. vi. 26).

Wilamowitz-Moellendorf. On text of S. i, 12. Hermes, xiv, p. 172.

Wilkins, A. S. Sketch of History of Rhetoric, Introduction to his edition of Cicero's *De Oratore*. Clarendon Press, 1895.

### Ancient Authors

The most important are:

**Quintilian. Institutio Oratoria, especially Books i and ii. The Declamations attributed to him, both the longer and the shorter.

*Calpurnius Flaccus. Declamationes. Lehnert, Teubner.

*Suetonius. De Grammaticis and De Claris Rhetoribus.

*Tacitus. Dialogus de Oratoribus.

*Q. Curtius Rufus and Arrian for the Suasoriae relating to Alexander.

*Cicero's Rhetorical Works, and the Philippics, especially the Second.

Petronius Arbiter. Satyricon.

Philostratus. Lives of the Sophists.

# LIST OF ABBREVIATIONS

A    = Codex Antverpiensis.
B    = Codex Bruxellensis.
C    = Codicum ABV consensus.
D    = Codex Bruxellensis.
T    = Codex Toletanus.
τ    = Corrector of the Codex Toletanus.
V    = Codex Vaticanus.
Br   = Codex Brugensis.

Schg. = Johannes Schultingh.
Gr    = J. F. Gronovius.
B⁰    = Henri Bornecque.
W     = Wernsdorf (Poetae Latini Minores).

In the references to Seneca's work:

C    = Controversiae.
S    = Suasoriae.

The notes refer to the text of this edition by page and line.

When the paragraphs are given they are those of Müller's edition of the text.

Müller's paragraphs are indicated at the side of the text and translation.

# SUASORIA I

## Deliberat Alexander an Oceanum naviget.

1 *...desinunt: cuicumque rei magnitudinem natura dederat, dedit et modum; nihil infinitum est nisi Oceanus. aiunt fertiles in Oceano iacere terras ultraque Oceanum rursus alia litora, alium nasci orbem, nec usquam rerum naturam desinere, 5 sed semper inde ubi desisse videatur novam exsurgere. facile ista finguntur quia Oceanus navigari non potest. satis sit hactenus Alexandro vicisse qua mundo lucere Soli satis est. intra has terras caelum Hercules meruit. stat immotum mare quasi deficientis in suo fine naturae pigra moles: novae ac 10 terribiles figurae, magna etiam Oceano portenta, quae profunda ista vastitas nutrit, confusa[1] lux alta caligine et interceptus tenebris dies, ipsum vero grave et defixum mare et aut nulla aut ignota sidera. ea[2] est, Alexander, rerum natura: post omnia Oceanus, post Oceanum nihil. 15

2 ARGENTARI

Resiste, orbis te tuus revocat; vicimus qua lucet. nihil tantum est quod ego Alexandri periculo petam.

POMPEI SILONIS

Venit ille dies, Alexander, exoptatus[3] quo tibi opera desset; 20 idem sunt termini et regni tui et mundi.

MOSCHI

Tempus est Alexandrum cum orbe et cum sole desinere. quod noveram vici; nunc concupisco quod nescio. quae tam ferae gentes fuerunt quae non Alexandrum posito genu 25 adorarint? qui tam horridi montes quorum non iuga victor miles calcaverit? ultra Liberi patris tropaea constitimus. non quaerimus orbem, sed amittimus. inmensum et humanae intemptatum experientiae pelagus, totius orbis vinculum terrarumque custodia, inagitata remigio vastitas, litora modo 30 saeviente fluctu inquieta, modo fugiente deserta; taetra caligo fluctus premit, et nescio qui, quod humanis natura subduxit oculis aeterna nox obruit.

---

* desinunt, Müller's correction of MSS. reading, sinunt, omitted in the translation, as little meaning can be got from it without the context.
[1] Müller and B° circumfusa.　　[2] B° haec.　　[3] B° exoptatus tuis.

MUSAE

Foeda beluarum magnitudo et inmobile profundum. testatum
est, Alexander, nihil ultra esse quod vincas; revertere.

ALBUCI SILI                                                    3

5 Terrae quoque suum finem habent, et ipsius mundi aliquis
occasus est; nihil infinitum est; modum tu magnitudini facere
debes, quoniam Fortuna non facit. magni pectoris est inter
secunda moderatio. eundem Fortuna victoriae tuae quem
naturae finem facit: imperium tuum cludit Oceanus. o quan-
10 tum magnitudo tua rerum quoque naturam supergressa est!
Alexander orbi magnus est, Alexandro orbis angustus est.
aliquis etiam magnitudini modus est; non procedit ultra spatia
sua caelum, maria intra terminos suos agitantur. quidquid ad
summum pervenit incremento non relinquit locum. non magis
15 quicquam ultra Alexandrum novimus quam ultra Oceanum.

MARULLI

Maria sequimur, terras cui tradimus? orbem quem non novi
quaero, quem vici relinquo.

FABIANI                                                       4

20 Quid? ista toto pelago infusa caligo navigantem tibi videtur
admittere, quae prospicientem quoque excludit? non haec
India est nec ferarum terribilis ille gentium conventus. in-
manes propone beluas, aspice, quibus procellis fluctibusque
saeviat, quas ad litora undas agat. tantus ventorum concursus,
25 tanta convulsi funditus maris insania est; nulla praesens
navigantibus statio est, nihil salutare, nihil notum; rudis et
inperfecta natura penitus recessit. ista maria ne illi quidem
petierunt qui fugiebant Alexandrum. sacrum quiddam terris
natura circumfudit Oceanum. illi[1] qui iam siderum colle-
30 gerunt meatus et annuas hiemis atque aestatis vices ad certam
legem redegerunt, quibus nulla pars ignota mundi est, de
Oceano tamen dubitant utrumne terras velut vinculum circumfluat an in suum colligatur orbem et in hos per quos
navigatur sinus quasi spiramenta quaedam magnitudinis suae
35 exaestuet; ignem post se, cuius augmentum ipse sit, habeat
an spiritum. quid agitis, conmilitones? domitoremne generis
humani, magnum Alexandrum, eo dimittitis quod adhuc quid
sit disputatur? memento, Alexander: matrem in orbe victo
adhuc magis quam pacato relinquis.

---

[1] B⁰ illi etiam.

5 DIVISIO

Aiebat Cestius hoc genus suasoriarum alibi aliter declamandum esse. non eodem modo in libera civitate dicendam sententiam quo apud reges, quibus etiam quae prosunt ita tamen ut delectent suadenda sunt. et inter reges ipsos esse 5 discrimen: quosdam minus, alios magis osos veritatem; facile Alexandrum ex iis esse quos superbissimos et supra mortalis animi modum inflatos accepimus. denique, ut alia dimittantur argumenta, ipsa suasoria insolentiam eius coarguit; orbis illum suus non capit. itaque nihil dicendum aiebat nisi cum summa 10 veneratione regis, ne accideret idem quod praeceptori[1] eius, amitino Aristotelis, accidit, quem occidit propter intempestive liberos sales; nam cum se deum vellet videri et vulneratus esset, viso sanguine eius philosophus mirari se dixerat quod non esset ἰχώρ, οἷός πέρ τε ῥέει μακάρεσσι θεοῖσιν. ille se ab 15 hac urbanitate lancea vindicavit. eleganter in C. Cassi epistula quadam ad M. Ciceronem missa positum: multum iocatur de stultitia Cn. Pompei adulescentis, qui in Hispania contraxit exercitum et ad Mundam acie victus est; deinde ait, "nos quidem illum deridemus, sed timeo ne ille nos gladio 20 ἀντιμυκτηρίσῃ." in omnibus regibus haec urbanitas ex

6 timescenda est. aiebat itaque apud Alexandrum esse sic dicendam sententiam ut multa adulatione animus eius permulceretur, servandum tamen aliquem modum ne non veneratio videretur sed adulatio, et accideret tale aliquid quale 25 accidit Atheniensibus, cum publicae eorum blanditiae non tantum deprehensae sed[2] castigatae sunt. nam cum Antonius vellet se Liberum patrem dici et hoc nomen statuis suis subscribi iuberet, habitu quoque et comitatu Liberum imitaretur, occurrerunt venienti ei Athenienses cum coniugibus 30 et liberis et Διόνυσον salutaverunt. belle illis cesserat, si nasus Atticus ibi substitisset. [3]dixerunt despondere ipsos in matrimonium illi Minervam suam et rogaverunt ut duceret; Antonius ait ducturum, sed dotis nomine imperare se illis mille talenta. tum ex Graeculis quidam ait: "κύριε, ὁ Ζεὺς 35 τὴν μητέρα σου Σεμέλην ἄπροικον εἶχεν." huic quidem impune fuit[4] sed Atheniensium sponsalia mille talentis aestimata sunt. quae cum exigerentur complures contumeliosi

---

[1] B⁰ censori ejus, amitino Aristotelis praeceptoris.
[2] B⁰ sed et.　　　　　[3] B⁰ sed dixerunt.
[4] B⁰ fuit ausum.

libelli proponebantur, quidam etiam ipsi Antonio tradebantur: sicut ille qui subscriptus statuae eius fuit, cum eodem tempore et Octaviam uxorem haberet et Cleopatram: "'Οκταουία καὶ 'Αθηνᾶ 'Αντωνίῳ· 'res tuas tibi habe'". bellissimam tamen **7**
5 rem Dellius dixit, quem Messala Corvinus desultorem bellorum civilium vocat, quia ab Dolabella ad Cassium transiturus salutem sibi pactus est, si Dolabellam occidisset, a Cassio deinde transit ad Antonium, novissime ab Antonio transfugit ad Caesarem. hic est Dellius cuius epistulae ad
10 Cleopatram lascivae feruntur. cum Athenienses tempus peterent ad pecuniam conferendam nec exorarent, Dellius ait, "at tamen dicito illos tibi annua, bienni, trienni die debere". longius me fabellarum dulcedo produxit; itaque ad propositum revertar. aiebat Cestius magnis cum laudibus **8**
15 Alexandri hanc suasoriam esse dicendam, quam sic divisit ut primum diceret, etiamsi navigari posset Oceanus, navigandum non esse; satis gloriae quaesitum; regenda esse et disponenda quae in transitu vicisset; consulendum militi tot eius[1] victoriis lasso; de matre illi cogitandum; et alias causas
20 complures subiecit. deinde illam quaestionem subiecit, ne navigari quidem Oceanum posse. Fabianus philosophus **9** primam fecit quaestionem eandem; etiamsi navigari posset Oceanus navigandum non esse. at rationem aliam primam fecit; modum inponendum esse rebus secundis. hic dixit
25 sententiam, "illa demum est magna felicitas quae arbitrio suo constitit." dixit deinde locum de varietate fortunae, et cum descripsisset nihil esse stabile, omnia fluitare et incertis motibus modo attolli, modo deprimi, absorberi terras et maria siccari, montes subsidere, deinde exempla regum ex
30 fastigio suo devolutorum, adiecit "sine potius rerum naturam quam fortunam tuam deficere". secundam quoque quae- **10** stionem aliter tractavit; divisit enim illam sic ut primum negaret ullas in Oceano aut trans Oceanum esse terras habitabiles. deinde: si essent, perveniri tamen ad illas non
35 posse; hic difficultatem navigationis, ignoti maris naturam non patientem navigationis. novissime: ut posset perveniri tanti tamen non esse. hic dixit incerta peti, certa deseri; descituras gentes si Alexandrum rerum naturae terminos supergressum enotuisset; hic matrem, de qua dixit: quo
40 modo illa trepidavit etiam quod Granicum transiturus esset!

---

[1] B⁰ suis.

11 Glyconis celebris sententia est: τοῦτο οὐκ ἔστι Σιμόεις οὐδὲ
Γράνικος· τοῦτο εἰ μή τι κακὸν ἦν οὐκ ἂν ἔσχατον ἔκειτο.
hoc omnes imitari voluerunt. Plution dixit: καὶ διὰ τοῦτο
μέγιστόν ἐστιν, ὅτι αὐτὸ μὲν μετὰ πάντα, μετὰ δὲ αὐτὸ οὐθέν.
Artemon dixit: βουλευόμεθα, εἰ χρὴ περαιοῦσθαι. οὐ ταῖς 5
Ἑλλησποντίαις ἠόσιν ἐφεστῶτες οὐδ' ἐπὶ τῷ Παμφυλίῳ
πέλαγει τὴν ἐμπρόθεσμον καραδοκοῦμεν ἄμπωσιν· οὐδὲ
Εὐφράτης τοῦτ' ἐστιν, οὐδὲ Ἰνδός, ἀλλ' εἴτε γῆς τέρμα, εἴτε
φύσεως ὅρος, εἴτε πρεσβύτατον στοιχεῖον, εἴτε γένεσις θεῶν,
ἱερώτερόν ἐστιν ἢ κατὰ ναῦς ὕδωρ. Apaturius dixit: ἐντεῦθεν 10
ἡ ναῦς ἐκ μιᾶς φορᾶς εἰς ἀνατολάς, ἔνθα δὲ εἰς τὰς ἀοράτους
δύσεις. Cestius descripsit sic: "fremit Oceanus quasi indig-
12 netur quod terras relinquas". corruptissimam rem omnium
quae umquam dictae sunt, ex quo homines diserti insanire
coeperunt, putabant Dorionis esse in metaphrasi dictam 15
Homeri, cum excaecatus Cyclops saxum in mare reiecit,
*οὖρος ἀποσπᾶται καὶ χείρια βάλλεται νῆσσος. haec quo
modo ex corruptis eo perveniant ut et magna et tamen sana
sint, aiebat Maecenas apud Vergilium intellegi posse. tumidum est: ὄρους ὄρος ἀποσπᾶται. Vergilius quid ait? rapit      20
                haud partem exiguam montis.
ita magnitudini studet ut non inprudenter discedat a fide.
est inflatum: καὶ χείρια βάλλεται νῆσσος. Vergilius quid ait
de navibus?[1]            credas innare revolsas                25
                Cycladas.
non dicit hoc fieri, sed videri. propitiis auribus accipitur
quamvis incredibile sit, quod excusatur antequam dicitur.
13 multo corruptiorem sententiam Menestrati cuiusdam, de-
clamatoris non abiecti suis temporibus, nactus sum in hac 30
ipsa suasoria, cum describeret beluarum in Oceano nascentium magnitudinem:.... efficit haec sententia ut ignoscam
Musae qui dixit ipsis Charybdi et Scylla maius portentum:
"Charybdis ipsius maris naufragium" et, ne in una re semel
insaniret: "quid ibi potest esse salvi ubi ipsum mare perit?" 35
Damas ethicos induxit matrem loquentem, cum describeret
adsidue prioribus periculis nova supervenisse:.... Barbarus
dixit, cum introduxisset excusantem se exercitum Mace-
14 donum, hunc sensum:.... Fuscus Arellius dixit: "testor ante
orbem tibi tuum deesse quam militem." Latro sedens[2] hanc 40

* Accepting Gertz's restoration of the Greek.
[1] B⁰ quod ait quidem de navibus.                [2] B⁰ sequens.

dixit: non excusavit militem, sed dixit: "duc, sequor;[1] quis
mihi promittit hostem, quis terram, quis diem, quis aerem?
da ubi castra ponam, ubi signa inferam. reliqui parentes,
reliqui liberos, commeatum peto; numquid inmature ab
5 Oceano?" Latini declamatores in descriptione Oceani non 15
nimis viguerunt; nam aut minus descripserunt aut nimis
curiose. nemo illorum potuit tanto spiritu dicere quanto
Pedo, qui in navigante Germanico dicit:

iamque vident[2] post terga diem solemque relictum
10    iam pridem[3] notis extorres finibus orbis
per non concessas audaces ire tenebras
ad rerum metas extremaque litora mundi;
nunc illum pigris immania monstra sub undis
qui ferat Oceanum, qui saevas undique pristis
15    aequoreosque canes, ratibus consurgere prensis.
accumulat fragor ipse metus. iam sidere limo
navigia et rapido desertam flamine classem
seque feris credunt per inertia fata marinis
iam non felici laniandos sorte relinqui.
20    atque aliquis prora caecum sublimis ab alta
aera pugnaci luctatus rumpere visu,
ut nihil erepto valuit dinoscere mundo,
obstructa in talis effundit pectora voces:
quo ferimur? fugit ipse dies orbemque relictum
25    ultima perpetuis claudit natura tenebris.
anne alio positas ultra sub cardine gentes
atque alium flabris intactum quaerimus orbem?
di revocant rerumque vetant cognoscere finem
mortales oculos: aliena quid aequora remis
30    et sacras violamus aquas divumque quietas
turbamus sedes?

ex Graecis declamatoribus nulli melius haec suasoria pro- 16
cessit quam Glyconi; sed non minus multa corrupte dixit
quam magnifice;[4] utrorumque faciam vobis potestatem. et
35 volebam vos experiri non adiciendo iudicium meum nec
separando a corruptis sana; potuisset enim fieri ut vos magis
illa laudaretis quae insaniunt. at nihilo minus poterit fieri,
quamvis distinxerim. illa belle dixit:....sed fecit, quod
solebat, ut sententiam adiectione supervacua atque tumida
40 perderet; adiecit enim:....illud quosdam dubios iudici sui
habet—ego non dubito contra sententiam ferre—: 'ὑγίαινε
γῆ, ὑγίαινε ἥλιε· Μακεδόνες ἄρα χάος εἰσάσσουσι.'

¹ Bᵒ sequar.                    ² Bᵒ and Müller, iam pridem.
³ Bᵒ and Müller, iamque vident.    ⁴ So Bᵒ after Thomas.

# SUASORIA II

Trecenti Lacones contra Xersen missi, cum treceni
ex omni Graecia missi fugissent, deliberant an
et ipsi fugiant.

ARELLI FUSCI PATRIS

1 At, puto, rudis lecta aetas et animus qui frangeretur metu, 5
insuetaque arma non passurae manus hebetataque senio aut
vulneribus corpora. quid dicam? potissimos Graeciae? an
Lacedaemoniorum electos?[1] an repetam tot acies patrum
totque excidia urbium, tot victarum gentium spolia? et nunc
produntur condita sine moenibus[2] templa? pudet consilii 10
nostri, pudet, etiamsi non fugimus, deliberasse talia. at cum
tot milibus Xerses venit. o Lacedaemonii, ite[3] adversus
barbaros; non refero opera vestra, non avos, non patres,
quorum vobis exemplo ab infantia surgit ingenium. pudet
Lacedaemonios sic adhortari: en,[4] loco tuti sumus. licet 15
totum classe Orientem trahat, licet metuentibus[5] explicet
inutilem[6] navium numerum: hoc mare quod tantum ex vasto[7]
patet, urguetur in minimum, insidiosis excipitur angustiis
vixque minimo aditus navigio est, et huius quoque remigium
arcet inquietum omne quod circumfluit mare, fallentia cursus 20
vada altioribus internata, aspera scopulorum et cetera quae
navigantium vota decipiunt. pudet, inquam, Lacedaemonios
2 et armatos quaerere quemadmodum tuti sint. non referam
Persarum spolia? certe super spolia nudus cadam. sciet et
alios habere nos trecentos qui sic non fugiant et sic cadant. 25
hunc sumite animum: nescio an vincere possimus; vinci non
possumus. haec non utique perituris refero; sed, si cadendum
est, erratis si metuendam creditis mortem. nulli natura in
aeternum spiritum dedit statque nascentibus in finem vitae
dies. ex inbecilla enim nos materia deus orsus est; quippe 30
minimis succidunt corpora. indenuntiata sorte rapimur; sub
eodem pueritia fato est, eadem iuventus causa cadit. optamus
quoque plerumque mortem; adeo in securam quietem recessus

---

[1] B⁰ and Müller, an Lacedaemonios? an electos?
[2] B⁰ his de manubiis.            [3] B⁰ ita.
[4] B⁰ hoc loco.                    [5] B⁰ and Müller, intuentibus.
[6] Müller, ingentem.               [7] B⁰ and Müller, ex vasto urguetur.

ex vita est. at gloriae nullus finis est proximeque deos sic
cadentes colunt;[1] feminis quoque frequens hoc in mortem
pro gloria iter est. quid Lycurgum, quid interritos omni
periculo quos memoria sacravit viros referam? ut unum
5 Othryadem excitem, adnumerare trecentis exempla possum.

TRIARI                                                                    3

Non pudet Laconas ne pugna quidem hostium, sed fabula
vinci? magnum est,[2] alimentum virtutis est nasci Laconem.
ad certam victoriam omnes remansissent; ad certam mortem
10 tantum Lacones. ne sit Sparta lapidibus circumdata: ibi
muros habet ubi viros. melius revocabimus fugientes trecenos
quam sequemur. sed montes perforat, maria contegit. numquam solido stetit superba felicitas, et ingentium imperiorum
magna fastigia oblivione fragilitatis humanae conlapsa sunt.
15 scias licet ad finem bonum non pervenisse quae ad invidiam
perducta sunt. maria terrasque, rerum naturam statione
mutavit sua: moriamur trecenti ut hic primum invenerit
quod mutare non posset. si tam demens placiturum consilium erat, cur non potius in turba fugimus?

20 PORCI LATRONIS                                                    4

In hoc scilicet morati sumus ut agmen fugientium cogeremus.
erimus inter fortes fugacissimi, inter fugaces tardissimi.
rumori terga vertitis? sciamus saltem quam fortis sit iste
quem fugimus. vix vel victoria dedecus elui potest: ut omnia
25 fortiter fiant, feliciter cadant, multum tamen nomini nostro
detractum est: iam Lacones an fugeremus deliberavimus.
atenim moriemur! quantum ad me quidem pertinet, post
hanc deliberationem nihil aliud timeo quam ne revertar.
arma nobis fabulae excutiunt? nunc, nunc pugnemus;
30 latuisset virtus inter trecenos. ceteri quidem fugerunt. si me
quidem interrogatis quid sentiam, et in nostrum et in
Graeciae patrocinium loquar: electi sumus, non relicti.

GAVI SABINI                                                           5

Turpe est cuilibet viro fugisse, Laconi etiam deliberasse de
35 fuga.

MARULLI

In hoc restitimus ne in turba fugientium lateremus. habent

---

1 Müller, proximique deos sic †ageses agunt.
2 B⁰ deletes *est*.

quemadmodum se excusent Graeciae treceni : " tutas Thermopylas putavimus cum relinqueremus illic Laconas ".

CESTI PII

Quam turpe esset fugere iudicastis, Lacones, tam diu non
fugiendo. omnibus sua decora sunt. Athenae eloquentia 5
inclitae sunt, Thebae sacris, Sparta armis. ideo hanc Eurotas
amnis circum fluit, qui pueritiam indurat ad futurae militiae
patientiam? ideo[1] Taygeti nemoris difficilia nisi Laconibus
iuga? ideo Hercule gloriamur deo operibus caelum merito?
6 ideo muri nostri arma sunt? o grave maiorum virtutis 10
dedecus! Lacones se numerant, non aestimant. videamus
quanta turba sit, ut habeat certe Sparta etiamsi non fortes
milites at nuntios veros. ita ne bello quidem, sed nuntio
vincimur? merito, hercules, omnia contempsit quem Lacones
audire non sustinent. si vincere Xersen non licet, videre 15
liceat; volo scire quid fugiam. adhuc non sum ex ulla parte
Atheniensium similis, non muris[2] nec educatione; nihil prius
illorum imitabor quam fugam?

7 POMPEI SILONIS

Xerses multos secum adducit, Thermopylae paucos recipiunt. 20
nihil refert quantas gentes in orbem nostrum Oriens effuderit
quantumque nationum secum Xerses trahat; tot ad nos per-
tinent quot locus ceperit.

CORNELI HISPANI

Pro Sparta venimus, pro Graecia stemus; vincamus hostes, 25
socios iam vicimus; sciat iste insolens barbarus nihil esse
difficilius quam Laconis armati latus fodere. ego vero quod
treceni discesserunt gaudeo; liberas nobis reliquere Thermopylas; nil erit quod virtuti nostrae se apponat, quod se in-
serat; non latebit in turba Laco; quocumque Xerses aspexerit, 30
Spartanos videbit.

8 BLANDI

Referam praecepta matrum: "aut in his aut cum his?"
minus turpe est a bello inermem reverti quam armatum
fugere. referam captivorum verba? captus Laco: "occide", 35
inquit, "non servio". potuit[3] non capi si fugere voluisset.
(describite terrores Persicos); omnia ista, cum mitteremur,

---

[1] B⁰ and Müller insert *enitimur in.*
[2] B⁰ moribus.        [3] Müller, non potuit.

audivimus. videat trecentos Xerses et sciat quanti bellum
aestimatum sit, quanto aptus numero locus. revertamur ne
nuntii quidem nisi novissimi. quis fugerit nescio; hos mihi
Sparta commilitones dedit. (descriptio Thermopylarum.)
5 nunc me delectat quod fugerunt treceni; angustas mihi
Thermopylas fecerunt.[1]

CONTRA. CORNELI HISPANI                              9

At ego maximum video dedecus futurum rei publicae nostrae,
si Xerses nihil prius in Graecia vicerit quam Laconas. ne
10 testem quidem virtutis nostrae habere possumus; id de nobis
credetur quod hostes narraverint. habetis consilium meum;
id est autem meum quod totius Graeciae. si quis aliud
suadet, non fortes vos vult esse sed perditos.

CLAUDI MARCELLI

15 Non vincent nos, sed obruent. satis fecimus nomini, ultumi
cessimus; ante nos rerum natura victa est.

DIVISIO                                             10

Huius suasoriae feci mentionem non quia in ea subtilitatis
erat aliquid quod vos excitare posset, sed ut sciretis quam
20 nitide Fuscus dixisset vel quam licenter; ipse sententiam non
feram; vestri arbitrii erit utrum explicationes eius luxuriosas
putetis an vegetas. Pollio Asinius aiebat hoc non esse suadere,
sed ludere. recolo nihil fuisse me iuvene tam notum quam
has explicationes Fusci, quas nemo nostrum non alius alia
25 inclinatione vocis velut sua quisque modulatione cantabat.
at[2] quia semel in mentionem incidi Fusci, ex omnibus
suasoriis celebres descriptiunculas subtexam, etiamsi nihil
occurrerit quod quisquam alius nisi suasor dilexerit. divisione 11
autem in hac suasoria Fuscus usus est illa volgari ut diceret
30 non esse honestum fugere, etiamsi tutum esset: deinde: aeque
periculosum esse fugere et pugnare; novissime: periculosius
esse fugere: pugnantibus hostes timendos, fugientibus et
hostes et suos. Cestius primam partem sic transit[3] quasi
nemo dubitaret an turpe esset fugere; deinde illo transit, an
35 non esset necesse. "haec sunt," inquit, "quae vos confundunt:
hostes,[4] sociorum fuga, vestra ipsorum paucitas." non quidem
in hac suasoria sed in hac materia disertissima illa fertur
sententia Dorionis, cum posuisset hoc dixisse trecentis

---

[1] B⁰ fecerant.                    [2] B⁰ *et.*
[3] B⁰ tractavit.                   [4] B⁰ hostium copia, vestrorum paucitas.

Leonidam, quod puto etiam apud Herodotum esse: ⟨ἀριστο-
12 ποιεῖσθε ὡς ἐν" Ἀιδου δειπνησόμενοι⟩,.. Sabinus Asilius, venustissimus inter rhetoras scurra, cum hanc sententiam Leonidae
rettulisset, ait: "ego illi ad prandium promisissem, ad cenam
renuntiassem." Attalus Stoicus, qui solum vertit a Seiano 5
circumscriptus, magnae vir eloquentiae, ex his philosophis
quos vestra aetas vidit longe et subtilissimus et facundissimus,
cum tam magna et nobili sententia certavit et mihi dixisse
videtur animosius quam prior:....occurrit mihi sensus in
eiusmodi materia a Severo Cornelio dictus tamquam de 10
Romanis nescio an parum fortiter. edicta in posterum diem
pugna epulantes milites inducit et ait:

stratique per herbam
"hic meus est", dixere, "dies".

elegantissime quidem adfectum animorum incerta sorte pen- 15
dentium expressit, sed parum Romani animi servata est
magnitudo; cenant enim tamquam crastinum desperent.
quantum illis Laconibus animi erat qui non poterant[1] dicere:
13 "hic dies est meus". illud Porcellus grammaticus arguebat
in hoc versu quasi soloecismum, quod cum plures induxisset, 20
diceret: "hic meus est dies", non: "hic noster est", et in
sententia optima id accusabat quod erat optimum. muta enim
ut "noster" sit, peribit omnis versus elegantia, in quo hoc
est decentissimum quod ex communi sermone trahitur; nam
quasi proverbii loco est: "hic dies meus est"; et, cum ad 25
sensum rettuleris, ne grammaticorum quidem calumnia ab
omnibus magnis ingeniis summovenda habebit locum: dixerunt enim non omnes simul tamquam in choro manum
ducente grammatico, sed singuli ex iis: "hic meus est dies".
14 sed ut revertar ad Leonidam et trecentos, pulcherrima illa 30
fertur Glyconis sententia:....in hac ipsa suasoria non sane
refero memoria dignam ullam sententiam Graeci cuiusquam
nisi Damae: ποῖ φεύξεσθε, ὁπλῖται, τείχη; de positione loci
eleganter dixit Haterius, cum angustias loci facundissime
descripsisset: "natus trecentis locus". Cestius cum de- 35
scripsisset honores quos habituri essent si pro patria cecidis-
sent, adiecit: "per sepulchra nostra iurabitur". Nicetes longe
disertius hanc phantasiam movit et adiecit:....[2] nitide nisi

[1] Bº poterant non dicere.
[2] Müller,...nisi antiquior Xerses fuisset quam Demosthenes †CIPTOY
cui dicere.

antiquior Xerses fuisset quam ut illum Demosthenis ὅρκου
hic dicere liceret. hanc suam dixit sententiam aut certe non
deprehensam, cum descripsisset oportunitatem loci et tuta
undique pugnantium latera et angustias a tergo positas, sed
5 adversas hostibus.... Potamon magnus declamator fuit Mity- 15
lenis, qui eodem tempore viguit quo Lesbocles magni nominis
et nomini respondentis ingenii; in quibus quanta fuerit
animorum diversitas in simili fortuna puto vobis indicandum,
multo magis quia ad vitam pertinet quam si ad eloquentiam
10 pertineret. utrique filius eisdem diebus decessit: Lesbocles
scholam solvit; nemo umquam postea declamantem audivit;
ampliore animo se gessit Potamon: a funere filii contulit
se in scholam et declamavit. utriusque tamen adfectum
temperandum puto: hic durius tulit fortunam quam patrem
15 decebat, ille mollius quam virum. Potamon, cum suasoriam 16
de trecentis diceret, tractabat quam turpiter fecissent Lacones
hoc ipsum quod deliberassent de fuga, et sic novissime
clausit:.... insanierunt in hac suasoria multi circa Othryadem: Murredius qui dixit: "fugerunt Athenienses: non
20 enim Othryadis nostri litteras didicerant". Gargonius dixit:
"Othryades qui periit ut falleret, revixit ut vinceret". Licinius
Nepos: "eius exemplo vobis etiam mortuis vincendum fuit".
Antonius Atticus inter has pueriles sententias videtur palmam
meruisse; dixit enim: "Othryades paene a sepulchro victor
25 digitis vulnera pressit ut tropaeo Laconem inscriberet.
o dignum Spartano atramentum! o virum, cuius ne litterae
quidem fuere sine sanguine!" Catius Crispus, municipalis
orator, cacozelos dixit post relatum exemplum Othryadis:
"aliud ceteros, aliud Laconas decet: nos sine deliciis educamur,
30 sine muris vivimus, sine vita vincimus". Seneca fuit, cuius 17
nomen ad vos potuit pervenisse, ingenii confusi ac turbulenti,
qui cupiebat grandia dicere adeo ut novissime morbo huius
rei et teneretur et rideretur; nam et servos nolebat habere
nisi grandes et argentea vasa non nisi grandia. credatis mihi
35 velim non iocanti, eo pervenit insania eius ut calceos quoque
maiores sumeret, ficus non esset nisi mariscas, concubinam
ingentis staturae haberet. omnia grandia probanti inpositum
est cognomen vel, ut Messala ait, cognomentum, et vocari
coepit Seneca Grandio. aliquando iuvene me is in hac
40 suasoria, cum posuisset contradictionem: "at omnes qui missi
erant a Graecia fugerunt", sublatis manibus, insistens summis

digitis—sic enim solebat quo grandior fieret—exclamat:
"gaudeo, gaudeo". mirantibus nobis quod tantum illi bonum
contigisset, adiecit: "totus Xerses meus erit". item dixit: "iste
qui classibus suis maria subripuit, qui terras circumscripsit,
dilatavit profundum, novam rerum naturae faciem imperat, 5
ponat sane contra caelum castra, commilitones habebo deos".

18 Senianus multo inpotentius[1] dixit: "terras armis obsidet,
caelum sagittis, maria vinculis: Lacones, nisi succurritis,
mundus captus est". decentissimi generis stultam sententiam
referam Victoris Statori, municipis mei, cuius fabulis memoria 10
dignissimis aliquis delectetur. is huius suasoriae occasione
sumpsit contradictionem: "at", inquit, "trecenti sumus"; et
ita respondit: "trecenti, sed viri, sed armati, sed Lacones, sed

19 ad Thermopylas; numquam vidi plures trecentos". Latro in
hac suasoria, cum tractasset omnia quae materia capiebat, 15
posse ipsos et vincere, posse certe invictos reverti ait beneficio
loci; tum illam sententiam: "si nihil aliud, erimus certe
belli mora". postea memini auditorem Latronis Arbronium
Silonem, patrem huius Silonis qui pantomimis fabulas scripsit
et ingenium grande non tantum deseruit sed polluit, recitare 20
carmen, in quo agnovimus sensum Latronis in his versibus:

> ite agite, O Danai, magnum paeana canentes,
> ite triumphantes: belli mora concidit Hector.

tam diligentes tunc auditores erant, ne dicam tam maligni,
ut unum verbum surripi non posset; at nunc cuilibet 25
20 orationem in Verrem tuto licet dicere pro sua. sed, ut
sciatis sensum bene dictum dici tamen posse melius, notate
prae ceteris quanto decentius Vergilius dixerit hoc quod
valde erat celebre, "belli mora concidit Hector":

> quidquid ad adversae cessatum est moenia Troiae,       30
> Hectoris Aeneaeque manu victoria Graium
> haesit.

Messala aiebat hic Vergilium debuisse desinere: quod sequitur

> et in decimum vestigia rettulit annum

explementum esse, Maecenas hoc etiam priori conparabat. 35
sed ut ad Thermopylas revertar, Diocles Carystius dixit...
21 Apaturius dixit...Corvo rhetori testimonium stuporis red-
dendum est, qui dixit: "quidni, si iam Xerses ad nos suo
mari navigat, fugiamus antequam nobis terra subripiatur?"

---

[1] Müller, potentius.

hic est Corvus qui, cum temperaret scholam Romae, Sosio
illi qui Iudaeos subegerat declamavit controversiam de ea
quae apud matronas disserebat liberos non esse tollendos et
ob hoc accusatur rei publicae laesae. in hac controversia
5 sententia eius haec ridebatur: "inter pyxides et redolentis
animae medicamina constitit mitrata contio". sed, si vultis,
historicum quoque vobis fatuum dabo. Tuscus ille qui  22
Scaurum Mamercum, in quo Scaurorum familia extincta est,
maiestatis reum fecerat, homo quam inprobi animi, tam in-
10 felicis ingenii, cum hanc suasoriam declamaret, dixit: "ex-
pectemus, si nihil aliud, hoc effecturi ne insolens barbarus
dicat: 'veni, vidi, vici '", cum hoc post multos annos Divus
Iulius victo Pharnace dixerit. Dorion dixit: ἄνδρες....aiebat
Nicocrates Lacedaemonius insignem hanc sententiam futuram
15 fuisse, si media intercideretur. sed ne vos diutius infatuem,  23
quia dixeram me Fusci Arelli explicationes subiecturum, hic
finem suasoriae faciam. quarum nimius cultus et fracta
conpositio poterit vos offendere cum ad meam aetatem
veneritis; interim non dubito quin nunc vos ipsa quae
20 offensura sunt vitia delectent.

# SUASORIA III

Deliberat Agamemnon an Iphigeniam immolet ne
gante Calchante aliter navigari fas esse

**1** ARELLI FUSCI PATRIS

Non in aliam condicionem deus fudit aequora quam ne omnis
ex voto iret dies; nec ea sors mari tantum est: caelum specta; 5
non sub eadem condicione sidera sunt? alias negatis imbribus
exurunt solum, et miseri cremata agricolae lugent semina, et
haec interdum anno lex est; alias serena clauduntur, et omnis
dies caelum nubilo gravat: subsidit solum, et creditum sibi
terra non retinet; alias incertus sideribus cursus est, et 10
variantur tempora, neque soles nimiś urguent neque ultra
debitum imbres cadunt: quidquid asperatum aestu est, quidquid nimio diffluxit imbre, invicem temperatur altero; sive
ista natura disposuit, sive, ut ferunt, luna cursu gerit—quae,
sive plena lucis suae est splendensque pariter adsurgit in 15
cornua, imbres prohibet, sive occurrente nubilo sordidiorem
ostendit orbem suum, non ante finit quam lucem reddit—sive
ne lunae quidem ista potentia est, sed flatus qui[1] occupavere,
annum tenent: quidquid horum est, extra iussum dei tutum
fuit adultero mare. at non potero vindicare adulteram: prior 20
est salus pudicae. ne quid huius virginitati timerem persequebar adulterum: victa Troia virginibus hostium parcam;
nihil adhuc virgo Priami timet.

**2** CESTI PII

Vos ergo, di immortales, invoco: sic reclusuri estis maria? 25
obserate potius. ne Priami quidem liberos immolaturus es.
describe nunc tempestatem: omnia ista patimur nec[2] parricidium fecimus. quod hoc sacrum est virginis deae templo
virginem occidere? libentius hanc sacerdotem habebit quam
victimam.                                                        30

CORNELI HISPANI

Infestae sunt, inquit, tempestates et saeviunt maria, neque
adhuc parricidium feci. ista maria, si numine suo deus
regeret, adulteris clauderentur.

---

[1] B⁰ qui caelum.               [2] B⁰ nec adhuc.

MARULLI

Si non datur nobis[1] ad bellum iter, revertamur ad liberos.

ARGENTARI

Iterum in malum familiae nostrae fatale revolvimur: propter
5 adulteram fratris liberi pereunt. ista mercede nolo illam
reverti. at Priamus bellum pro adultero filio gerit.

DIVISIO                                                          3

Hanc suasoriam sic divisit Fuscus ut diceret, etiamsi aliter
navigari non posset non esse faciendum. hoc sic tractavit
10 ut negaret faciendum, quia homicidium esset, quia parricidium, quia plus inpenderetur quam peteretur: peti
Helenam, inpendi Iphigeniam; vindicari adulterium, com-
mitti parricidium. deinde dixit, etiamsi non immolasset, navi-
gaturum; illam enim moram naturae maris et ventorum
15 esse: deorum voluntatem ab hominibus non intellegi. hoc
Cestius diligenter divisit; dixit enim deos rebus humanis non
interponere arbitrium suum; ut interponant, voluntatem
eorum ab homine non intellegi; ut intellegatur, non posse
fata revocari. si non sint fata, nesciri futura; si sint, non
20 posse mutari. Silo Pompeius, etiamsi quod esset divinandi 4
genus certum, auguriis negavit credendum: "quare ergo, si
nescit Calchas, adfirmat? primum scire se putat"—hic
communem locum dixit in omnes qui hanc adfectarent
scientiam—; "deinde irascitur tibi, invitus militat, quaerit
25 sibi tam magno testimonio apud omnes gentes fidem". in ea
descriptione quam primam in hac suasoria posui, Fuscus
Arellius Vergilii versus voluit imitari; valde autem longe
petit et paene repugnante materie,[2] certe non desiderante,
inseruit. ait enim de luna: "quae, sive plena lucis suae est
30 splendensque pariter assurgit in cornua, imbres prohibet, sive
occupata nubilo sordidiorem ostendit orbem suum, non ante
finit quam lucem reddit". at Vergilius haec quanto et 5
simplicius et beatius dixit:

luna, revertentes cum primum colligit ignes,
35      si nigrum obscuro comprenderit aera cornu,
maximus agricolis pelagoque parabitur imber.

et rursus:

sin ortu quarto, namque is certissimus auctor,
pura nec obtunsis per caelum cornibus ibit.

_____

[1] B⁰ nobis aliter.            [2] B⁰ materia.

solebat autem Fuscus ex Vergilio multa trahere ut Maecenati
imputaret: totiens enim pro beneficio narrabat in aliqua se
Vergiliana descriptione placuisse; sicut in hac ipsa suasoria
dixit: "cur iste¹ in interpretis ministerium placuit? cur hoc
os deus elegit? cur hoc sortitur potissimum pectus quod 5
tanto numine impleat?" aiebat se imitatum esse Vergilianum
6 "plena deo". solet autem Gallio noster hoc aptissime
ponere. memini una nos ab auditione Nicetis ad Messalam
venisse. Nicetes suo impetu valde Graecis placuerat. quaere-
bat a Gallione Messala quid illi visus esset Nicetes? Gallio 10
ait: "plena deo". quotiens audierat aliquem ex his declamatoribus quos scholastici caldos vocant, statim dicebat:
"plena deo". ipse Messala numquam aliter illum ab novi
hominis auditione venientem interrogavit quam ut diceret:
"numquid plena deo?" itaque hoc ipsi iam tam familiare 15
7 erat ut invito quoque excideret. apud Caesarem cum mentio
esset de ingenio Hateri, consuetudine prolapsus dixit: "et ille
erat plena deo". quaerenti deinde quid hoc esse vellet, versum
Vergilii rettulit, et quomodo hoc semel sibi apud Messalam
excidisset et numquam non postea potuisset excidere. 20
Tiberius ipse Theodoreus offendebatur Nicetis ingenio;
itaque delectatus est fabula Gallionis; hoc autem dicebat
Gallio Nasoni suo valde placuisse; itaque fecisse illum² quod
in multis aliis versibus Vergilii fecerat, non subrupiendi
causa, sed palam mutuandi, hoc animo ut vellet agnosci: esse 25
autem in tragoedia eius:

> feror huc illuc, vae, plena deo.

iam, si vultis, ad Fuscum revertar et descriptionibus eius
vos statim³ satiabo ac potissimum eis quas in verisimili-
tudinis⁴ tractatione posuit, cum diceret omnino non con- 30
cessam futurorum scientiam.

¹ B⁰ iste vates et ejus ministerium.
² B⁰ illum suum.                    ³ B⁰ affatim.
⁴ B⁰ in simili huic tractatione.

## SUASORIA IV

## Deliberat Alexander Magnus an Babylona intret, cum denuntiatum esset illi responso auguris periculum.

ARELLI FUSCI　　　　　　　　　　　　　　　　　I

5 Quis est qui futurorum scientiam sibi vindicet? novae oportet sortis is sit qui iubente deo canat, non eodem contentus utero quo inprudentes nascimur; quandam imaginem dei praeferat qui iussa exhibeat dei. sic est; tantum enim regem tantique rectorem orbis in metum cogit. magnus iste et supra
10 humanae sortis habitum sit cui liceat terrere Alexandrum: ponat iste suos inter sidera patres et originem caelo trahat, agnoscat suum vatem deus; non eodem vitae fine,[1] extra omnem fatorum necessitatem caput sit quod gentibus futura praecipiat. si vera sunt ista, quid ita non huic studio servit
15 omnis aetas? cur non ab infantia rerum naturam deosque qua licet visimus, cum pateant nobis sidera et interesse numinibus liceat? quid ita in inutili desudamus facundia aut periculosis atteritur armis manus? an melius alio pignore quam futuri scientia ingenia surrexerint? qui vero in media 2
20 se, ut praedicant, fatorum misere pignora, natales inquirunt et primam aevi horam omnium annorum habent nuntiam; quo ierint motu sidera, in quas discucurrerint partes, contrane durus[2] steterit an placidus adfulserit Sol: plenam lucem an initia surgentis acceperit, an abdiderit in noctem obscurum
25 caput Luna; Saturnus nascentem ad cultum agrorum, an ad bella Mars militem, an negotiosum in quaestus Mercurius exceperit, an blanda adnuerit nascenti Venus, an ex humili in sublime Iupiter tulerit, aestimant: tot circa unum caput tumultuantis deos! futura nuntiant: plerosque diu dixere 3
30 victuros, at nihil metuentis[3] oppressit dies; aliis dedere finem propincum, at illi superfuere agentes inutilis animas: felices nascentibus annos spoponderunt, at Fortuna in omnem properavit iniuriam. incertae enim sortis vivimus: unicuique ista pro ingenio finguntur, non ex fide scientiae[4] eruuntur.

---

[1] The MSS. after *fine* read *aetate magna* bracketed by Müller, emended to *non aetate maligna* by B⁰.

[2] B⁰ *dirus*.　　[3] B⁰ *mox oppressit*.　　[4] B⁰ *ex siderum scientia*.

erit aliquis orbe toto locus qui te victorem non viderit?
Babylon ei cluditur cui patuit Oceanus?

4 DIVISIO

In hac suasoria nihil aliud tractasse Fuscum scio quam
easdem quas supra rettuli quaestiones ad scientiam futuri 5
pertinentis. illud quod nos delectavit, praeterire non possum.
declamitarat Fuscus Arellius controversiam de illa quae,
postquam ter mortuos pepererat, somniasse se dixit ut in
luco pareret. valde in vos contumeliosus fuero, si totam
controversiam, quam ego intellego vos scire, fusius ex- 10
posuero¹....Fuscus, cum declamaret et a parte avi non
agnoscentis puerum tractaret locum contra somnia et deorum
providentiam et male de magnitudine eorum dixisset mereri
eum qui illos circa puerperas mitteret, summis clamoribus
illum dixit Vergili versum: 15

scilicet is superis labor est, ea cura quietos
sollicitat.

5 auditor Fusci quidam, cuius pudori parco, cum hanc suasoriam de Alexandro ante Fuscum diceret, putavit aeque
belle poni eundem versum et dixit: 20

scilicet is superis labor est, ea cura quietos
sollicitat.

Fuscus illi ait: "si hoc dixisses audiente Alexandro, scisses
apud Vergilium et illum versum esse:

capulo tenus abdidit ensem". 25

et quia soletis mihi molesti esse de Fusco, quid fuerit quare
nemo videretur dixisse cultius, ingeram vobis Fuscinas explicationes. dicebat autem suasorias libentissime et frequentius Graecas quam Latinas. Hybreas in hac suasoria
dixit: οἷον ἔσχηκε Βαβυλὼν μάντιν ὀχύρωμα. 30

¹ B⁰ and Müller, me dicere....Fuscus.

# SUASORIA V

## Deliberant Athenienses an tropaea Persica tollant, Xerse minante rediturum se nisi tollerentur

ARELLI FUSCI I

5 Pudet me victoriae vestrae, si sic fugatum creditis Xersem ut reverti possit. tot caesa milia, nihil ex tanta acie relictum minanti, nisi quod vix fugientem sequi possit; totiens mersa classis; quid Marathona, quid Salamina referam? pudet dicere: dubitamus adhuc an vicerimus. Xerses veniet?
10 nescio quomodo languet circa memoriam iacturae animus et disturbata arma non[1] repetit. prior enim metus futuri pignus est et amissa, ne audeat, amissurum monent. ut interdum in gaudio surgit animus et spem ex praesenti metitur, ita adversis frangitur: omnis deficit animum fides ubi ignominia
15 spem premit, ubi nullam meminit aciem nisi qua fugerit; haeret circa damna sua et quae male expertus est vota deponit. si venturus esset, non minaretur: suis ira ardet ignibus et in pacta non solvitur. non denuntiaret si venturus esset, neque 2 armaret nos nuntio nec instigaret victricem Graeciam nec
20 sollicitaret arma felicia: magis superveniret inprovidis; nam et antea arma indenuntiata moverat. quantumcumque Oriens valuit primo in Graeciam impetu effusum est: hoc ille numero ferox et in deos arma tulerat. extincta tot ante Xersen milia, tot sub ipso, iacent: nulli nisi qui fugerunt
25 supersunt. quid dicam Salamina? quid Cynaegiron referam et te, Polyzele? et hoc agitur an vicerimus? haec ego tropaea dis posui,[2] haec in totius conspectu Graeciae statui, ne quis timeret Xersen minantem. me miserum! pugnante Xerse tropaea posui: fugiente tollam? nunc Athenae vincimur: non
30 tantum credetur redisse, sed vicisse Xerses. non potest 3 Xerses nisi per nos tropaea tollere. credite mihi, difficile est attritas opes recolligere et spes fractas novare et ex paenitenda acie in melioris eventus fiduciam surgere.

CESTI PII

35 Inferam, inquit, bellum. alia mihi tropaea promittit. potest maior venire quam quom victus est?

---

[1] B⁰ omits *non*.                    [2] B⁰ deposui.

ARGENTARI

Non pudet vos? pluris tropaea vestra Xerses aestumat quam vos.

4 DIVISIO

Fuscus sic divisit: etiamsi venturus est Xerses, nisi tollimus, 5 non sunt tropaea tollenda: confessio servitutis est iussa facere. si venerit, vincemus: hoc non est diu colligendum; de eo dico "vincemus" quem vicimus. sed ne veniet quidem: si venturus esset non denuntiaret; fractus est et viribus et animo. Cestius et illud adiecit, quod in prima parte tractavit, 10 non licere Atheniensibus tropaea tollere: commune in illis ius totius Graeciae esse; commune bellum fuisse, communem victoriam. deinde ne fas quidem esse: numquam factum ut quisquam consecratis virtutis suae operibus manus adferret. "ista tropaea non sunt Atheniensium, deorum sunt: illorum 15 bellum fuit, illos Xerses vinculis, illos sagittis persequebatur". hic omnia ad impiam et superbam Xersis militiam pertinentia. 5 "quid ergo? bellum habebimus? habuimus et habebimus: si Xersem removeris, invenietur alius hostis: numquam magna imperia otiosa". (enumeratio bellorum prospere ab Athenien- 20 sibus gestorum.) deinde: "non erit bellum; Xerses enim non veniet". multo timidiores esse quom superbissimi fuerint. novissime: "ut veniat, cum quibus veniet? reliquias victoriae nostrae colliget; illos adducet quos priore bello quasi inutiles reliquit domi et si qui ex fuga conservati sunt. nullum habet 25 6 militem nisi aut fastiditum aut victum". Argentarius his duobus contentus fuit: aut non venturum Xersen aut non esse metuendum, si venerit. his solis institit et illud dixit, quod exceptum est: "'tollite' inquit 'tropaea'. si vicisti, quid erubescis? si victus es, quid imperas?" locum movit 30 non inutiliter: iudicare quidem se neque Xersen neque iam quemquam Persarum ausurum in Graeciam effundi; sed eo magis tropaea ipsis tuenda, si quis umquam illinc venturus hostis esset, ut conspectu tropaeorum animi militum accen- 7 derentur, hostium frangerentur. Blandus dixit: "repleat ipse 35 prius Atho et maria in antiquam faciem reducat. apparere vult posteris quemadmodum venerit; appareat quemad- modum redierit". Triarius omni dimissa divisione tantum exultavit quod Xersen audiret venire: adesse ipsis novam victoriam, nova tropaea. Silo Pompeius venusto genere 40 sententiae usus est: "nisi tollitis" inquit "tropaea, ego veniam". hoc ait Xerses: "nisi haec tropaea tollitis, alia ponetis".

Alteram partem solus Gallio declamavit et hortatus ad 8
5 tollenda tropaea dixit gloriae nihil detrahi; mansuram enim memoriam victoriae, quae perpetua esset; ipsa tropaea et tempestatibus et aetate consumi; bellum suscipiendum fuisse pro libertate, pro coniugibus, pro liberis: pro re supervacua et nihil nocitura si defieret, non esse suscipiendum. hic
10 dixit utique venturum Xersen et descripsit adversus ipsos deos tumentem; deinde habere illum magnas vires: neque omnes illum copias in Graeciam perduxisse nec omnes in Graecia perdidisse; timendam esse fortunae varietatem; exhaustas esse Graeciae vires nec posse iam pati alterum
15 bellum; illi esse inmensam multitudinem hominum. hoc loco disertissimam sententiam dixit dignam quae vel in oratione vel in historia ponatur: "diutius illi perire possunt quam nos vincere".

# SUASORIA VI

## Deliberat Cicero an Antonium deprecetur

**1** Q. HATERI

Sciant posteri potuisse Antonio servire rempublicam, non potuisse Ciceronem. laudandus erit tibi Antonius; in hac causa etiam Ciceronem verba deficient. crede mihi, cum 5 diligenter te custodieris, faciet tamen Antonius quod Cicero tacere non possit. si intellegis, Cicero, non dicit "roga ut vivas", sed "roga ut servias". quemadmodum autem hunc senatum intrare poteris, exhaustum crudeliter, repletum turpiter? intrare autem tu senatum voles in quo non Cn. 10 Pompeium visurus es, non M. Catonem, non Lucullos, non Hortensium, non Lentulum atque Marcellum, non tuos, inquam,[1] consules Hirtium ac Pansam? Cicero, quid in **2** alieno saeculo tibi? iam nostra peracta sunt. M. Cato, solus maximum vivendi moriendique exemplum, mori maluit quam 15 rogare—nec erat Antonium rogaturus—et illas usque ad ultimum diem puras a civili sanguine manus in pectus sacerrimum armavit. Scipio cum gladium in pectus abdidisset, quaerentibus qui in navem transierant militibus imperatorem "imperator", inquit, "bene se habet". victus vocem victoris 20 emisit. "vetat", inquis, "me Milo rogare iudices"; i nunc et Antonium roga.

**3** PORCI LATRONIS

Ergo loquitur umquam Cicero ut non timeat Antonius, loquitur umquam Antonius ut Cicero timeat? civilis sanguinis 25 Sullana sitis in civitatem redit, et ad triumviralem hastam pro vectigalibus civium Romanorum mortes locantur; unius tabellae albo Pharsalica ac Mundensis Mutinensisque ruina vincitur, consularia capita auro rependuntur: tuis verbis, Cicero, utendum est: "o tempora, o mores!". videbis[2] 30 ardentes crudelitate simul ac superbia oculos; videbis illum non hominis, sed belli civilis vultum; videbis illas fauces, per quas bona Cn. Pompei transierunt, illa latera, illam totius corporis gladiatoriam firmitatem: videbis illum pro tribunali locum quem modo magister equitum, cui ructare turpe erat, 35

---

[1] B⁰ tuos denique consules.    [2] B⁰ illos ardentes.

vomitu foedaverat: supplex accadens genibus deprecaberis?
eo ore cui se debet salus publica, humilia in adulationem verba
summittes? pudeat; Verres quoque proscriptus fortius perit.

CLAUDI MARCELLI AESERNINI                                    4
5 Occurrat tibi Cato tuus cuius a te laudata mors est: quicquam
ergo tanti putas ut vitam Antonio debeas?

CESTI PII
Si ad desiderium populi respicis, Cicero, quandoque perieris
parum vixisti; si ad res gestas, satis vixisti; si ad iniurias
10 Fortunae et praesentem rei publicae statum, nimium diu
vixisti; si ad memoriam operum tuorum, semper victurus es.

POMPEI SILONIS
Scias licet tibi non expedire vivere, si Antonius permittit ut
vivas. tacebis ergo proscribente Antonio et rem publicam
15 laniante, et ne gemitus quidem tuus liber erit? malo populus
Romanus mortuum Ciceronem quam vivum desideret.

TRIARI                                                      5
"Quae Charybdis est tam vorax? Charybdim dixi, quae si
fuit, animal unum fuit; vix me dius fidius Oceanus tot res
20 tamque diversas uno tempore absorbere potuisset". huic tu
saevienti putas Ciceronem posse subduci?

ARELLI FUSCI PATRIS
Ab armis ad arma discurritur; foris victores domi trucidamur,
domi nostro sanguini intestinus hostis incubat; quis non hoc
25 populi Romani statu Ciceronem ut non[1] vivat cogi putat?
rogabis, Cicero, turpiter Antonium, rogabis frustra. non te
ignobilis tumulus abscondet; nec idem virtutis tuae qui vitae
finis est. immortalis humanorum operum custos memoria,
qua magnis viris vita perpetua est, in omnia te saecula sacratum
30 dabit; nihil aliud intercidet quam corpus fragilitatis caducae, 6
morbis obnoxium, casibus expositum, proscriptionibus ob-
iectum; animus vero divina origine haustus, cui nec senectus
ulla nec mors, onerosi corporis vinculis exsolutus ad sedes
suas et cognata sidera recurret. et tamen, si ad aetatem
35 annorumque numquam observatum viris fortibus numerum
respicimus, sexaginta supergressus es, nec potes non videri
nimis vixisse qui moreris rei publicae superstes. vidimus

---

[1] B⁰ omits *non*.

furentia toto orbe civilia arma, et post Italicas Pharsaliasque
acies Romanum sanguinem hausit Aegyptus. quid indignamur in Ciceronem Antonio licere quod in Pompeium
Alexandrino licuit spadoni? sic occiduntur qui ad indignos
confugiunt.                                                        5

**7** CORNELI HISPANI

Proscriptus est ille qui tuam sententiam secutus est: tota
tabula tuae morti proluditur; alter fratrem proscribi, alter
avunculum patitur; quid habes spei? ut Cicero periret tot
parricidia facta sunt. repete agedum tot patrocinia, tot 10
clientelas et maximum beneficiorum tuorum, consulatum
ipsum: iam intelleges Ciceronem in mortem cogi posse, in
preces non posse.

ARGENTARI

Explicantur triumviralis regni delicata convivia, et popina 15
tributo gentium instruitur; ipse vino et somno marcidus
deficientes oculos ad capita proscriptorum levat. iam ad ista
non satis est dicere: hominem nequam!

**8** DIVISIO

Latro sic hanc divisit suasoriam; etiamsi impetrare vitam ab 20
Antonio potes, non est tanti rogare; deinde: impetrare non
potes. in priore illa parte posuit turpe esse cuilibet Romano,
nedum Ciceroni, vitam rogare; hoc loco hominum qui ultro
mortem adprehendissent exempla posuit. deinde: vilis illi
vita futura est et morte gravior detracta libertate. hic omnem 25
acerbitatem servitutis futurae descripsit. deinde: non futurum
fidei intemeratae beneficium. hic cum dixisset: [1] "aliquid
erit, quod Antonium offendat, aut factum tuum aut dictum
aut silentium aut vultus", adiecit sententiam: "haud enim[2]
**9** placiturus es". Albucius aliter divisit; primam partem fecit: 30
moriendum esse Ciceroni, etiamsi nemo proscriberet eum.
hic insectatio temporum fuit. deinde: moriendum esse illi
sua sponte, quom moriendum esset etiamsi mori noluisset;
graves odiorum causas esse; maximam causam proscriptionis
ipsum esse Ciceronem. et solus ex declamatoribus temptavit 35
dicere non unum illi esse Antonium infestum. hoc loco dixit
illam sententiam: "si cui ex triumviris non es invisus, gravis
es", et illam sententiam quae valde excepta est: "roga,

---

[1] B⁰ semper aliquid erit.
[2] Müller, aude perire; B⁰ haud enim.

Cicero, exora unum ut tribus servias". Cestius sic divisit: 10
mori tibi utile est, honestum est, necesse est, ut liber et
inlibatae dignitatis consummes vitam. hic illam sententiam
dixit audacem: "ut numereris cum Catone qui servire ne
5 Antonio quidem nondum domino potuit".[1] Marcellus hunc
sensum de Catone melius: "usque eone omnia cum fortuna
populi Romani conversa sunt ut aliquis deliberet utrum satius
sit vivere cum Antonio an mori cum Catone?" sed ad
divisionem Cesti revertamur. dixit mori illi utile esse ne
10 etiam cruciatus corporis pateretur: non simplici illum modo
periturum si Antonii manibus incidisset. in hac parte cum
descripsisset contumelias insultantium Ciceroni et verbera et
tormenta, dixit illam multum laudatam sententiam: "tu
mehercules, Cicero, cum veneris ad Antonium mortem
15 rogabis". Varius Geminus sic divisit: "hortarer te, si nunc 11
alterutrum utique faciendum esset, aut moriendum aut
rogandum, ut morereris potius quam rogares"; et omnia con-
plexus est, quae a ceteris dicta erant: sed addidit et tertium;
adhortatus est illum ad fugam: illic esse M. Brutum, illic
20 C. Cassium, illic Sex. Pompeium. et adiecit illam sententiam
quam Cassius Severus unice mirabatur: "quid deficimus? et
res publica suos triumviros habet". deinde etiam quas petere
posset regiones percucurrit: Siciliam dixit vindicatam esse
ab illo, Ciliciam a proconsule egregie administratam, familiares
25 studiis eius et Achaiam et Asiam, Deiotari regnum obligatum
beneficiis, Aegyptum et habere beneficii memoriam et agere
perfidiae paenitentiam. sed maxime illum in Asiam et in
Macedoniam hortatus est in Cassi et in Bruti castra. itaque
Cassius Severus aiebat alios declamasse, Varium Geminum
30 vivum[2] consilium dedisse.

Alteram partem pauci declamaverunt. nemo ausus est 12
Ciceronem ad deprecandum Antonium hortari; bene de
Ciceronis animo iudicaverunt. Geminus Varius declamavit
alteram quoque partem et ait: "spero me Ciceroni meo per-
35 suasurum ut velit vivere. quod grandia loquitur et dicit:
'mors nec immatura consulari nec misera sapienti', non
movet me: idiotam gerit; ego belle mores hominis novi:
faciet, rogabit. nam quod ad servitutem pertinet, non
recusabit; iam collum tritum habet; et Pompeius illum et
40 Caesar subegerunt: veteranum mancipium videtis". et com-

---

[1] See note.  [2] B⁰ unum.

13 plura alia dixit scurrilia, ut illi mos erat. divisit sic, ut diceret
non turpiter rogaturum, non frustra rogaturum. in priore
parte illud posuit, non esse turpe civem victorem rogari . a
victo. hic, quam multi rogassent C. Caesarem, hic et
Ligarium. deinde: ne iniquum quidem esse Ciceronem 5
satis facere, qui prior illum proscripsisset, qui hostem
iudicasset: a reo semper nasci satisfactionem; audacter
rogaret.[1] deinde: non pro vita illum, sed pro re publica
rogaturum: satis illum sibi vixisse, rei publicae parum.
in sequenti parte dixit exorari solere inimicos: ipsum ex- 10
oratum Vatinio Gabinioque reis adfuisse. facilius exorari
Antonium posse, qui cum tertio esset, ne quis e tribus hanc
tam speciosam clementiae occasionem praeriperet. fortasse
ei irasci Antonium, qui ne tanti quidem illum putasset quem
14 rogaret. fuga quam periculosa esset cum descripsisset, adiecit, 15
quocumque pervenisset serviendum illi esse: ferendam esse
aut Cassii violentiam aut Bruti superbiam aut Pompei
stultitiam.

   Quoniam in hanc suasoriam incidimus non alienum puto
indicare quomodo quisque se ex historicis adversus memoriam 20
Ciceronis gesserit. nam, quin Cicero nec tam timidus fuerit
ut rogaret Antonium, nec tam stultus ut exorari posse eum
speraret, nemo dubitat excepto Asinio Pollione, qui infestis-
simus famae Ciceronis permansit. et is etiam occasionem
scholasticis alterius suasoriae dedit: solent enim scholastici 25
declamitare: "deliberat Cicero an salutem promittente
Antonio orationes suas comburat". haec inepte ficta cuilibet
15 videri potest. Pollio vult illam veram videri: ita enim dixit
in ea oratione quam pro Lamia edidit.

ASINI POLLIONIS                                    30

   "Itaque numquam per Ciceronem mora fuit quin eiuraret
suas quas cupidissime effuderat orationes in Antonium;
multiplicesque numero et accuratius scriptas illis contrarias
edere ac vel ipse palam pro contione recitare pollicebatur":
adieceratque his alia sordidiora multo, ut ibi facile liqueret 35
hoc totum adeo falsum esse ut ne ipse quidem Pollio in
historiis suis ponere ausus sit. huic certe actioni eius pro
Lamia qui interfuerunt negant eum haec dixisse—nec enim
mentiri sub triumvirorum conscientia sustinebat—, sed postea
16 composuisse. nolo autem vos, iuvenes mei, contristari quod 40

---

[1] Bᵒ ac laesum rogari.

a declamatoribus ad historicos transeo. satis faciam vobis et
fortasse efficiam ut, his sententiis lectis, solidis et verum
habentibus accedatis aequiores;[1] hoc si tamen recta via
consequi non potero, decipere vos cogar, velut salutarem
5 daturus pueris potionem, summa parte poculi. T. Livius
adeo retractationis consilium habuisse Ciceronem non dicit,
ut neget tempus habuisse; ita enim ait.

T. LIVI                                                    17

"M. Cicero sub adventum triumvirorum urbe cesserat pro
10 certo habens, id quod erat, non magis Antonio eripi se quam
Caesari Cassium et Brutum posse; primo in Tusculanum
fugerat, inde transversis itineribus in Formianum ut ab
Caieta navem conscensurus proficiscitur. unde aliquotiens
in altum provectum cum modo venti adversi rettulissent,
15 modo ipse iactationem navis caeco volvente fluctu pati non
posset, taedium tandem eum et fugae et vitae cepit, regres-
susque ad superiorem villam, quae paulo plus mille passibus
a mari abest, 'moriar', inquit, 'in patria saepe servata'.
satis constat servos fortiter fideliterque paratos fuisse ad
20 dimicandum; ipsum deponi lecticam et quietos pati quod
sors iniqua cogeret iussisse. prominenti ex lectica praebentique
inmotam cervicem caput praecisum est. nec id satis stolidae
crudelitati militum fuit: manus quoque scripsisse aliquid in
Antonium exprobrantes praeciderunt. ita relatum caput ad
25 Antonium iussuque eius inter duas manus in rostris positum,
ubi ille consul, ubi saepe consularis, ubi eo ipso anno adversus
Antonium quanta nulla umquam humana vox cum admira-
tione eloquentiae auditus fuerat; vix attollentes lacrimis oculos
humentes intueri truncata membra civis poterant". Bassus 18
30 Aufidius et ipse nihil de animo Ciceronis dubitavit quin
fortiter se morti non praebuerit tantum sed obtulerit.

AUFIDI BASSI

"Cicero paulum remoto velo postquam armatos vidit, 'ego
vero consisto', ait; 'accede, veterane, et si hoc saltim potes
35 recte facere, incide cervicem'. trementi deinde dubitantique:
'quid, si ad me', inquit, 'primum venissetis?'" Cremutius 19
Cordus et ipse ait Ciceronem secum cogitasse utrumne
Brutum an Cassium an Sextum Pompeium peteret; omnia
illi displicuisse praeter mortem.

[1] See note.

CREMUTI CORDI

"Quibus visis laetus Antonius, cum peractam proscriptionem suam dixisset esse, quippe non satiatus modo caedendis civibus sed differtus quoque, super rostra exponit. itaque, quo saepius ille ingenti curcumfusus turba processerat, quae 5 paulo ante aures praebuerat piis orationibus[1] quibus multorum capita servaverat, eo tum per artus sublatus aliter ac solitus erat a civibus suis conspectus est, praependenti capiti orique eius inspersa sanie, brevi ante princeps senatus Romanique nominis titulus, tum pretium interfectoris sui. 10 praecipue tamen solvit pectora omnium in lacrimas gemitusque visa ad caput eius deligata manus dextera, divinae eloquentiae ministra; ceterorumque caedes privatos luctus excitaverunt, illa una communem".

**20**  BRUTTEDI NIGRI  15

"Elapsus interim altera parte villae Cicero lectica per agros ferebatur; sed, ut vidit adpropinquare notum sibi militem, Popillium nomine, memor defensum a se laetiore vultu aspexit. at ille victoribus id ipsum imputaturus occupat facinus caputque decisum nihil in ultimo fine vitae facientis 20 quod alterutram in partem posset notari, Antonio portat oblitus se paulo ante defensum ab illo". et hic voluit positi in rostris capitis miserabilem faciem describere, sed magni-
**21**  tudine rei obrutus est. "ut vero iussu Antonii inter duas manus positum in rostris caput conspectum est, quo totiens 25 auditum erat loco, datae gemitu et fletu maximo viro inferiae, nec, ut solet, vitam depositi in rostris corporis contio audivit, sed ipsa narravit. nulla non pars fori aliquo actionis inclutae signata vestigio erat; nemo non aliquod eius in se meritum fatebatur: hoc certe publicum beneficium palam erat, illam miser- 30 rimi temporis servitutem a Catilina dilatam in Antonium".

Quotiens magni alicuius viri mors ab historicis narrata est, totiens fere consummatio totius vitae et quasi funebris laudatio redditur. hoc, semel aut iterum a Thucydide factum, item in paucissimis personis usurpatum a Sallustio, T. Livius 35 benignus omnibus magnis viris praestitit; sequentes historici multo id effusius fecerunt. Ciceroni hoc, ut Graeco verbo
**22**  utar, ἐπιτάφιον Livius reddit. T. Livi. "Vixit tres et sexaginta annos, ut, si vis afuisset, ne inmatura quidem mors videri

[1] See note.

possit. ingenium et operibus et praemiis operum felix, ipse
fortunae diu prosperae; sed in longo tenore felicitatis magnis
interim ictus vulneribus, exilio, ruina partium pro quibus
steterat, filiae morte, exitu tam tristi atque acerbo, omnium
5 adversorum nihil ut viro dignum erat tulit praeter mortem,
quae vere aestimanti minus indigna videri potuit, quod a
victore inimico nihil crudelius passus erat quam quod eiusdem
fortunae conpos victo fecisset. si quis tamen virtutibus vitia
pensarit, vir magnus ac memorabilis fuit et in cuius laudes
10 exequendas Cicerone laudatore opus fuerit". ut est natura
candidissimus omnium magnorum ingeniorum aestimator
T. Livius, plenissimum Ciceroni testimonium reddidit. Cordi 23
Cremuti non est operae pretium referre redditam Ciceroni
laudationem; paene[1] nihil enim in ea Cicerone dignum est ac
15 ne hoc quidem quod[2] maxime tolerabile est: "proprias enim
simultates deponendas interdum putabat, publicas numquam
vi decernendas: civis non solum magnitudine virtutum sed
multitudine quoque conspiciendus".

AUFIDI BASSI

20 "Sic M. Cicero decessit, vir natus ad rei publicae salutem, quae
diu defensa et administrata in senectute demum e manibus
eius elabitur, uno ipsius vitio laesa, quod nihil in salutem eius
aliud illi quam si caruisset Antonio placuit. vixit sexaginta
et tres annos ita ut semper aut peteret alterum aut invicem
25 peteretur, nullamque rem rarius quam diem illum quo nullius
interesset ipsum mori vidit". Pollio quoque Asinius, qui 24
Verrem, Ciceronis reum, fortissime morientem tradidit,
Ciceronis mortem solus ex omnibus maligne narrat, testimonium tamen quamvis invitus plenum ei reddidit.

30 ASINI POLLIONIS

"Huius ergo viri tot tantisque operibus mansuris in omne
aevum praedicare de ingenio atque industria supervacuum
est. natura autem atque Fortuna pariter obsecuta est ei, si
quidem facies decora ad senectutem prosperaque permansit
35 valetudo; tum pax diutina, cuius instructus erat artibus,
contigit; namque ad priscam severitatem iudiciis exactis
maxima noxiorum multitudo provenit, quos obstrictos patro-
cinio incolumes plerosque habebat; iam felicissima consulatus
ei sors petendi et gerendi magna, munere deum, consilio

---

[1] B⁰ omits *paene* and *enim*.      [2] B⁰ inserts *per se.*

industriaque. utinam moderatius secundas res et fortius adversas ferre potuisset! namque utraeque cum evenerant ei,
mutari eas non posse rebatur. inde sunt invidiae tempestates
coortae graves in eum certiorque inimicis adgrediendi fiducia;
maiore enim simultates adpetebat animo quam gerebat. sed 5
quando mortalium nulli virtus perfecta contigit, qua maior
pars vitae atque ingenii stetit ea iudicandum de homine est.
atque ego ne miserandi quidem exitus eum fuisse iudicarem
25 nisi ipse tam miseram mortem putasset." adfirmare vobis
possum nihil esse in historiis eius hoc quem rettuli loco 10
disertius, ut mihi tunc non laudasse Ciceronem, sed certasse
cum Cicerone videatur. nec hoc deterrendi causa dico ne
historias eius legere concupiscatis; concupiscite et poenas
Ciceroni dabitis. nemo tamen ex tot disertissimis viris melius
Ciceronis mortem deploravit quam Severus Cornelius. 15

26 CORNELI SEVERI

"Oraque magnanimum spirantia paene virorum
in rostris iacuere suis; sed enim abstulit omnis,
tamquam sola foret, rapti Ciceronis imago.
tunc redeunt animis ingentia consulis acta 20
iurataeque manus deprensaque foedera noxae
patriciumque nefas extinctum: poena Cethegi
deiectusque redit votis Catilina nefandis.
quid favor aut coetus, pleni quid honoribus anni
profuerant? sacris exculta quid artibus aetas? 25
abstulit una dies aevi decus, ictaque luctu
conticuit Latiae tristis facundia linguae.
unica sollicitis quondam tutela salusque,
egregium semper patriae caput, ille senatus
vindex, ille fori, legum ritusque togaeque, 30
publica vox saevis aeternum obmutuit armis.
informes voltus sparsamque cruore nefando
canitiem sacrasque manus operumque ministras
tantorum pedibus civis proiecta superbis
proculcavit ovans nec lubrica fata deosque 35
respexit. nullo luet hoc Antonius aevo.
hoc nec in Emathio mitis victoria Perse,
nec te, dire Syphax, non fecit in hoste Philippo;
inque triumphato ludibria cuncta Iugurtha
afuerunt, nostraeque cadens ferus Annibal irae 40
membra tamen Stygias tulit inviolata sub umbras".

non fraudabo municipem nostrum bono versu, ex quo hic   **27**
multo melior Severi Corneli processit:

> conticuit Latiae tristis facundia linguae.

Sextilius Ena fuit homo ingeniosus magis quam eruditus,
5 inaequalis poeta et plane quibusdam locis talis quales esse
Cicero Cordubenses poetas ait, pingue quiddam sonantis atque peregrinum. is hanc ipsam proscriptionem recitaturus
in domo Messalae Corvini Pollionem Asinium advocaverat et
in principio hunc versum non sine assensu recitavit:

10
> deflendus Cicero est Latiaeque silentia linguae.

Pollio Asinius non aequo animo tulit et ait: " Messala, tu quid
tibi liberum sit in domo tua videris; ego istum auditurus non
sum cui mutus videor ". atque ita consurrexit. Enae inter-
fuisse recitationi Severum quoque Cornelium scio, cui non
15 aeque displicuisse hunc versum quam Pollioni apparet quod
meliorem quidem sed non dissimilem illi, et ipse conposuit.
si hic desiero, scio futurum ut vos illo loco desinatis legere
quo ego a scholasticis recessi; ergo, ut librum velitis usque
ad umbilicum revolvere, adiciam suasoriam proximae similem.

# SUASORIA VII

## Deliberat Cicero an scripta sua conburat promittente Antonio incolumitatem si fecisset

**1** Q. HATERI

Non feres Antonium; intolerabilis in malo ingenio felicitas est nihilque nocere cupientis magis accendit quam prosperae 5 turpitudinis conscientia.[1] difficile est; non feres, inquam, et iterum inritare inimicum in mortem tuam cupies. quod ad me quidem pertinet, multum a Cicerone absum; tamen non taedet tantum me vitae meae sed pudet. ne propter hoc quidem ingenium tuum amas, quod illud Antonius plus odit 10 quam te? remittere ait se tibi ut vivas, commentus quemadmodum eripiat etiam quod vixeras. crudelior est pactio Antonii quam proscriptio. ingenium erat in quod nihil iuris haberent triumviralia arma. commentus est Antonius quemadmodum quod non poterat cum Cicerone proscribi a 15 Cicerone proscriberetur. hortarer te, Cicero, ut vitam magni aestimares, si libertas suum haberet in civitate locum, si suum in libertate eloquentia, si non civili ense cervicibus illuderetur;[2] nunc, ut scias nihil esse melius quam mori, vitam tibi Antonius promittit. pendet nefariae proscriptionis 20 tabula: tot praetorii, tot consulares, tot equestris ordinis viri periere; nemo relinquitur nisi qui servire possit. nescio an hoc tempore vivere velis, Cicero; nemo est cum quo velis. merito hercules illo tempore vixisti quo Caesar ultro te rogavit ut viveres sine ulla pactione, quo tempore non quidem stabat 25 res publica, sed in boni principis sinum ceciderat.

**2** CESTI PII

Numquid opinio me fefellit? intellexit Antonius salvis eloquentiae monumentis non posse Ciceronem mori. ad pactionem vocaris, qua pactione melior ante te pars tui petitur. 30 adcommoda mihi paulisper eloquentiam tuam; Ciceronem periturum rogo. si te audissent Caesar et Pompeius neque inissent turpem societatem neque diremissent; si uti umquam consilio tuo voluissent neque Pompeius Caesarem deseruisset neque Pompeium Caesar. quid referam consulatum salu- 35

---

[1] B⁰ illi continere se difficile est.
[2] B⁰ civibus luderetur: Müller, cervicibus luerentur.

tarem urbi, quid exilium consulatu honestius, quid provocatam inter initia adulescentiae libertate tirocinii tui Sullanam
potentiam, quid Antonium avulsum a Catilina, rei publicae
redditum? ignosce, Cicero, si diu ista narravero: forsitan
5 hoc die novissime audiuntur. si occidetur Cicero, iacebit 3
inter Pompeium patrem filiumque et Afranium, Petreium,
Q. Catulum, M. Antonium, illum indignum hoc successore
generis; si servabitur, vivet inter Ventidios et Canidios et
Saxas: ita dubium est utrum satius sit cum illis iacere an cum
10 his vivere? pro uno homine iactura publica pacisceris. scio
omne pretium iniquum esse quod ille constituit: non emo
tanti Ciceronis vitam quanti vendit Antonius. si hanc tibi
pactionem ferret: "vives, sed eruentur oculi tibi; vives, sed
debilitabuntur pedes"; etiamsi in alia damna corporis prae-
15 stares patientiam, excepisses tamen linguam. ubi est sacra
illa vox tua: "mori enim naturae finis est, non poena?" hoc
tibi uni non liquet? at videris Antonio persuasisse. adsere
te potius libertati et unum[1] crimen inimico adice: fac
moriendo Antonium nocentiorem.

20 P. ASPRENATIS                                      4

Ut Antonius Ciceroni parcat, Cicero in eloquentiam suam
ipse animadvertet? quid autem tibi sub ista pactione pro-
mittitur? ut Cn. Pompeius et M. Cato et ille antiquos resti-
tuatur rei publicae senatus, dignissimus apud quem Cicero
25 loqueretur? multos care victuros animi sui contemptus
oppressit; multos perituros parati ad percundum animi ipsa
admiratio eripuit et causa illis vivendi fuit fortiter mori velle.
permitte populo Romano contra Antonium polliceri. scripta
tua si combusseris Antonius paucos annos tibi promittit:
30 at, si non combusseris, amor populi Romani omnes.

POMPEI SILONIS                                       5

Quale[2] est, ut perdamus eloquentiam Ciceronis, fidem se-
quamur Antonii? misericordiam tu istam vocas, supplicium
sumptum de Ciceronis ingenio? credamus Antonio, Cicero,
35 si bene illi pecunias crediderunt faeneratores, si bene
pacem Brutus et Cassius. hominem et vitio naturae et
licentia temporum insanientem, inter scaenicos amores sanguine civili luxuriantem: hominem qui creditoribus suis
oppigneravit rem publicam, cuius gulae duorum principum

---

[1] B° novum.                          [2] B° grave est.

bona, Caesaris ac Pompei, non potuerunt satis facere! tuis
utar, Cicero, verbis: "cara est cuiquam salus quam aut dare
aut eripere potest Antonius?" non est tanti servari Ciceronem
ut servatum Antonio debeam.

6 TRIARI

Conpulsus aliquando populus Romanus in eam necessitatem
est, ut nihil haberet praeter Iovem obsessum et Camillum
exulem; nullum tamen fuit Camilli opus maius quam quod
indignum putavit viros Romanos salutem pactioni debere.
o gravem vitam, etiamsi sine pretio daretur! Antonius hostis
a re publica iudicatus nunc hostem rem publicam iudicat.
Lepidus, ne quis illum putet male Antonio collegam placuisse,
alienae semper dementiae accessio, utriusque collegae mancipium, noster dominus est.

7 ARGENTARI

Nihil Antonio credendum est. mentior? quid enim iste non
potest qui occidere Ciceronem potest, qui servare nisi crudelius
quam occidat non potest? ignoscere tu illum tibi putas qui
ingenio tuo irascitur? ab hoc tu speras vitam cui nondum
verba tua exciderunt? ut corpus, quod fragile et caducum
est, servetur, pereat ingenium, quod aeternum est? ego
8 mirabar si mors crudelior esset Antonii venia. P. Scipionem
a maioribus suis desciscentem generosa mors in numerum
Scipionum reposuit. mortem tibi remittit, ut id pereat quod
in te solum inmortale est. qualis est pactio? aufertur Ciceroni
ingenium sine vita; promittuntur pro oblivione nominis tui
pauci servitutis anni. non ille te vivere vult, sed facere te
ingenii tui superstitem: videlicet Cicero audiat Lepidum,
Cicero audiat Antonium, nemo Ciceronem. poteris perferre
ut, quod Cicero optimum habet, ante se efferat? sine durare
post te ingenium tuum, perpetuam Antonii proscriptionem.

ARELLI FUSCI PATRIS

Quoad humanum genus incolume manserit, quamdiu suus
litteris honor, suum eloquentiae pretium erit, quamdiu rei
publicae nostrae aut fortuna steterit aut memoria duraverit,
admirabile posteris vigebit ingenium tuum, et uno proscriptus
saeculo proscribes Antonium omnibus. crede mihi, vilissima
pars tui est quae tibi vel eripi vel donari potest; ille verus est
Cicero, quem proscribi Antonius non putat nisi a Cicerone
9 posse. non ille tibi remittit proscriptionem, sed tolli desiderat

suam. si fidem deceperit Antonius, morieris; si praestiterit,
servies. quod ad me attinet, fallere eum malo. per te,
M. Tulli, per quattuor et sexaginta annos pulchre actos, per
salutarem rei publicae consulatum, per aeternam, si pateris,
5 ingenii tui memoriam, per rem publicam, quae, ne quid te
putes carum illi relinquere, ante te perit, oro et obtestor ne
moriaris confessus quam nolueris mori.

Huius suasoriae alteram partem neminem scio declamasse; 10
omnes pro libris Ciceronis solliciti fuerunt, nemo pro ipso;
10 cum adeo illa pars non sit mala, ut Cicero si haec condicio
lata ei fuisset deliberaturus non fuerit. itaque hanc suasoriam
nemo declamavit efficacius quam Silo Pompeius; non enim
ad illa speciosa se contulit, ad quae Cestius, qui dixit hoc
gravius esse supplicium quam mortem, et ideo hoc Antonium
15 eligere; brevem vitam esse homini, multo magis seni: itaque
memoriae consulendum, quae magnis viris aeternitatem
promitteret, non qualibet mercede vitam redimendam esse.
hic condiciones intolerabiles. nihil tam intolerabile esse quam
monumenta ingenii sui ipsum exurere. iniuriam illum factu-
20 rum populo Romano, cuius linguam in locum principem
extulisset, ut insolentis Graeciae studia tanto antecederet
eloquentia quanto fortuna; iniuriam facturum generi humano.
paenitentiam illum acturum tam care spiritus empti, cum in
servitute senescendum fuisset et in hoc unum eloquentia
25 utendum ut laudaret Antonium. male cum illo agi: dari
vitam, eripi ingenium.

Silo Pompeius sic egit, ut diceret Antonium non pacisci, 11
sed inludere: non esse illam condicionem, sed contumeliam:
combustis enim libris nihilominus occisurum; non esse tam
30 stultum Antonium ut putaret ad rem pertinere libros a
Cicerone conburi, cuius scripta per totum orbem terrarum
celebrarentur, nec hoc petere eum quod posset ipse facere,
nisi forte non esset in scripta Ciceronis ei ius cui esset in
Ciceronem; quaeri nihil aliud, quam ut ille Cicero multa
35 fortiter de mortis contemptu locutus ad turpes condiciones per-
ductus occideretur. Antonium illi non vitam cum condicione
promittere, sed mortem sub infamia quaerere. itaque quod
turpiter postea passurus esset, nunc illum debere fortiter
pati.

40 Et haec suasoria. . . . insignita est. dixit enim sententiam
cacozeliae genere humillimo et sordidissimo, quod detractu

aut adiectione syllabae facit sensum,[1] "pro facinus indignum!
peribit ergo quod Cicero scripsit, manebit quod Antonius
12 proscripsit?" apud Cestium Pium rhetorem declamabat hanc
suasoriam Surdinus, ingeniosus adulescens, a quo Graecae
fabulae eleganter in sermonem Latinum conversae sunt. 5
solebat dulces sententias dicere, frequentius tamen praedulces
et infractas. in hac suasoria, cum iusiurandum bellis sensibus
prioribus complexus esset, adiecit: "ita te legam". Cestius,
homo nasutissimus, dissimulavit exaudisse se, ut adules-
centem ornatum, quasi inpudens esset, obiurgaret: "quid 10
dixisti? quid? ita te fruar?" erat autem Cestius nullius
quidem ingenii nisi sui amator, Ciceroni etiam infestus, quod
13 illi non inpune cessit. nam cum M. Tullius, filius Ciceronis,
Asiam obtineret, homo qui nihil ex paterno ingenio habuit
praeter urbanitatem, cenabat apud eum Cestius. M. Tullio 15
et natura memoriam ademerat, et ebrietas, si quid ex ea
supererat, subducebat; subinde interrogabat quid ille vo-
caretur qui in imo recumberet, et cum saepe subiectum illi
nomen Cestii excidisset, novissime servus, ut aliqua nota
memoriam eius faceret certiorem, interroganti domino quis ille 20
esset qui in imo recumberet, ait: "hic est Cestius qui patrem
tuum negabat litteras scisse"; adferri ocius flagra iussit et
Ciceroni, ut oportuit, de corio Cestii satis fecit. erat autem
14 etiam ubi pietas non exigeret scordalus. Hybreae, disertissimi
viri, filio male apud se causam agenti ait: ἡμεῖς οὖν πατέ- 25
ρων ⟨μέγ᾽ ἀμείνονες εὐχόμεθ᾽ εἶναι;⟩ et, cum in quadam
postulatione Hybreas patris sui totum locum ad litteram
omnibus agnoscentibus diceret, "age", inquit, "non putas
me didicisse patris mei: 'quousque tandem abutere, Catilina,
patientia nostra?'" Gargonius, fatuorum amabilissimus, in 30
hac suasoria dixit duas res, quibus stultiores ne ipse quidem
umquam dixerat; unam in principio: nam, cum coepisset
scholasticorum frequentissimo iam more a iureiurando et
dixisset multa, ait: "itaque primum tantum Antonium[2]
timeat quantum potest; ita aut totus vivat Cicero aut totus 35
moriatur, ut ego quae hodie pro Ciceronis ingenio dixero
nulla pactione delebo". alteram rem dixit cum exempla
referret eorum qui fortiter perierant: "Iuba et Petreius mutuis
vulneribus concurrerunt et mortes faeneraverunt".

---

[1] B⁰ sententiam.        [2] B⁰ Antonius.

## "Alexander considers whether he should sail the Ocean"

\* \* \* \* \* \* \* \* \* \*

In nature everything that has magnitude has limits too: there 1
is nothing boundless except Ocean. It is commonly said that
there lie fertile lands in the Ocean, that beyond the Ocean
again other shores, another world arises, and there is no end
to created things, but ever a new world begins where the old
seems to end. It is easy to invent such tales since one cannot
sail the Ocean. Let Alexander be content with having conquered that portion of the world where the sun is content to
shine. Within the limits of these lands Hercules won his place
in heaven. There lies the motionless sea, a lifeless bulk of
nature, as it were, which here has its appointed end. There are
strange and frightful shapes, great monsters in the Ocean also,
which that deep abyss rears. The light is mingled in dense
gloom: the dark makes a curtain for the day; in ponderous
bulk fast-rooted lie the waters; of stars there are none or they
are unknown. Such, Alexander, is the constitution of nature.
Beyond everything is the Ocean, beyond the Ocean nothing.

ARGENTARIUS                                                     2

Stop, your own world calls you back. All that the sun shines
on we have conquered. No aim is so important that for it
I would endanger Alexander's safety.

POMPEIUS SILO

That day has come, Alexander, that long-desired day, on
which your toil should cease: the bounds of your kingdom
are the bounds of the world.

MOSCHUS

It is time that Alexander should stop where the world ends
and the sun ceases to shine. I have conquered the known: now
I desire the unknown. What tribes were so savage as not to
adore Alexander on bended knee? What mountains so dreadful that his victorious soldiers have not trod their ridges?
We have halted beyond the trophies of Father Bacchus. In

this search for a new world we lose the old. Boundless and
unexplored by man is the sea: it girdles the whole earth: it
guards the lands: it is a waste of waters untroubled by the
oar: now its shores are unquiet under the raging billow, now
they are desolate when the billow withdraws: a horror of
darkness weighs on its waters, and, I know not how, what
nature has denied to human eyes eternal night overwhelms.

MUSA

Loathsome and huge are the monsters: deep and immovable
the abyss. The case is plain: there is nothing more to
conquer: retrace your steps.

3 ALBUCIUS SILUS

The lands too have their own boundary, and the universe
itself ends somewhere: everything is finite: you must set a
limit to your greatness since fortune sets none. Self-control
in success is the mark of a great heart. Fate bounds your
victorious march with the bounds of the world. Your empire
is closed by the ocean. Your grandeur has far transcended the
majesty of nature. To the world Alexander is great: to
Alexander the world is narrow. But even the greatest things
are finite. The spacious sky moves within its own paths, the
restless seas observe their boundaries. Whatever has reached
its zenith can increase no farther. We know nothing greater
than Alexander: we know nothing beyond Ocean.

MARULLUS

In our quest of the seas to whom are we to give over the dry
lands? A world unknown is my goal, the conquered world
I abandon.

4 FABIANUS

Another point. Do you think that if the eye cannot pierce the
darkness that broods on all these waters the ship can cleave its
waves? This is not India, nor its dreadful hosts of savage
peoples. Imagine the awful monsters in the sea, observe the
storms and billows with which it rages, the waves it drives to
the shore: such is the warring of its winds: such the mad rage
of the sea when stirred from its lowest depths: there is no
anchorage at hand, no safety: all is unknown: far within
its depths all that is monstrous and imperfect in nature has
found a refuge. Not even those who fled from Alexander

sought those seas. The Ocean that nature has poured round the world is something sacred.

Those who defined the courses of the stars, and reduced to fixed law the annual alternations of winter and summer, to whom no part of the world is unknown, nevertheless have no sure knowledge of the Ocean. They know not whether it surrounds the earth like a girdle, or forms a circle by itself, and surges out into these navigable bays, which are as it were the breathing vents of its immensity. They doubt whether it has fire or air behind it fed by its exhalations. What do you mean, fellow-soldiers? Will you allow the conqueror of the human race, the great Alexander, to embark on that element whose nature is still unknown? Remember, Alexander, you are leaving your mother in a world that is only conquered not pacified.

### DIVISIO 5

Cestius used to say that in suasoriae as a class the tone must vary with the situation. Opinion in a free state should not be expressed in the same manner as at the courts of kings. Unpalatable counsel must not be given to these even for their good. Even kings differ in character. They all hate truth more or less. Alexander clearly was one of the haughtiest kings in history with a spirit too arrogant for a mortal. Finally to abandon other evidences the suasoria in itself makes clear his arrogance: the world is his own, yet he is not satisfied. On these grounds, Cestius used to say, all argument must be couched in a tone of the highest respect for the king, if one would avoid the fate of his teacher, Aristotle's cousin, whom Alexander slew for the ill-timed frankness of his wit. It was Alexander's wish to be considered a god, and, on one occasion when he was wounded, the philosopher said on seeing the blood flow that he was surprised that it was not "that limpid stream that flows in the veins of the blessed gods". Alexander took revenge for this sally with his spear. C. Cassius in a letter to Cicero makes a neat point which recalls this story. After many jests about the folly of young Cn. Pompey (who gathered an army in Spain and was beaten at Munda) he concludes by saying: "We may have a laugh at his expense, but his reply, I fear, will be a sword-thrust". With all kings such wit is to be dreaded. And so Cestius said 6 that in the case of Alexander the arguments must both soothe and flatter: yet as the appearance must be one of reverence not of flattery we must exercise restraint: otherwise we may meet some such fate as befell Athens, when its flattery of Antony was exposed and punished. Antony wanted to be called Father Liber and gave orders that this title should be inscribed on his statues. He also imitated Bacchus in dress and retinue. The Athenians with their wives and children met him on his arrival, and greeted him as "Dionysus". All would have gone well if their Attic wit had stopped there, but they proceeded to offer him in marriage their goddess Minerva, and to entreat him to wed her. Antony said he would marry her, but exacted 1000 talents as dowry: whereupon one of the Greeks said: "Sire, Zeus had your mother, Semele, to wife without a dowry". This jest passed unpunished, but the betrothal cost the Athenians 1000 talents. During the exaction of the money a great number of lampoons were published, some were even delivered to Antony himself: such as the one which was written under his statue, for at the same time he had both Octavia and Cleopatra to wife, "Octavia

7 and Athene to Antonius: 'Take your own property and begone'". In this connection a very witty thing was said by Dellius, whom Messala Corvinus calls the acrobat of the civil wars, because when he was on the point of deserting Dolabella for Cassius he bargained for his own safety on condition of killing Dolabella: then deserted from Cassius to Antony, lastly abandoned Antony for Caesar. The same Dellius wrote those wanton letters to Cleopatra which are current. When the Athenians asked for time to collect the money, and asked in vain, Dellius said to Antony: "Since they have divorced you, tell them to pay it in three annual instalments". The pleasure of story-telling has taken me too far: so I shall

8 return to my subject. Cestius used to say that this suasoria must be expressed in terms of high compliment to Alexander. He arranged the argument thus: first he said, even if the Ocean could be navigated it should not be navigated: enough glory had been won: Alexander must consolidate the conquests he had made on his march. He must have some regard for his soldiers worn out with his many victories: he should think of his mother: and he added several other reasons. Then he put this point, that the Ocean could not be navigated.

Fabianus, the philosopher, put the same proposition first: 9 namely that even if the Ocean could be, it ought not to be navigated: but he put a different reason first—a limit must be set to success. Here he gave expression to this maxim: "Supreme good fortune stops of its own accord". Then he commented generally on the fickleness of fortune, describing how nothing in the world is stable, all things are in a state of flux, rising and falling at random, lands are swallowed by the Ocean, seabeds become dry, mountains subside: finally he quoted examples of kings cast down from their high estate. Then he added, "Let the dry land come to an end sooner than your prosperity". He treated the second proposition also in 10 a different manner. This is how he put it: first he denied that there were any habitable lands either in the Ocean or beyond the Ocean. Then he said if there were, it was impossible to reach them: in this connection he described the difficulty of the voyage: the sea was uncharted, and could not be navigated because its nature was unknown. Finally granting that these lands could be reached, yet they were not worth the pains. He pointed out that they were abandoning what was certain for what was uncertain: the nations would revolt if once it was known that Alexander had passed beyond the limits of the world: here he mentioned Alexander's mother of whom he said: "Just think how she trembled when you were merely on the point of crossing the Granicus." Glyco's 11 aphorism on this is famous: "This water is not Simoeis nor even Granicus: if Ocean had not been an evil thing, it would not be the limit of the world." Everybody wanted to imitate this. Plution said: "For this reason it is the greatest thing, because it comes after everything, and after it there is nothing". Artemon said: "We are considering if we ought to try the passage. We are not standing on the shores of the Hellespont nor even by the Pamphylian sea waiting eagerly for the ebb before its time: neither is this Euphrates nor Indus, but whether it is the end of the land, the boundary of nature, the oldest element, or the cradle of the gods, it is a water too holy for ships". Apaturius said: "Thence the ship without changing its course shall go to the rising place of the sun, and then to the unseen lands of its setting". Cestius thus described the scene: "The Ocean roars as if indignant at your leaving the dry lands". They thought that Dorio's para- 12 phrase of Homer's lines describing how the blinded Cyclops hurled back the rock into the sea, was in worse taste than anything ever written since taste began to deteriorate: "He tears up a mountain, and takes an island in his hand and hurls it". How such expressions, instead of being in bad taste, lose their extravagance while retaining all their emphasis, could be understood, Maecenas said, from the pages of Vergil— "Mountain is torn from mountain", is an example of bombast. Vergil represents his hero as seizing "no small part of a mountain". He secures the effect of greatness without carelessly violating truth. It is turgid to say, "He takes an island in his hand and hurls it". Vergil describing the ships says merely, "One might think that the Cyclades were torn up and swimming on the sea". He does not say this actually happens, only that it seems to happen. The reader accepts the statement with indulgence, although it is impossible, because the apology precedes the expression.

13 I found in this very suasoria an aphorism of Menestratus, no mean rhetorician in his day, which shows still worse taste. When he was describing the size of the monsters born in the Ocean he said:....This expression makes us inclined to excuse Musa, who spoke of a wonder greater even than Charybdis and Scylla: "Charybdis where the sea itself is ship-wrecked", and not content with being extravagant once in one subject proceeded to say: "What can be safe there where the sea itself perishes?" Damas dramatically introduced a speech by the king's mother, when he was describing how without intermission one danger after another had arisen....

Barbarus used this expression when he had introduced
14 the Macedonian army excusing itself:....Fuscus Arellius said: "I call you to witness that your own world ends before your soldiers fail". Latro while still seated spoke thus—he did not make apologies for the soldiers but said—"Lead and I follow: but who guarantees me an enemy, who guarantees me land, or daylight, or air? Give me somewhere to place my camp, to set my standards. I have abandoned my parents, I have abandoned my children, I ask for my discharge. Is it
15 too soon to ask that on the edge of the Ocean?" Latin rhetoricians in describing the Ocean have not been too vigorous: their descriptions have been either too vague or too detailed. None of them have been so spirited as Pedo, who

says in "The voyage of Germanicus": "Already they see day
and sun left far behind, long exiled as they are from the well-
known limits of the world, daring to go through gloom
forbidden to the bounds of creation, and the farthest shores
of the universe: and now they behold the Ocean, which has
huge monsters beneath its sluggish waves, which bears on all
sides savage sharks and dogs of the sea, seizing their ships
and rising high in wrath. (The very crashing of its billows
swells their fear.) Now they feel their ships settling on a
shoal and their fleet abandoned by the swift winds, and
believe that they are left at last by the careless fates to be
mangled in a doom unhappy by the wild beasts of the sea.
And one aloft on the high prow striving to pierce the dark
mist with straining eye, when his strength availed not to
discern anything amid the loss of the world, poured out his
imprisoned soul in words like these: 'Whither are we borne?
Day itself flees, and nature at the limit of her sway shrouds
the abandoned world in eternal gloom. Do we mean to
search for races that dwell beyond this under another sky,
and for a world untouched by the blasts of the storm? The
gods are calling us back, and forbid mortal eyes to know the
end of things. Why are we violating alien seas and sacred
waters with our oars and troubling the calm abodes of the
gods?'"

Of the Greek rhetoricians none had greater success with **16**
this suasoria than Glyco: but he has as many instances of bad
taste as of splendid diction. I shall give you the means of
testing both. I wanted to try you without giving you my
opinion and without separating what is in good taste from
what is in bad—for you might rather have praised the extravagant things—but you may happen to do so all the same,
even if I do discriminate. The following was finely said:....
but as usual he ruined the expression by a superfluous and
bombastic addition, for he added:....Critics hesitate whether
to approve or condemn the following—I do not hesitate to
give my verdict against it—"Farewell O world, Farewell O
Sun: the Macedonians are rushing into chaos".

# SUASORIA II

"The three hundred Lacedaemonians sent against
Xerxes, when the contingents of three hundred from
each of the Greek cities had fled, deliberate
whether they too should flee"

1 ARELLIUS FUSCUS THE FATHER

But, I suppose, it is raw recruits that have been chosen, and
men whose courage can be broken by fear, with hands that
cannot support unfamiliar arms, and frames grown torpid
with age or wounds. What shall I call you? The chosen of
Greece, or the elect of the Spartans? Think of the many
battles fought by your sires, the many cities they destroyed,
the spoils of their many conquests. Do you now betray your
temples which are built without ramparts to defend them?
Our deliberations put me to shame: even if we have not fled,
I am ashamed to have thought of such a thing. "But," you
will say, "Xerxes comes with thousands". O Spartans, on
against the barbarians! I do not appeal to your achievements,
to your grandsires, or to your fathers. Their example has
inspired your souls from childhood. No, it is a shame so to
encourage Spartans. See, the position is secure. Let him
bring all the Orient in his fleet, let him deploy before your
fearful gaze his useless host: this broad arm of the mighty
ocean contracts into the narrowest of channels, then a
treacherous passage succeeds, with scarce an entrance for the
smallest vessel, and even the smallest vessel is kept away by
the stormy sea that flows all round, by the treacherous shoals
that rise here and there amid the deeper waters, the sharp
rocks and all other dangers that betray the sailor's hopes.
I am ashamed, I say, that Spartans, and armed Spartans, look
2 for a way of safety. I shall not, you say, carry home the spoils
of the Persians? Well then, I shall fall naked on the spoils.
Let him know that we are not the only three hundred of our
race who will stand and die like us. Say this to your souls:
"I know not whether we can conquer: conquered we cannot
be". I do not say this, as though we must perish in any case:
but, if we must fall, you are wrong in thinking death terrible.

To none has nature given the breath of life for ever; our life's last day is fixed at birth. God created us of frail material: a trifle destroys us: death takes us without warning. Such is the lot of boyhood, so youth perishes. Most of our time we pray for death: so calm and untroubled a retreat it is from the cares of life. But glory knows no death, and those who fall thus men worship as likest gods. Women too have found this path to death a path of glory. Why should I name Lycurgus, why those men, undaunted in all danger, whose memory we revere? Though I should name Othryades alone, yet I can name examples for three hundred.

TRIARIUS 3

Surely we Spartans are ashamed to be beaten by the tongue of rumour and not by the sword of the foe. It is a great thing, it is the very sustenance of valour to be born a Spartan. For certain victory all would have remained, for certain death Spartans alone. Sparta needs no stone walls around it: its walls are its men. We shall do better if we recall, rather than follow the contingents that have fled. But, I am told, he tunnels the hills, he bridges the seas. Never did haughty success stand on a solid foundation, and towering empires have sunk in ruin through forgetfulness of human frailty. Clearly powers that have reached an envious height have arrived at no happy end. He has moved from their appointed place the seas, the lands, the worlds. We are but three hundred, yet let us die, that here first he may find something that he could not change. If we meant to approve of that mad design of retreating, why did we not rather flee in the crowd?

PORCIUS LATRO 4

This forsooth is why we remained—to bring up the rear of the fugitives. Among the brave we are readiest to flee, in the flight we are laggards. Do you flee before an idle tale? Let us know at least how brave he is whom we flee. Even victory can hardly wipe out the stain on our honour: though we show perfect valour, though we win complete success, yet much has been taken from our renown: we are Spartans, and have thought of flight. But, you say, we shall perish. For myself, after this debate the one thing I fear is return from the battle. Do old wives' tales dash the arms from our hands? Now, if ever, let us fight: our valour would have been hidden among the contingents. The rest have fled. If you ask my opinion, I shall speak for ourselves and for Greece: We are chosen champions: we have not been deserted.

**5 GAVIUS SABINUS**

It is a shame for any man to flee, for a Spartan even to think of flight.

**MARULLUS**

This is why we have remained—to avoid being hidden in the crowd of fugitives. The others have an excuse to offer: "We thought Thermopylae secure, since we left the Spartans there".

**CESTIUS PIUS**

Spartans, you have shown the dishonour of retreat by refraining from retreat so long. Every state has its peculiar glory. Athens is famous for eloquence, Thebes for religion, Sparta for arms. Is it for this the river Eurotas flows round it, a river that disciplines our boyhood to the endurance of future warfare? For this are the wooded ridges of Taygetus difficult to all but Spartans? Is it for this we glory in Hercules who won a place in heaven by his prowess? Is it for this we **6** have no bulwarks but our armed men? Deep is the stain on the valour of our ancestors! Spartans regard their numbers, not their valour. Let us see the size of the host, that Sparta may have, if not gallant soldiers, at least true messengers. Are we then conquered not by arms but by tidings of the foe? Rightly, by Hercules, has Xerxes despised all the world, since Spartans cannot stand before the news of his approach. If you may not conquer Xerxes you may look at him; I want to know what it is that I flee. Hitherto I have not been like the Athenians in anything. I dwelt in no walled city: my training was not the same. Is their flight the first thing I shall copy?

**7 POMPEIUS SILO**

Xerxes is bringing a host with him: Thermopylae has room only for a handful. It matters not how populous the races poured by the Orient on our world, how numerous the tribes Xerxes drags in his train: we have to do only with those who can find room in the pass.

CORNELIUS HISPANUS

We came for Sparta, let us stand for Greece. We have triumphed over our allies; let us triumph over the enemy. The insolent barbarian shall know that nothing is more difficult than to pierce the breast of an armed Spartan. I rejoice that our allies have left Thermopylae: they have cleared the field for us: no one shall rival or share in our exploits. No crowd of combatants shall hide the Spartan's prowess. Look where Xerxes may, it is Spartans he shall see.

BLANDUS    8

Shall I repeat to you what our mothers say as we receive our shields, "Return either with these or on these?" It is less dishonour to return without arms from war than to flee in arms. Shall I remind you of the sayings of captured Spartans? The Spartan prisoner said: "Slay me, I cannot be a slave". Had he chosen to flee he could have avoided capture. Recount the terrors that the Persians inspire. We heard all that when we were leaving Sparta. Let Xerxes behold our three hundred and see how lightly we esteem the war: let him see just how many the pass can hold. Let us not go home even as messengers, unless we go last of all. I know not who has fled. It was these men here that Sparta gave me as comrades in arms. (Description of Thermopylae.) Now I rejoice that the contingents have retreated: they made Thermopylae too small for me.

On the other side. CORNELIUS HISPANUS    9

I foresee the greatest dishonour to our country if Spartans are the first in Greece to be conquered by Xerxes. We cannot have even a true record of our valour; there will be no report to believe but the report of the foe. I have given you my decision: all Greece concurs in it. If anyone gives different counsel, he wishes not to hearten, but to destroy you.

CLAUDIUS MARCELLUS

They will not conquer, they will overwhelm us. We have done enough for our renown; we are the last to retreat: before we were conquered nature was subdued.

DIVISIO    10

I have mentioned this suasoria, not because there was in it some refinement of thought and style capable of inspiring you,

but that you might understand the brilliance or, if you will,
the licence of the style of Fuscus. I shall not give you my
criticism: it will be open to you to decide whether in your
opinion his developments are in an animated or in a pampered
style. Asinius Pollio used to say that this was playing with
words not genuine suasoria. I remember that nothing was so
popular in my young days as these descriptive flights of
Fuscus, which every one of us used to roll out each in his own
tone, each with his own rhythm. And now that I have
happened to mention Fuscus I shall add famous little descriptive passages from all his suasoriae, even if they have
11 been admired by none but writers of such. Fuscus employed
in this suasoria the usual division of the argument; he said
it was not honourable to flee even if it were safe; then, to flee
and to fight were equally dangerous; lastly, it was more
dangerous to flee—combatants need fear only the enemy, fugitives both the enemy and their own men. Cestius passed over
the first part, as if no one doubted that it was dishonourable
to flee: then he took up this question whether it was not
necessary. "This is what troubles you" he said, "the enemy,
the flight of your allies, your small numbers". There is an
eloquent expression of Dorio's, not indeed in this suasoria,
but quoted in this connection. He represents Leonidas as
saying, (and I think the remark is found also in Herodotus),
12 "Eat a good lunch, for we are to dine in Hades". Sabinus
Asilius, the most charming and witty of rhetoricians, when he
had recalled this saying of Leonidas, said: "I should have
accepted the lunch, but declined the dinner". Attalus, the
Stoic, who went into exile on finding himself the object of
Sejanus's plots, was an eloquent speaker, and of the philosophers alive in your day by far the most gifted in expression
and the most profound in thought. He tried to rival the
greatness and nobility of this maxim of Dorio's, and seems
to me to have spoken with even more spirit than the former:
. . . . In a similar connection I remember an idea expressed by
Severus Cornelius. As it was spoken of Romans I rather
think it lacks courage. He introduces some soldiers feasting
on the eve of battle, and says: "Stretched on the grass they
say, 'This day at least is mine'". In this he has expressed with
fine taste the feelings of minds doubtful of their fate, but the
thought is unworthy of the greatness of the Roman soul: for

they dine as if in despair of the morrow. How much spirit
had those Spartans who could not say, "This day at least is
mine". Porcellus, the grammarian, criticised this as un- 13
grammatical, because he had introduced more than one, and
yet made them say, "This is my day", not, "This is our day".
In doing so he really attacked the best point in an excellent
expression, for change "my" to "our" and all the fine finish
of the line will be lost: the most appropriate touch in the line
is just this phrase which is taken from ordinary speech:
"This day is mine" is almost a proverb, and if you refer to
the general sense, you will see that even the grammarians'
pedantic criticism, to which great minds must not be sub-
jected, is out of place. They said, "This day is mine", each
individually, not simultaneously, like a class conducted by a
teacher. But to return to Leonidas and his three hundred: 14
t iere is a very fine saying from Glyco: .... In this very suasoria
indeed I do not actually recall any idea worth remembering
of any Greek except Damas: "Whither will you flee,
soldiers? you are the bulwarks of Sparta". When Haterius
had described the pass in eloquent terms he neatly summed
up the position as ground "meant by nature for three
hundred". Cestius, after describing the honours that would
be paid to them if they fell in battle for their country, added:
·'Men will swear by our tombs". Nicetes portrayed this idea
far more eloquently and added: .... Brilliantly said were it
not that Xerxes is too early in date for this oath of Demosthenes to be possible. The following idea of his is original, or
at any rate not identified. After describing the advantage of
the position, and how their flanks were safe, and the defile in
their rear, an obstacle only to the enemy (he said): ....
Potamon was a great rhetorician at Mitylene who flourished 15
at the same time as the famous Lesbocles whose genius was
equal to his reputation. I think I must point out to you how
great was the difference in their spirits in a similar misfortune seeing that the point affects not merely eloquence but
life itself. Each lost a son at the same time. Lesbocles closed
his school; and after that no man ever heard him declaim.
Potamon showed a loftier spirit; from the funeral of his son
he betook himself to his school, and delivered a declamation.
In my opinion the feeling of each should have been modified:
in his misfortune the one showed too little feeling for a

**16** father, the other too little fortitude for a man. Potamon in delivering a suasoria about the three hundred described the dishonour incurred by the Spartans in even thinking of flight, and closed the argument thus:.... In this suasoria many lost all discretion in speaking about Othryades: Murredius spoke thus: "The Athenians fled because they had never learned the A B C of our Othryades (with their blood)". Gargonius said: "Othryades who died to deceive, came to life to conquer the foe". Licinius Nepos: "Inspired by his example you ought to have conquered even in death".[1] Antonius Atticus seems to have carried off the palm for childishness, for he said: "Victor almost from the tomb Othryades pressed his wounds with his fingers, to inscribe the name of Sparta on the trophy. The ink was worthy of a Spartan: surely he was a hero who even wrote in blood". Catius Crispus, a provincial orator, after quoting Othryades as an example, imitated this idea in a far-fetched way: "We Spartans differ from all the world in our standards of honour: no luxury surrounds our upbringing: no walls protect our lives:
**17** no death prevents our victory". Seneca, whose name perchance has reached your ears, had a disorderly and uncontrolled talent. He always tried to talk in a lofty style, and at last this desire became a disease and made him a laughing-stock; for he refused to have any slaves except tall ones and any vessels of silver but large ones. Believe me, I am not jesting, his madness came to such a pass that he had his shoes made too large for him, he ate no figs except the large kind (*mariscae*), and took a giantess for his mistress. Since he approved of big things only he received the surname or, as Messala says, the "supername" of Grandio, and was called Seneca the Grand. Once in my young days when he had stated in this suasoria the objection: "But, you will say, all the troops sent by ·Greece have fled", raising his hands, standing on tiptoe, so he was wont to do, to look taller, he calls out: "I rejoice, I rejoice!" As we marvelled what great good luck had befallen him, he added: "Xerxes will be entirely mine". He said also: "He has stolen the seas with his fleet, he has narrowed the lands, he has enlarged the deep, and commanded nature to take a new shape: let him set his

[1] One thinks of "*Debout les morts!*" at the battle of Verdun—an instance of practical rhetoric on the battlefield.

camp against heaven, I shall have the gods as my comrades-in-arms". What Senianus said was much more extravagant: "He besets the land with his arms, the sky with his arrows, 18 the sea with his chains: to the rescue, Spartans, or the universe is taken". I shall now quote to you a saying of Victor Statorius which although in good style is foolish in idea. He was a townsman of mine and wrote some charming fables not unworthy of preservation. In this suasoria he took up the objection: "But we are only three hundred", and replied: "Yes, only three hundred, but men, but armed men, but Spartans, and at Thermopylae: never did three hundred seem to me more numerous". In this suasoria Latro, after 19 discussing all possible arguments, said that they could win, at any rate thanks to their position they could return un-defeated, and then added the following: "If we do no more, we shall at least stay the advance of the war". Some time afterwards I remember Arbronius Silo, one of Latro's pupils, father of the Silo who wrote pieces for the ballet dancers, so not only neglecting but degrading his great abilities, read aloud a poem in which we recognised Latro's idea in these lines: "On, ye Danai, singing aloud the battle-song; on, in triumph, fallen is Hector, who stayed the advance of the war". So diligent were pupils then, not to mention so critical, that even one word could not be plagiarised: but now anyone you like can with safety give the speech against Verres as his own. But to show you that an idea though well-expressed can yet 20 be expressed better, mark with how much more grace Vergil has expressed this famous idea, "Fallen is Hector, who stayed the advance of the war". "In all our delay before the obstinate Trojan city, it was Hector and Aeneas whose hand stayed the Grecian victory".[1] Messala used to say that Vergil ought to have stopped here, for the line that follows, "and bore back its advance to the tenth year", is mere padding. Maecenas thought that it could be compared for excellence even with the preceding lines. But to return to Thermopylae, Diocles Carystius said:....Apaturius said:....I must give 21 Corvus the rhetorician a certificate for his stupidity when he said: "Well, if Xerxes is now sailing to attack us after making the sea his own, let us flee before he steals the land from us". This Corvus when he conducted a school at Rome declaimed,

---

[1] Mackail's translation.

in the presence of that Sosius who subdued the Jews, a controversia about her who argued in the presence of married women that they should rear no children, and on this account was accused of injuring the commonwealth. In this controversia the following sentence of his was ridiculed: "amid ointment-boxes and drugs to scent the breath stood the snooded

22 throng". But if you like I shall show you folly in a historian too. Tuscus, who indicted for treason Scaurus Mamercus the last of the family of the Scauri, was without principle as a man or felicity as an author. In delivering this suasoria he said: "Let us make a stand for this, if for nothing else, that the arrogant barbarian may not say, 'I came, I saw, I conquered'", although the late Julius said this many years after on the occasion of his victory over Pharnaces. Dorion said: "Men...." Nicocrates, the Spartan, used to say that this argument would have been noteworthy if it had been halved.

23 But I won't make fools of you any longer, and I shall end this suasoria here because I promised to show you how Arellius Fuscus developed his subjects. You may possibly be offended by his excessive ornament and jerky style when you reach my time of life: meanwhile I do not doubt that now you will be pleased with those very faults which some day you will dislike.

# SUASORIA III

"Agamemnon deliberates whether he should sacrifice
Iphigenia since Calchas declares that otherwise
it is a sin to sail"

ARELLIUS FUSCUS THE FATHER                              1

When God spread out the waters of the sea, he did not
ordain that at all times they should be obedient to our
prayers: nor is it so only with the sea. Observe the sky: are
not the stars governed by the same conditions? At one time
they withhold the rain, and parch the ground, and poor
farmers mourn the destruction of their seeds (these conditions sometimes prevail for a year). At another time the clear
blue is hidden, and every day sees the sky heavy with cloud:
the soil sinks down, and the earth does not retain what has been
entrusted to it. Again the stars become inconstant in their
motions, the conditions keep changing: the sun's heat is not
too oppressive, nor fall the rains beyond what is due: whatever harshness the heat has caused, whatever excess of
moisture the streaming rains have brought, the one is
tempered by the other. Whether such is the order of nature,
or, as men say, these changes are controlled by the course of
the moon—which if its light is undimmed and its brilliant
crescent steadily waxing, keeps away the rains, or if cloud
obscures it, and its circle is duller, makes no end of rain until
it regains its light—or, whether the moon has no such
influence, but it is the winds that seize and dominate the
season; no matter which of these causes is the true one, it
was no order of a god that made the sea safe for an adulterer.
Even if you urge that I cannot punish the adulteress (unless
I offer this sacrifice), surely the chaste maiden has the prior
claim. I pursued the adulterer to safeguard her purity. If
I conquer Troy I shall spare the maidens of the enemy. As
yet Priam's virgin daughter has nothing to fear.

CESTIUS PIUS                                           2

For these reasons I appeal to the immortal gods. Are these
the terms on which you will open the seas? Nay close them
rather. Even Priam's children you do not mean to sacrifice.

(Describe now the storm): we have shed no kindred blood, yet these are our sufferings. Is it an appropriate sacrifice to slay a virgin in the temple of a virgin goddess? She will receive her more gladly as priestess than as victim.

CORNELIUS HISPANUS

Against us, he cries, fierce are the storms and the seas rage and yet up till now I have shed no kindred blood. Those seas if the will of God controlled them would be closed to adulterers.

MARULLUS

If our path to the war is blocked, let us go home to our children.

ARGENTARIUS

For the second time an evil fate descends upon our house. For the sake of an adulteress a brother's children perish. At such a price I would not wish her back. But Priam, you tell me, wages war to defend an adulterous son.

3 DIVISIO

This is the analysis of the argument adopted by Fuscus. He said, the maiden must not be sacrificed even if otherwise they could not sail. It must not be done, because it was a shedding of blood, because it was a shedding of kindred blood, because they were losing more than they gained; losing Iphigenia to gain Helen. They were punishing adultery by shedding kindred blood. He added that he would sail even without that sacrifice: the delay was natural, due to the sea and the winds. The will of the gods was hidden from men. This last point was carefully analysed by Cestius. He said: the gods do not interpose their will in human affairs: even if they do interpose it their will is not known to man: granting that it is known what is once decreed cannot be altered: if there is no such thing as fate the future is unknown:

4 if there is, it cannot be changed. Silo Pompeius said that even if there were some means of knowing the future, still augury was unworthy of belief. "You may ask in reply, 'why does Calchas claim to know if he is ignorant?'". To which I answer, "Firstly, he thinks he knows"—here he handled the stock argument against all who claimed this knowledge—then he said, "He is angry with you: he is averse to the war:

he wants to win the confidence of the world by a proof so convincing". In the description which I placed first in this suasoria Fuscus Arellius wished to imitate some lines of Vergil. The passage is far-fetched, and he inserted it although the matter is almost irrelevant and certainly unnecessary. He speaks of the moon "which, if its light is undimmed, and its brilliant crescent steadily waxing, keeps away the rains, or if a cloud obscures it, and its circle is duller, makes no end of rain until it regains its light". How much more simply and 5 happily has Vergil expressed this: "When first the moon's light returns and gathers strength, if the points of the crescent are dull and dark with mist, rain and storm are threatening on land and sea". And again, "But if at her fourth rising (and this is the surest sign), she sails through the heavens with crescent bright and clear". Fuscus used often to borrow ideas from Vergil to win the approval of Maecenas; he was so given to claiming credit for having succeeded in some description modelled on Vergil. For example in this suasoria he said: "Why was Calchas the favoured interpreter of the gods? Why did the god choose him as his mouthpiece? Why did the god choose this man's heart to fill with his divine inspiration?" In this he said he had imitated Vergil's well-known phrase, *plena deo* (full of divine frenzy). My friend Gallio has a habit of 6 quoting this phrase just in the right place. I remember our going together to the house of Messala, after listening to Nicetes. The latter's fiery delivery had greatly pleased the Greeks. Messala asked Gallio what he thought of Nicetes to which Gallio replied: "O, he's full of divine frenzy". As often as he heard one of these rhetoricians whom the students of rhetoric call "impassioned", he immediately said, "He's full of divine frenzy". Whenever Gallio came from hearing a new rhetorician Messala always used the same form of question: "Is he full of divine frenzy?" This phrase became so common with Gallio that it often slipped from him involuntarily. Once in Caesar's presence when the genius of 7 Haterius was mentioned, dropping into his usual habit he said: "He too was full of divine frenzy". When the Emperor asked what he meant, he quoted the line of Vergil, and told how he had once let fall the phrase in the presence of Messala, and could never after prevent its slipping out. Tiberius being a pupil of Theodorus, didn't like Nicetes' style, and so was charmed with this story of Gallio's. The latter used to tell how his friend Ovid was greatly pleased with this story, and, as he had done with many other lines of Vergil, borrowed the idea, not desiring to deceive people but to have it openly recognised as borrowed. He said it could be found in one of Ovid's tragedies: "Alas, I am driven hither and thither, full of divine frenzy." Now, if you like, I shall return to Fuscus, and I will at once glut you with descriptive passages of his, and especially with those which he put in his treatment of the Probable, when he maintained that a knowledge of the future was absolutely impossible.

"Alexander the Great deliberates whether he should enter Babylon, since an oracle had threatened him with danger if he did so"

ARELLIUS FUSCUS                                              I

Who is he who claims a knowledge of the future? Singular must be his lot in life, who is bidden by a god to prophesy: he must disdain that womb from which *we* come who do not know the future. He must boast some likeness to a god who proclaims a god's commands. It must be so: since he inspires fear in a king so powerful, ruler of so vast a world. Great must *he* be, and raised beyond the limits of a mortal lot, who has the power to strike terror into Alexander. He may set his sires amid the stars, and claim descent from heaven, the god must acknowledge his own seer. No narrow span of years can be his: *his* soul must be exempt from all decrees of fate, who proclaims the future's secret to the world. If these auguries are true, why then do we not devote all our days to the pursuit of this lore? Why do we not from our earliest years pierce into the heart of things, and visit the gods, since the path is clear; since the stars are an open book to us, and we may hold converse with divinities? If this is so, then why do we thus labour in the pursuit of an eloquence which is useless, why do we waste our strength in the practice of arms which are perilous? Surely genius will thrive best on this knowledge of the future. Can there be a better guarantee of its growth? Those, who, as they assert, have probed to the 2 secrets of fate, enquire into the days of our birth, and count the first hour of our life the index of all the years to come: they calculate the motions of the stars at that hour, the direction of their various paths, decide if the sun stood steadily adverse, or shone calmly upon us: if the moon was full, or its light only waxing, or if it hid its head in the gloom of night; whether Saturn welcomed us at birth to the life of a farmer, or Mars as warriors to a life of arms, or Mercury to the busy pursuit of wealth, whether with sweet smile Venus beckoned to us, or Jupiter raised us from low to high estate— all those gods thronging and crowding round one single head!

**3** The future is the burden of the message. To many these seers have foretold long life: and while they thought of no danger the day of doom overwhelmed them: to some they have announced that death was near, yet these have long survived to useless days: to others they have promised happy years, yet every form of misfortune fell swiftly on their head. Our life's destiny is unknown. These predictions are but arbitrary fictions of the seers; no treasures from the mine of true knowledge. Shall there be then, Alexander, one spot in the whole world which has not beheld thee as victor? Is Babylon barred to him to whom the Ocean lay open?

**4** DIVISIO

In this suasoria I know that Fuscus treated only those questions I have reported above relating to the knowledge of the future. Because of the pleasure it gave us I cannot pass over the following quotation. Fuscus Arellius delivered a declamation about the woman who had three times given birth to a dead child and then said she had dreamed that she must bring forth in a grove. I should insult your intelligence if I set down at length the whole controversy with which I am aware you are well acquainted:.... When Fuscus was declaiming on the side of the grandfather who refused to recognise the child, he handled the stock argument against dreams and the existence of a divine providence. Then after declaring that he who represented the gods as attending upon women in childbirth, wronged their majesty, he quoted amid great applause the following line of Vergil:

> Is that forsooth a task for gods above?
> Are such the cares that irk their calm repose?

**5** A certain pupil (to spare his feelings I will not name him) was delivering this suasoria about Alexander in the presence of Fuscus and thought to quote the same line with equally good effect. So he said:

> Is that forsooth a task for gods above?
> Are such the cares that irk their calm repose?

Then says Fuscus to him: "If you had said this in the presence of Alexander, you would have learned that in Vergil there is also this line:

> He buried his sword as far as the hilt."

Since you are always worrying me about Fuscus and asking
the reason of his unique reputation for elegance of style, I
shall inflict on you examples of the way in which Fuscus
developed his subject. He was always delighted to deliver
suasoriae, and rendered them oftener in Greek than in Latin.
In his handling of this suasoria Hybreas said: "What a bul-
wark Babylon has found in this seer!"

# SUASORIA V

'The Athenians deliberate whether they should remove the trophies of their victory over the Persians, since Xerxes threatens that he will return if they are not removed"

**1** ARELLIUS FUSCUS

I blush for your victory if you deem that Xerxes can return from such a rout. After the slaughter of so many thousands, there is scarcely enough of his great army left (for all his threats) to form an escort for his flight. His many fleets are beneath the sea. No need to remind you of Marathon and Salamis. I blush to say it: we still doubt the reality of our victory. Shall Xerxes come? Words fail me to tell the depression of his soul at the memory of his loss, his aversion from the thought of his shattered armies. The panic he felt before presages future terror: his past losses bode further disaster and forbid enterprise. Sometimes there is joy and exultation in his soul when the present is the basis of his hopes, then his spirit is shattered as he thinks of past disasters. All confidence fails his soul when dishonour lies heavy on his hopes, when he remembers he was routed on every field. He is benumbed by his losses, and abandons those ill-starred ambitions. If he meant to come he would use no threats: the flame of his anger burns fiercely, it is not extinguished in **2** thoughts of negotiation. He would send no warning if he meant to come, nor would he arm us by his tidings, nor goad Greece in her victory, nor provoke her successful arms: rather would he come upon us unprepared. Formerly he sent no warning before putting his armies in motion. In that first assault all the strength of the Orient poured into Greece. In proud reliance on that host he had raised his weapons even against the gods. Low lie all those thousands, as many blotted out before his reign as were destroyed under his command: none survive except the fugitives. No need to recall Salamis, or Cynaegiros, or thee, Polyzelos! And yet we question our victory! I raised these trophies in honour of the gods, I raised them in the sight of all Greece that none should fear the threats of Xerxes. O, the pity of it! I set up trophies when Xerxes was in the field; shall I remove them now that he has fled? Now, Athenians, we are conquered: men will not believe merely that Xerxes has come back: they will believe that he is the victor. By our aid only can Xerxes **3** remove these trophies. Believe me, it is difficult to rally forces ground to the dust, to renew shattered hopes, and from a field of battle that you rue to rise to confident hopes in a better issue.

CESTIUS PIUS

I shall invade, says Xerxes; he is only promising me more trophies. Can he come in greater power than when we defeated him?

ARGENTARIUS

Are you not ashamed? Xerxes sets a higher value on your trophies than on you.

DIVISIO **4**

Fuscus analysed the argument thus: Even if Xerxes meant to come unless we removed the trophies they ought not to be removed. To carry out his commands is to confess ourselves his slaves. If he comes we shall defeat him. This statement needs no long proof: I say, "We shall defeat him", of the man whom we have defeated before. But he will not even come: if he meant to come, he would not announce his coming: his strength and spirit are alike broken. Cestius also added the following argument, which he dealt with in the first part, "The Athenians have no right to remove the trophies: the right in them is common to all Greece: all shared in the war: all shared in the victory": finally, he said it was even a sin against the gods. "Never has anyone dared to lay hands on the memorials in which his valour was enshrined. Those trophies do not belong to the Athenians; they belong to the gods: theirs was the war: Xerxes' bonds, Xerxes' weapons were aimed at them". Here he introduced everything relevant to the irreligious and proud warfare of Xerxes. "But in that case", you say, "we shall have war". **5** "Well, we have had war already, and shall have it again; remove Xerxes, you will find another foe; great empires are never at rest". (Enumeration of the wars successfully waged by the Athenians.) Next he said, "there will not be war; for Xerxes will not come." The most tyrannical are always most

fearful. "Lastly, granting that he comes, with whom will he come? He will gather together what your victory left: he will bring those whom he left behind in the last war as useless: or those who escaped from the rout. Every soldier he has was
6 either despised by himself or beaten by us." Argentarius was content with these two points: either Xerxes will not come, or need not be feared if he does. On these two alone he based his argument: here he made this striking statement: "'Remove the trophies', says he: but I reply, 'If you are the victor, why do you blush? If you are defeated, why do you give commands?'" Then he raised the following point with good effect: in his judgment neither Xerxes nor any Persian would dare to invade Greece; but in case an enemy came from that quarter they must guard the trophies all the more, that the sight of them might inspire their own soldiers, and break the
7 spirit of the enemy. Blandus said: "Let him first fill up Athos, and restore the seas to their original form. He wishes posterity to know him as he came, let them rather know him as he returned." Triarius neglected all analysis of the question, and merely expressed his exultation at the news that Xerxes was returning: soon they would have a fresh victory, fresh trophies. This statement of Silo Pompeius is both neat and witty: "Unless you remove the trophies", says Xerxes, "I shall come back", that is to say, "Unless you remove these trophies, you will raise others".
8     Gallio was the only one who argued on the opposite side. He exhorted them to remove the trophies: that would not diminish their glory: the memory of their victory would remain for ever, while weather and time would destroy the trophies: the war had had to be undertaken for liberty, for their wives and for their children: it was wrong to undertake another for an idle thing and one the loss of which would do no harm. Here he said Xerxes would most certainly come, and he described Xerxes' pride that braved the gods themselves: he had great resources: he had not brought all his forces against Greece, nor lost them all in Greece: they must fear the fickleness of fortune: the strength of Greece was exhausted, and could not now endure a second war: Xerxes had inexhaustible supplies of men. Here he delivered this sentence eloquent enough for either oratory or history: "We shall be exhausted with victories before they are exhausted with defeats".

# SUASORIA VI

## "Cicero considers whether he should beg Antony for life"

QUINTUS HATERIUS         1

Let future generations know that the commonwealth not Cicero could bow the knee to Antony. You will have to write eulogies on Antony; on such a theme even Cicero's eloquence will ·fail. Believe me, however carefully you guard your tongue, Antony will do what Cicero cannot pass in silence. If you understand aright, Cicero, he does not say "Ask for life", but "Ask for bondage". How will you bring yourself to enter this senate depleted by cruelty, recruited with dishonour? . Will you have the heart to enter a senate in which you are not to see Cn. Pompey, nor M. Cato, nor the Luculli, nor Hortensius, nor Lentulus and Marcellus, nor your own peculiar consuls, Hirtius and Pansa? What has Cicero in common with an alien generation? Now our days are over. Marcus Cato, alone our noblest pattern in life and in death, 2 chose to die rather than beg for mercy—yet it was no Antony he had to petition—and armed those hands of his, to the last unstained by Roman blood, against his own noble breast. When Scipio had buried the sword deep in his bosom he replied to the soldiers who had boarded his vessel and were searching for the commander, "With the commander all is well". Triumphant in defeat he spoke like a conqueror. You yourself said, "Milo forbids me to ask mercy from the jury". Go, then, and ask mercy from Antony.

PORCIUS LATRO         3

Does then Cicero ever speak without striking terror into Antony? Does Antony ever speak to strike terror into Cicero? A thirst like Sulla's for his country's blood arises in the state again, and under the triumvirs' spear not taxes but the lives of Roman citizens are bought and sold. By the white wax of one tablet the disasters of Pharsalia, Munda and Mutina are surpassed: the lives of consuls are bartered for gold: your own words are all that we can utter: "Alas for the degeneracy of the age!" You shall see eyes burning at once with

cruelty and pride: no human countenance shall you see, but
the very visage of the Fury of civil war: you shall behold those
jaws that devoured the wealth of Cn. Pompey, that brawny
chest, that gladiator's strength of frame: you shall see that
spot before the seat of justice which lately as Master of the
Horse, who ought to be a pattern of dignity[1], he had defiled
in the most shameful manner. Will you fall as a suppliant
there and beg for life on bended knee? With that tongue
that saved the state will you utter humble words of flattery?
Shame! Even Verres when proscribed died more gallantly.

**4 CLAUDIUS MARCELLUS AESERNINUS**

Remember Cato whose death you extolled: do you think
anything in the world so precious that you should be indebted to Antony for life?

**CESTIUS PIUS**

If you think of the people's desire, the people's grief, no
matter when you die, you die untimely. In the light of your
services you have lived long enough: but looking to the
wrongs inflicted by Fortune, and your country's plight, you
have lived too long: as regards your works and their memory
you are destined to be immortal.

**POMPEIUS SILO**

You may know that for you longer life is not expedient, if you
live only by Antony's reprieve. Will you then keep silence
while Antony issues his proscriptions and mangles his country?
Shall not even your groans be free? I had rather the Roman
people mourned Cicero in death than in life.

**5 TRIARIUS**

What Charybdis so rapacious as he? Charybdis, said I? If
Charybdis ever was, she was only one monster: scarcely, by
heavens, could the sea itself have gulped down so many
diverse things at once. And you would snatch Cicero from
this madman's rage?

**ARELLIUS FUSCUS, THE FATHER**

We rush from strife to strife: victors abroad we are butchered
at home; at home an intestine enemy gloats upon our blood.
Since this is the plight of the Roman people, who does not

---

[1] A paraphrase: the literal Latin is too coarse for English.

think that Cicero must die? Your prayers to Antony will be shameful and in vain. In no obscure tomb can you be shrouded from men's eyes: your virtues will not perish with your life. Undying Memory, the guardian of human achievements, which makes great men's lives immortal, will make your name sacred to all generations. All that will pass away is the **6** frail, perishable body, subject to disease, liable to mischances, exposed to proscription: but the soul, of birth divine, which knows neither age nor death, freed from the heavy bonds of the flesh, will hasten to its familiar home among the stars. Yet, if we regard your age and the number of your years, which gallant men never reckon, you have passed sixty, and your life cannot but seem too long since by lingering you survive your country. We have seen civil war raging through the whole world, and after the stricken fields of Italy and Pharsalia, now even Egypt has drunk its fill of Roman blood. Why should we be wroth that Antony may do to Cicero what the Alexandrian eunuch did to Pompey? So miserably *they* perish who flee for refuge to the unworthy.

CORNELIUS HISPANUS     **7**

*He* was doomed to die who only supported your motion. The whole list of the proscribed is but the prelude to your death: the one permits the proscription of a brother, the other of an uncle: what hope have you? Those bloody deeds have but one object—the death of Cicero. Recall to mind, I pray you, all those your eloquence defended, all those your power protected, recall your consulate itself, the greatest of your services: then you will understand that Cicero may be constrained to die but never to beg for life.

ARGENTARIUS

The triumvirs act the king: they parade before us the luxury of their revels, a cookshop stocked with the tribute of the world. Antony himself, haggard with wine and watching, lifts his drowsy eyes to the heads of the proscribed. The reproach of "worthless creature" no longer meets the case.

DIVISIO     **8**

Latro arranged this suasoria thus: Even if you can obtain life from Antony it is not worth while to ask it; secondly: you cannot obtain it. In the former part he laid it down that it was

dishonourable for any Roman, all the more for Cicero, to ask
for life: here he introduced examples of those who had died
of their own accord; next he said that further life was worthless to him; and, without liberty, more grievous than death.
Here he described all the bitterness of the servitude that was
in store for him. The pledge would not be kept inviolate.
Then after saying "Something in you will offend Antony,
some deed, some word, your silence, or a look:" he con-
cluded thus: "You will hardly win *his* favour".

9      Albucius's arrangement was different: firstly, he said that
Cicero must die even if no one proscribed him (here he
inveighed against the age). Then, he must die of his own free
will, since he would have to die, even if he did not want to:
he had roused deadly hatred. Cicero was himself the chief
motive for the proscription. He was the only rhetorician who
dared to say that Antony was not alone in his hostility to him.
In this passage he expressed the following: "If not a personal
enemy of each, you are obnoxious to them all"; and the
following which was much admired: "If, Cicero, you ask
mercy of one and obtain it, you will be the slave of
three".

10     This was the arrangement of Cestius: "For you death is
expedient, honourable and necessary, that in freedom and
with honour untarnished, you may put the crown upon your
life". Here he expressed the daring idea: "that you may be
numbered with Cato, who could not be a slave though Antony
was not yet tyrant". Marcellus expressed this idea about
Cato still better: "Have all things changed so utterly with the
overthrow of the Roman people that one should debate
whether it is better to live with Antony or die with Cato?"
But let us return to Cestius and his analysis of the argument.
He said death was expedient to avoid physical torture: Cicero
would not merely die if he fell into the hands of Antony.
When he had described here the mockery and the insults that
would be heaped on him, the scourgings and tortures, he gave
expression to a sentiment that has been much admired: "By
heavens, Cicero, when you come to Antony you will beg not
11 for life, but for death". Varius Geminus thus arranged the
arguments: "I should exhort you, if you must in any case
choose one of the alternatives, death or entreaty, to die rather
than beg for life": and he included all the arguments used by

the others: but he added a third, he exhorted him to flee. He said here was M. Brutus, there C. Cassius, in that place Sex. Pompeius: then he continued with that appeal which was admired in the highest degree by Cassius Severus, "Why do we falter? The free state too has its triumvirs". He went on to survey rapidly the regions he might go to. He instanced his defence of Sicily, his excellent administration of Cilicia in his proconsulate, his student days in Asia and Achaia, his services to the kingdom of Deiotarus, the benefits he had conferred on Egypt, where they were not forgotten, and which was now doing penance for its treachery to Pompey. But most of all he urged him to go to Asia and Macedonia to the camp of Brutus and Cassius. And so Cassius used to say that where others had declaimed, Varius Geminus had given genuine counsel.

Few have declaimed on the other side. No one dared to **12** exhort Cicero to entreat Antony for life. They judged Cicero's spirit well. Geminus Varius declaimed on the opposite side also. He said: "I hope I shall persuade my dear Cicero to be willing to live. Those lofty sentiments he uttered long ago do not weigh with me—'No consular can die untimely, no wise man in misery'. He holds no office now. I know well the character of the man. He will do it: he will ask for mercy. As regards servitude he will make no objection to that. He is quite used to harness. Pompey and Caesar both broke him in. You see in him a slave grown old in service." And he added many other jests as was his manner. He arranged his arguments thus: Cicero would not be dis- **13** honoured in begging for mercy: he would not even beg in vain. Firstly he said it was not disgraceful to beg mercy of a countryman who had defeated you. He instanced the numbers that had petitioned Caesar, he mentioned Ligarius. It was quite right that Cicero should give satisfaction to Antony, since Cicero had proscribed him first, and had judged him a traitor. It is the wrongdoer that always makes reparation: he should beg boldly for life: his petition would not be for his own sake, but for his country's: for him personally his life had been long enough: for his country all too short. In the second part he said personal enemies usually grant these petitions: Cicero had forgiven Vatinius and Gabinius, and had defended them on their trial. Since he

was one of three, Antony would be more easily induced not
to allow one of the other triumvirs to deprive him of so
handsome an opportunity for clemency. The cause of
Antony's resentment might be that Cicero did not think him
14 worth entreaty. When he had described the dangers of flight,
he added that Cicero must be in subjection no matter where he
went. He would have to endure the violent temper of Cassius,
or the arrogance of Brutus, or the folly of Pompey (the younger).

Since I have chanced on this suasoria I do not think it
irrelevant to point out how each of the historians has treated
the memory of Cicero. All are agreed that Cicero was not
cowardly enough to petition Antony, nor foolish enough to
hope that his petition would be successful. We must make an
exception of Asinius Pollio, who showed persistent hostility
to Cicero's reputation. Thus he gave the rhetoricians a
subject for a second suasoria. The rhetoricians often declaim
on this subject: "Cicero deliberates whether he should burn
his speeches, since Antony promises him life on these terms".
15 Anyone can see that this is a stupid fiction. Pollio means it to
be taken for truth. This is what he said in the speech he published in defence of Lamia.

ASINIUS POLLIO

"And so Cicero never hesitated to deny the authorship of
the speeches against Antony, in spite of the passion with
which he had delivered them: and he promised to write many
times that number with far more care, in direct contradiction
of them, and even to deliver them in public". Pollio made
other accusations still more dishonourable, and it was quite
evident that the whole story was so false that even Pollio had
not the courage to insert it in his historical writings. Certainly those who heard his speech in defence of Lamia say
that he did not make the above statements but concocted them
afterwards—for he could not support the lie, since the
16 triumvirs knew the truth. I don't want to vex you, my young
friends, by passing from rhetoricians to historians. I shall
make amends to you, and perhaps cause you after reading
these extracts to approach with greater favour the solid truths
of history: if, however, I cannot achieve this purpose directly
I shall be compelled to cheat you at the first sip, just as we do
with children when giving them medicine. So far is Livy from

stating that Cicero intended to retract that he says Cicero had
no time; here is what he says:

### LIVY    17

"Marcus Cicero, shortly before the arrival of the triumvirs,
had left the city, convinced, and rightly, that he could no
more escape Antony than Cassius and Brutus could escape
Caesar: at first he had fled to his Tusculan villa, then he set
out by cross-country roads to his villa at Formiae, intending
to take ship from Caieta. He put out to sea several times but
was driven back by contrary winds. At last since he could no
longer put up with the tossing of the ship, as there was a
heavy ground swell, he became weary of flight and of life, and
returning to his villa on the high ground, which was little more
than a mile from the sea, 'Let me die' says he, 'in my own
country, which I have often saved'. It is quite true that his
slaves were ready to fight for him with bravery and fidelity:
but he ordered them to set down the litter, and quietly to
suffer the hard necessity of fate. As he leaned from the litter
and kept his neck still for the purpose, his head was struck
off. But that did not satisfy the callous brutality of the
soldiers: they cut off his hands too, reviling them for
having written something against Antony. So the head was
brought to Antony and by his order was set between the two
hands on the rostra where he had been heard as consul, often
as consular, where in that very year his eloquent invectives
against Antony had commanded unprecedented admiration.
Men were scarce able to raise their tearful eyes and look upon
the mangled remains of their countryman". Bassus Aufidius, 18
too, had no doubt about Cicero's spirit, and that he not only
submitted bravely to death, but courted it.

### AUFIDIUS BASSUS

"After he saw the armed men Cicero slightly drew aside the
curtain of the litter and said: 'I go no further: approach,
veteran soldier, and, if you can at least do so much properly,
sever this neck'. Then as the soldier trembled and hesitated,
he added: 'What would you have done had you come to me
as your first victim?'" Cremutius Cordus also says that 19
Cicero debated whether he should go to Brutus or Cassius or
Sextus Pompeius, but every course displeased him except
death.

CREMUTIUS CORDUS

"On seeing the head and hands of Cicero Antony was delighted and displayed them on the rostra, saying that his share of the proscription was now complete, for he was not only sated but glutted with the blood of his countrymen. And so in that spot to which he had often gone attended by a huge throng, which shortly before had lent its ears to those devoted speeches by which he had saved the lives of many, with what a mournful change his mangled remains raised aloft were seen by his countrymen, the head drooping and the lips sprinkled with gore, he who but yesterday was the leader of the senate and the glory of the Roman name, now a source of profit to his assassin. But especially the hearts of all melted to tears and groans at the sight of the right hand nailed beside the head, the right hand that had wielded that divine pen. The murder of the other victims stirred only private grief, Cicero's death alone plunged the whole state into mourning."

**20** BRUTTEDIUS NIGER

"Meanwhile slipping out from the other side of the villa Cicero was carried in a litter through the fields: but when he saw Popillius approaching, a soldier well-known to him, remembering that he had defended him, his countenance brightened. But Popillius to gain favour with the conquerors made haste to do the deed and cut off his head. In that last moment of his life there is nothing to be censured in Cicero's conduct. Popillius, regardless that he had shortly before been defended by his victim, carried the head to Antony". Here Bruttedius meant to describe the pitiful sight when the head was set on the rostra, but the greatness
**21** of the task overwhelmed him. "But when the head was set on the rostra between the two hands at the command of Antony, and when the citizens saw it in that place where so often his eloquence had been heard, with groans and tears all did honour to the great man who was dead. No dead body lay on the rostra: no customary eulogy was pronounced to the assembled citizens, but they told the story of his life to one another. There was no spot in the forum but was marked by the memory of some famous pleading of his: no one who had not some service to acknowledge rendered

by Cicero: certainly this service to the state was known to all—that he had postponed that wretched time of slavery from the days of Catiline to those of Antony."

Whenever historians describe the death of a great man they usually sum up his whole life, and pronounce a sort of funeral oration. This was done once or twice by Thucydides, and adopted in a very few instances by Sallust; Titus Livius generously applied it to all great men: subsequent historians have done it much more freely. This is the "epitaph", to use a Greek word, that Livius wrote for Cicero: "He lived **22** sixty-three years, so that even if he had not died by violence his death cannot seem untimely. The rich products of his genius were amply rewarded; he enjoyed long years of prosperity: but his long career of good fortune was interrupted from time to time by serious disasters—exile, the ruin of the party he championed, the sad and untimely death of his daughter. Of all these disasters he bore as became a man none except his death. A true judgment might have found this less undeserved in that he suffered at the hands of his enemy no more cruel fate than he would himself have inflicted had he been equally fortunate. Yet if one weighs his virtues with his faults he deserves a place in history as a truly great man, and another Cicero would be required to praise him adequately." With that impartial judgment with which he weighs all men of genius Titus Livius has rendered the amplest tribute to Cicero. It is not worth while to quote the **23** eulogy pronounced on Cicero by Cremutius Cordus. There is hardly anything in it worthy of Cicero, not even the following, although it is passable.

CREMUTIUS CORDUS

"He thought that private animosities should sometimes be forgotten, political feuds should never be decided by force of arms. He was a man conspicuous not merely for the greatness but also for the number of his virtues."

AUFIDIUS BASSUS

"So died M. Cicero, the born saviour of his country. He long defended and guided it, but in his old age at last it slipped from his grasp, injured by this one mistake that he approved of no other course to save it than the removal of Antony. He lived sixty-three years, always attacking some political

opponent, or himself the object of attack, and nothing was
rarer in his experience than a day on which it was to no one's
**24** interest that he should die." Pollio Asinius, too, who described the gallant death of Verres whom Cicero impeached,
is the only author who paints the death of Cicero in grudging
terms: yet even in spite of himself he does him ample
justice.

ASINIUS POLLIO

"His numerous and imperishable works make it superfluous
to recount the genius and industry of this great man. Nature
and happy chance were alike his servants, since he preserved
his handsome features and robust health into old age. His
life fell fortunately on a time of long peace, in the arts of
which he was accomplished, for when justice was admini-
stered with antique rigour, there came into being a very large
number of accused, very many of whom he successfully
defended, and so secured their friendship. He was very
fortunate in his candidature for the consulship, and in the
god-given chance of doing great deeds in it with wisdom and
energy. Would that he had been able to endure prosperity
with greater self-control, and adversity with greater fortitude!
For whenever either had fallen to his lot, he thought it could
not change. Hence arose those violent storms of unpopu-
larity, and hence his personal enemies had greater confidence
in attacking him: for he invited enmity with greater spirit
than he fought it. But since no mortal is blessed with perfect
virtue, a man must be judged by that virtue on which the
greater part of his life and genius has been based. And I
should not have thought that his end was to be pitied had not
**25** he himself thought death so great a misfortune." I can assure
you that there is nothing in Pollio's historical works more
eloquent than this passage which I have quoted; in fact he
seems not then to have extolled Cicero, but to have entered
into rivalry with him. Nor do I say this to deter you from the
desire of reading his histories. Indulge your desire and you
will make amends to Cicero. Yet of all these eloquent men
none has lamented the death of Cicero in better terms than
Cornelius Severus.

**26** CORNELIUS SEVERUS

"And the heads of great-hearted men, the lips almost breathing

still, lay low on their own rostra: but all eyes were irre-
sistibly drawn to the countenance of Cicero in death, as if that
head lay there alone. Then come back to the minds of men
the great deeds of his consulate, the host of conspirators, the
discovery of the guilty pact, and the stamping out of the sin
of the nobles: the punishment of Cethegus is recalled, and
Catiline disappointed of his unholy desires. What had
availed the favouring throngs, his years full of honours, or his
polished and accomplished age? One day swept away the
age's glory, and, smitten with grief, silent and sad, fell the
eloquence of the Latin tongue. Once sole protector and
saviour of the distressed, ever the illustrious leader of his
country, champion of the senate, of the forum, of the laws
of religion and of the ways of peace. The voice of the free
state fell dumb for ever under the savagery of arms. His
countenance defiled, his grey hairs sprinkled with blood
unholy, his noble hands that wielded that mighty pen, his
countryman in his triumph threw down and spurned with
haughty feet, nor regarded slippery fate and the gods.
In no lapse of time shall Antony wash away this stain. The
gentle victor had not done this with Emathian Perses, nor
with thee, dread Syphax, nor when Philip was the foe: in
the triumph over Jugurtha all mockery was absent, and fierce
Hannibal, when he fell to our wrath, yet carried his limbs
inviolate to the Stygian shades."

I shall not rob our countryman of a good line that in- **27**
spired this much better one of Cornelius Severus:

> Silent and sad fell the eloquence of the Latin tongue.

Sextilius Ena was a gifted rather than a learned man, unequal
as a poet, and no doubt sometimes showing the defects that
Cicero ascribes to the poets of Cordova, "who have something thick and foreign in their utterance". He intended to
read aloud in the house of Messala Corvinus this very poem
on the proscription, and had invited Asinius Pollio. In the
beginning he read this line with much approval:

> We must weep for Cicero and the silence of the Latin tongue.

This roused Pollio Asinius who said: "Messala, you may do
what you like in your own house: I do not intend to listen to
a man who thinks me dumb". And with this he rose and

went out. I know that Cornelius, too, was present at that
recital, and clearly he was not as vexed with this line as
Pollio, because he too composed a line better indeed but not
unlike it. If I end here I know that you will stop reading just
there where I left the rhetoricians: and so to make you
willing to turn over the roll to the end I shall add a suasoria
similar to the last.

# SUASORIA VII

## "Cicero considers whether he should burn his writings as Antony promises him life if he does so"

QUINTUS HATERIUS                                                    I

You will not endure Antony. In a bad nature success is intolerable; nothing inflames evil desire more than the consciousness of prosperous villainy. The effort is too great: you will not put up with him, I tell you, and you will have the desire to goad once more your enemy to kill you. For myself, I am far from being a Cicero, yet I am not only weary but ashamed of my life. Is this not the reason why you prize your genius—that Antony hates it more than he hates you? Ostensibly he grants you life, but his design is to make you as if you had not lived. Antony's conditions are more cruel than the proscription. Your genius is the one thing beyond the reach of the triumvirs' swords. Antony's aim is to secure Cicero's assistance in destroying that part of Cicero which proscription cannot reach. I should now exhort you to hold your life dear, if liberty still had its home in our state, and eloquence its source in liberty, if our necks were not the sport of our countryman's sword: but, as it is, Antony promises you life to convince you that there is nothing better than death. There hangs the announcement of the infamous proscription: all that multitude of praetorians, of consulars, of members of the equestrian order, has perished: none is left save those who can stoop to slavery. I know not, Cicero, whether after all that has happened you still desire to live. Not one person is left to justify that desire. You did right in deciding against death when Caesar of himself made the request that you should live, and imposed no conditions; when the state, though no longer free, had at least fallen into the hands of a benevolent despot.

CESTIUS PIUS                                                       2

Unless my judgment is at fault, Antony has seen clearly that Cicero cannot die while the records of his eloquence are safe. The bargain proposed assails the noblest part of your soul

before assailing you: lend me your eloquence for a moment;
I crave this boon of Cicero before he dies. If Caesar and
Pompey had listened to you, they would not have formed their
dishonourable alliance, nor have broken it: if they had ever
been willing to hearken to your advice, Pompey would not
have abandoned Caesar nor Caesar Pompey. No need to
recall your consulate that saved the state, your exile still more
honourable than your consulate, your frank challenge to the
despotism of Sulla, in the dawn of youth on the threshold of
your public life, no need to recall how you tore Antonius from
the side of Catiline and restored him to his country. Pardon
me, Cicero, if I dwell on these achievements; perchance after
3 to-day they will be invoked no more. If Cicero is slain he will
lie in death with Pompey the father and Pompey the son, with
Afranius, Petreius, Q. Catulus, and M. Antonius, who deserved a less degenerate successor: if Cicero survives he will
live among the Ventidii, the Canidii, and the Saxae: is it so
doubtful whether it is better to lie in death with those or live
with these? You gain one life, your own, by your bargain; you
inflict a national loss. I know that every price that he fixes is
unjust; at Antony's price I do not buy even Cicero's life. If
this were his proposal, "You will live, but eyeless, you will
live, but crippled": even if you could have brought yourself
to endure other bodily losses, yet you would have excepted
your tongue. Have you forgotten that noble utterance of
yours, "Death is the natural close of life, no punishment"?
Do you alone doubt its truth? But you urge, you think you
have persuaded Antony. Rather take your stand firmly on the
side of liberty, and add one more crime to your enemy's
score: by your death plunge Antony still deeper in guilt.

4 PUBLIUS ASPRENAS

In order to gain life from Antony does Cicero himself mean
to destroy the records of his eloquence? What are you offered
in Antony's proposal? the restoration of Cn. Pompey, and
M. Cato, and of the old senate, the only fit audience for
Cicero? Many who were about to pay too dear for life, have
died through the contempt they inspired; many at the point
of death have been saved by the admiration their courage
extorted, and have found their salvation in this brave willing-
ness to die. As against Antony's proposal hear what the
Roman people have to offer. In return for the burning of

your writings Antony offers you a few years of life: if you
refuse, the Roman people, in their love, offer you immortality.

POMPEIUS SILO                                               5

What shall we call it if we destroy the eloquence of Cicero to
secure the protection of Antony? Is this an act of grace, this
penalty inflicted on your genius? If the money-lenders did
well in giving him their money, if Brutus and Cassius did well
in giving him peace, then let us, Cicero, put our faith in
Antony—a madman whose natural inclination to vice finds
scope in the licence of the age, who interrupts his amours
with actresses to wanton in Roman blood; a bankrupt who
pledged the free commonwealth with his creditors, a creature
of avarice insatiable, even when gorged with the wealth
of two leaders of the state, Caesar and Pompey! Let me
use your own words, Cicero, "Does anyone prize a life that
Antony can give or take away?" Cicero's safety is not so
precious that we should accept Antony as the saviour.

TRIARIUS                                                    6

Once the Roman people was brought to such a pass that it had
lost all but Jove who was himself beleaguered, and Camillus
who was in exile: yet nothing in Camillus was nobler than his
indignation that Romans should owe their safety to a treaty.
A grievous burden is that life which Antony offers even if no
price were exacted. Antony, judged an enemy by the state,
now judges the state his enemy. In order that Antony's
approval of his colleague may be patent to all, Lepidus, ever
the abettor of another's madness, the tool of both his colleagues, has become our master.

ARGENTARIUS                                                 7

Antony must not be trusted in anything: surely I speak the
truth: of what crime is he not capable who has the heart to
slay Cicero, and who shows more cruelty in granting than in
refusing life? It is your genius that stirs his wrath: do you
think he forgives you that? Do you look for mercy from him
in whose soul your words still rankle? Shall oblivion fall on
your immortal genius to save your frail and perishable body?
I should marvel if there were more cruelty in death than in
pardon from Antony. Publius Scipio, degenerate scion of his 8

house, by a noble death was restored to the number of the
Scipios. He grants you life with the object of destroying
your all of immortality. This is the nature of the compact:
he spares your life and robs you of your genius. At the price
of oblivion to your name he offers you a few years of slavery.
His design is that you should live on as the silent survivor of
your genius. Cicero, it seems, is to listen to Lepidus and
Antony, but no one is to hear the voice of Cicero. Will you
have the heart to look with your own eyes on the burial of the
noblest thing you have? Rather let the records of your genius
survive you, to the eternal condemnation of Antony.

ARELLIUS FUSCUS, THE FATHER
As long as the human race endures, as long as literature has
its due honour, and eloquence is prized, as long as the fortune
of our state stands sure, or its memory survives, your genius
will live in the admiration of posterity, and though yourself
proscribed in one age you will proscribe Antony to all ages.
Believe me, it is only the most worthless part in you which
he can spare or take away: the true Cicero, as Antony well
9 knows, only Cicero can proscribe. It is not you he is ex-
empting from the proscription: he seeks to save himself from
your condemnation. If Antony breaks faith you will die: if
he keeps his word you will be a slave. For my part I prefer
him to break his word. I beseech you earnestly, M. Tullius,
by your own soul, by your noble life of sixty-four years, by
your consulate that saved your country, by the memorials
of your genius, whose immortality none but you can destroy,
by the free state which perishes before you, that you may
not think you are leaving to his mercy anything you love,
I implore you not to confess before your death such great
unwillingness to die.

10    No one to my knowledge argued on the other side in this
suasoria: all were anxious about Cicero's books, none about
Cicero personally; yet this side is not so bad that if Cicero
had actually been offered this condition he would have refused
to consider it. And so no one presented this case more
convincingly than Silo Pompeius: he did not employ, like
Cestius, the plausible arguments, that this proposal involved
a heavier penalty than death itself, and that was why Antony

adopted it. He argued that to every man life was short: much more so to an old man: he (Cicero) must think of fame which offered immortality to the great: life should not be ransomed at any cost: the terms were intolerable: nothing was so intolerable as that Cicero should burn with his own hands the records of his genius. He would be wronging the Roman people whose language he had made supreme, so that its eloquence as far surpassed the proud achievements of Greece as did its fortune: he would wrong the human race. If he bought life at such a price he would repent it: he would have to grow old in slavery, and employ his eloquence in extolling Antony and in nothing else. He was being infamously treated: he was granted life, but was bereft of genius.

Silo Pompeius argued that Antony's proposal was a **11** mockery. It was not an offer but an insult: even if he burned his books Antony would put him to death all the same. Antony was not foolish enough to think that there was any object to be gained in Cicero's burning his books, since his writings were renowned throughout the whole world; that was not Antony's aim: that was within his own power: unless perchance it was believed that the man who had Cicero at his mercy, had not Cicero's writings in his power too: Antony's only object was this, that the great Cicero after his many brave words about despising death should be brought to accept dishonourable terms and then slain. Antony was not promising him life on a condition, but death with dishonour. And so he must now endure with fortitude the fate that he must in any case suffer afterwards with dishonour. The bad taste of Senianus was shown in a remarkable manner in this suasoria too. He used an expression that sprang from affectation of the lowest and most vulgar type, I mean the type that secures its point by the addition or subtraction of a syllable, "What a shameful deed! Shall then Cicero's script perish and Antony's proscript remain?" A talented **12** youth named Surdinus who made a tasteful Latin translation of some Greek plays was delivering a declamation on this subject in the presence of Cestius Pius, the rhetorician. It was his manner to utter pleasing sentiments, but too often their strength was lost in their sweetness. In this suasoria after expressing some pretty sentiments in the form of an oath, he added: "So shall I read thee". Cestius, who was a very satirical fellow, pretended that he had not quite heard, and reproved the accomplished young man as if he had said something improper. "What did you say? What? So shall I enjoy thee?" Now Cestius cared for no one's talent but his own and went so far as to attack Cicero's, for which he

13 was properly punished. M. Tullius, Cicero's son, who had none of his father's ability except his wit, was governor of Asia, and Cestius happened to be dining in his house. Tullius was not gifted with a good memory, and drunkenness was gradually destroying any that he had. From time to time he kept asking the name of the guest who reclined on the lowest couch. He was told several times that it was Cestius, but as often forgot it. Finally the slave to imprint the name more deeply on his memory said to his master, when he asked who he was who reclined on the lowest couch, "This is the Cestius who said that your father was not a man of letters". Young Cicero ordered rods to be brought with speed, and Cestius's hide, as it deserved, yielded satisfaction to Cicero. But the younger Cicero was quick to take

14 offence even when filial piety did not demand it. Hybreas was a very good speaker and when his son in a case tried by Cicero was making a poor display the latter said: "Do we actually boast that we are better than our sires?" In a certain action when Hybreas delivered a whole passage of his father's verbatim, and everybody recognised it, Cicero said: "Come, don't you think that I have learned my father's 'How long, O Catiline, will you abuse our patience?'?" Gargonius, the most charming of simpletons, said in this suasoria two things than which even he never said anything more foolish: one in the exordium; when he had begun with an oath, which is now a very common practice in the schools, after a flood of words, he said: "So for the first time let him fear Antony with all the power of his soul; so may Cicero either wholly live or wholly die, as I shall never agree to destroy what I shall say to-day about Cicero's genius". He made the other statement in quoting examples of men who had died gallantly: "Juba and Petreius rushed together inflicting mutual wounds and lent death to one another".

# SUASORIA I

## NOTES

*References to the text of the present edition are to page and line*, e.g. **4**, 1.

The rhetor speaks in each case as one of a council of war held by Alexander the Great to determine whether having conquered Asia and India he should proceed to explore the Ocean, on whose shores he now stands.

The first part of the book of Suasoriae is lost. Even the title has been restored by conjecture. In C. VII, 7, 19, Seneca mentions a suasoria with this title: "illa suasoria in qua deliberat Alexander, an Oceanum naviget, cum exaudita vox esset: 'quousque invicte?'" Quintilian makes frequent reference to this or similar subjects. In III, 8, 16, he mentions the question, "an Alexander terras ultra Oceanum sit inventurus". See also VII, 2, 5. In VII, 4, 2, he says a similar subject was sometimes handled in suasoriae, "haec et in suasoriis aliquando tractari solent, ut, si Caesar deliberet, an Britanniam impugnet? quae sit Oceani natura?"

In *Ad Her.* IV, 22, Cornificius implies that Alexander had decided to make the voyage but was prevented by death, "Alexandro si vita longior data esset, Oceanum manus Macedonum transvolasset". So Lucan, x, 36:

> "Oceano classes inferre parabat
> exteriore mari. . . .
> occurrit suprema dies, naturaque solum
> tunc potuit finem vesano ponere regi".

Possibly the original title ran "Deliberat Alexander, an Oceanum naviget, cum exaudita vox esset: 'quousque invicte?'" In the passage quoted above, C. VII, 7, 19, Cestius is reported to have advised his pupils not to have recourse to such quotations (when they were given in the subject of debate) to secure an effective beginning or conclusion. He called the trick of beginning and closing in this way, "Echo", and made many jokes about it. Thus, for example, in this suasoria one of the pupils began his declamation with "quousque invicte?" and ended with it. Cestius said to him at once when he finished,

$$\text{ἔν σοι μὲν λήξω, σέο δ' ἄρξομαι.}$$

To another who finished a description of Alexander's victories with the same words, he at once retorted, "tu autem quousque?" In itself there seems no real reason to object to such a method of beginning and ending, but Cestius probably ruled it out as hackneyed.

**1, 2. natura.** This term denotes either the spirit that animates the universe (*mundus*), or the universe of created things itself, when it is usually accompanied by *rerum*. It may also mean the essential nature or endowment of any thing. This spirit seems to fail on the borders of the Ocean. The creative spirit dies out as we approach the limit of the lands, and its last imperfect manifestations, the monstrosities or monsters (*rudis et imperfecta natura*) take refuge in the depths of the sea. Sometimes the sea is represented as controlled by it, sometimes as outside the limits of its sway. Fabianus says in § 4 (**2**, 28): "sacrum quiddam terris natura circumfudit Oceanum". Nature here is represented as the agency that spread Ocean round the lands. In § 1 (**1**, 10), "quasi deficientis in suo fine naturae pigra moles", Ocean is called a lifeless bulk of nature as it were (*quasi*) which here reaches its appointed end and dies, i.e. an inert mass attached to or belonging to nature. (See Munro's Lucretius, I, 25, note.)

3. **aiunt**: "it is commonly believed"; but the rhetorician, quoted here, does not believe the statement. He says, "facile ista finguntur", etc. So also St Augustine, *De Civ. Dei*, 16, 9, rejects the idea that there are lands and men at the antipodes.

5. **rerum naturam**. See the note above. It seems simpler here to take this in the sense of 'created things' or 'world', and *novam exsurgere* as 'a new world arises'. Here also however there is the sense of agency about *natura*, and it may well be translated as 'the vital force in things never ceases, but ever where it seems to cease, there it rises with new vigour'.

8. **hactenus**. Alexander must not seek to go beyond the ordered universe or *mundus*. The sun shines only on the lands, the Ocean is enveloped in darkness. (See **1**, 12.)

9. **caelum Hercules meruit**. Hercules in his labours had not attempted to penetrate the Ocean; even to win divinity Alexander need not do so. Alexander is frequently compared with Hercules and Bacchus in the narratives of Arrian and Q. Curtius, and also in Sen. phil. This is sufficient evidence that such ideas were common in the schools of rhetoric. Below, § 2, Moschus says, "ultra Liberi patris tropaea constituimus". So Q. Curtius, IX, 4, 21, represents Alexander as saying to his soldiers, "Herculis et Liberi patris terminos transituros". Sen. phil. tells how Alexander laughed when the Corinthians offered him the citizenship of their city, but accepted it (*quia Herculi aequabatur*) when one of the ambassadors pointed out that they had never offered it to anyone else but Hercules (*De Ben.* I, 13, 1). Later (§ 2) the same author uses the phrase in reference to Alexander, "Herculis Liberique vestigia sequens". (See also Arrian, IV, 8, 3; IV, 10, 6; V, 2, 1; V, 3, 2.)

On the reference to Liber see Seyffert, *Dictionary of Classical Antiquities*: "The worship of Dionysus passed into Egypt and far into Asia. Hence arose a fable founded on the story of Alexander's campaigns, that the god passed victoriously through Egypt, Syria and India as far as the Ganges with his array of Sileni, Satyrs and inspired women". Arrian knows this story, but suspends judgment on its credibility (v, 3, 4).

**stat immotum mare.** *immotum*, 'unmoved' or 'immovable'. Cf. *ipsum vero grave et defixum mare* (1, 13) and *inmobile profundum* (2, 2). So Tac., *Germ.* XLV, calls it "pigrum ac prope immotum"; *Agric.* x, "mare pigrum et grave remigantibus". Pliny, *Nat. Hist.* IV, 16, 30, calls it even "mare concretum". It seems strange to us to have the sea called unmoved, but the sense is the same as in Byron's *Childe Harold*, IV, clxxxii,

"Unchangeable, save to thy wild waves' play".

This suasoria throws vivid light on the ancient conception of the sea. The rhetoricians are impressed by its eternal, unchanging nature. It is a *pigra moles*; it is outside the paths of stars and sun, and therefore shrouded in darkness (cf. Q. Curtius, IX, 4, 18, "trahi extra sidera et solem, cogique adire, quae mortalium oculis natura subduxerit"); it is unknown; it is something holy, forbidden to man's eyes. Cf. Hor. *Odes*, I, 3, 24:

"non tangenda rates transiliunt vada".

It is full of monsters strange, frightful, portentous. It cannot be navigated. It is boundless. It flows all round the earth, it is the warden of the lands. It is subject to frightful tempests. It is fathomless, yet full of shoals. Nature's power ends on its shores, save for the fact that the monsters it has created find refuge beneath Ocean's waves. It is the end of all things: after it there is nothing.

10. **deficientis.** For use of *deficio* cf. Calp. Flac. *Decl.* II, 14, "ex altera parte qua convexus et deficiens mundus vicinum mittit orientem (*sc.* solem)", 'on the other side where the heavens slope to their ending and launch the rising sun, their neighbour'. Cf. also Q. Curtius, IX, 4, 18, "caliginem ac tenebras et perpetuam noctem profundo incubantem mari, repletum immanium beluarum gregibus fretum, immobiles undas (unchanging waves), in quibus emoriens natura defecerit" ('in which the spirit of nature dies out utterly and ends').

**suo**, emphatic, 'proper' or 'appointed end'. Cf. "terrae quoque suum finem habent" (2, 5).

**pigra moles.** See note on **1**, 2 and 9. *piger* denotes what is without life, motion, energy, hence 'inert', 'sluggish'.

11. **figurae.** Sen. phil. describes them further in *Ad Marciam*, 18, 4: "videbis his inquietis et sine vento fluctuantibus aquis immani et excedenti terrestria magnitudine animalia, quaedam gravia et alieno se magisterio moventia, quaedam velocia, concitatis perniciora remigiis, quaedam haurientia undas, et magno praenavigantium periculo efflantia". Pliny the elder also, IX, 4, may be compared: "maximum animal in Indico mari pristis et balaena est, in Gallico oceano physeter, ingentis columnae modo se attollens altiorque navium velis diluviem quandam eructans, in Gaditano oceano arbor, in tantum vastis dispansa ramis, ut ex ea causa fretum numquam intrasse credatur. apparent et

rotae appellatae a similitudine, quaternis distinctae hae radiis, modiolos earum oculis duobus utrimque claudentibus".

12. **confusa.** The light mingles with a dense mist first, then it is completely cut off by darkness. There seems no reason to change *confusa*, which is given by all the MSS., to *circumfusa* with Müller, or *offusa* with Kiessling.

17. **Resiste.** Müller compares schol. B ad Luc. *Phars.* III, 233, "Alexander magnus, cum Oceanum pernavigare vellet, subito vocis sonitu monitus est: desiste". Hence he suggests *desiste*, but there seems no sufficient reason to change the MSS. reading.

**nihil tantum est**: flattery of the king. In Q. Curtius, IX, 6, 6–16, Craterus protests against Alexander's exposing himself to danger so rashly. He asks him to reserve himself for enterprises worthy of his renown. He is the sole safety and glory (*columen ac sidus*) of the Macedonians.

20. **exoptatus.** In Q. Curtius, IX, 2, 11, Alexander is represented as reflecting that his soldiers are now longing for immediate reward of their toils: "militem labore defatigatum, proximum quemque fructum finito tandem periculo expetere". Again, IX, 9, 4, Alexander encourages his soldiers as they approach the Ocean by saying, "adesse finem laboris omnibus votis expetitum".

21. **idem sunt termini.** In Arrian, *Anab.* V, 26, 2, Alexander is represented as using a similar expression: καὶ ὅροι τῆς ταύτῃ ἀρχῆς οὕσπερ καὶ τῆς γῆς ὅρους ὁ θεὸς ἐποίησε. The figure is familiar in Latin literature even before this time. Cicero in *Pro Sestio*, 31, 67, refers to Pompey, "qui omnibus bellis terra marique compressis imperium populi Romani orbis terrarum terminis definisset". Ovid has it also, *Fasti*, II, 684:

"gentibus est aliis tellus data limite certo;
Romanae spatium est urbis et orbis idem".

23. **cum orbe et cum sole.** Where the *orbis terrarum* ends, there the light of the sun ends too. The Ocean, as we have seen above, is shrouded in darkness. The idea of seeking a new world beyond this one is also found in Vell. Pater. II, 46, 1: "alterum paene imperio nostro ac suo quaerens orbem" (of Caesar). So in Florus, I, 45, 16: "omnibus terra marique peragratis respexit Oceanum et, quasi hic Romanis orbis non sufficeret, alterum cogitavit". Cf. also Sen. phil. Ep. 119, 8: "quaerit (*sc.* Alexander) quod suum faciat, scrutatur maria ignota, in Oceanum classes mittit novas, et, ut ita dicam, mundi claustra perrumpit". Cicero, too, says twice that the deeds of Pompey extend not merely to the end of the lands, but as far as the sun's power goes. In *Cat.* III, 11, 26, "quorum alter (Pompeius) finis vestri imperi non terrae sed caeli regionibus terminaret"; IV, 10, 21, "anteponatur omnibus Pompeius cuius res gestae atque virtutes isdem quibus solis cursus regionibus ac terminis continentur".

26. **adorarint**: a reference to the custom of prostration before the Persian king. Cf. Nepos, *Conon*, 3, 3, "necesse est enim, si in conspectu veneris, venerari te regem (quod προσκύνησιν illi vocant)". It was just this adoption of Persian customs which caused so much discontent among the Macedonians towards the end of Alexander's campaigns. Callisthenes lost his life through opposing this movement too frankly. See § 5, and note on **3**, 11.

27. **tropaea**. See note on **1**, 9. The rhetorician represents Alexander as having gone already farther than the god Dionysus in his victorious progress through Asia. Bornecque compares Napoleon's grandiloquent statement: "Je trouverai en Espagne les colonnes d'Hercule, mais non des limites à mon pouvoir".

29. **intemptatum**: a sea as yet to human experience unexplored. Cf. Sen. phil. *Ad Marciam*, 18, 5: "videbis nihil humanae audaciae intentatum". Horace has the idea (*Odes*, 1, 3, 21) that it should not be explored:

> "nequiquam deus abscidit
> prudens Oceano dissociabili
>    terras, si tamen impiae
> non tangenda rates transiliunt vada.
>    audax omnia perpeti
> gens humana ruit per vetitum nefas".

**totius orbis vinculum**. Cf. note on **1**, 9, *stat...mare*. Sen. phil. *Ad Marciam*, 18, 4, uses a similar expression, "vinculum terrarum Oceanus", and again in *Medea*, 375:

> "venient annis saecula seris,
>    quibus Oceanus vincula rerum
> laxet, et ingens pateat tellus",

a prophecy of a new world beyond the seas. Aulus Gellius has the idea too (XII, 13, 20): "cum vero (Oceanus) omnis terras omnifariam et undique versum circumfluat...undarum illius ambitu terris omnibus convallatis in medio eius sunt omnia...".

31. **deserta**: obviously a reference to stormy tides. Similarly Q. Curtius (IX, 9, 9) refers to the trouble caused to Alexander and his men by the tidal inrush on the Indus: "identidem intumescens mare et in campos paulo ante siccos descendere superfusum".

32. **premit**. Cf. Q. Curtius, IX, 4, 18, quoted in note on **1**, 9, *deficientis*. See also VII, 3, 11, "obscura coeli verius umbra quam lux, nocti similis premit terram", etc.

**nescio qui**: *qui*, old ablative.

**subduxit**. The phrase of Curtius is strikingly similar: "quae mortalium oculis natura subduxerit" (IX, 4, 18, quoted in note on *immotum mare*, **1**, 9). Florus, I, 33, 12, also expresses the idea that it is sinful to explore the ocean: "Decimus Brutus...peragratoque victor Oceani litore non prius signa convertit quam cadentem in maria solem obrutumque aquis ignem non sine quodam sacrilegii metu et horrore deprendit".

**2, 2. testatum**: passive, 'a proven truth'. Forcellini defines it as "ab omnibus cognitus, receptus, admissus, confessus, indubitatus, exploratus, quasi omnes vulgo testes de eo sint". Müller compares Cic. *Pro Murena*, 9, 20, "publicis litteris testata sunt omnia"; *Ad Att.* VIII, 9, 1, "ut testatum esse velim de pace quid senserim"; Livy, XXXIV, 41, 3, "testata quoque ipso Nemeorum die voce praeconis libertas est Argivorum". Cf. also *Pro Flac.* 26; *Act. I In Verr.* 48. [The MSS. read *testatus es* or *testantur*. F. Walter (*Berliner Philologische Wochenschrift*, 1918, No. 10) wishes to read *testatur ecce. testatum est* is Müller's emendation.]

**5. suum**: emphatic, 'their appointed end'. Cf. "deficientis in suo fine naturae" (1, 10).

**8. moderatio.** Cf. Arrian, *Anab.* v, 27, 9, Καλὸν δέ, ὦ βασιλεῦ, ... καὶ ἡ ἐν τῷ εὐτυχεῖν σωφροσύνη.

**eundem...finem facit.** The same idea as in "idem sunt termini et regni tui et mundi".

**11. angustus.** Cf. Juv. x, 169, "aestuat infelix angusto limite mundi".

**12. magnitudini.** A repetition of the idea at the beginning of the suasoria.

**13. maria...agitantur.** Cf. Sen. phil. *Nat. Quaest.* III, 30, 6, "natura pelagus stare aut intra terminos suos furere coget".

**quidquid ad summum pervenit.** Alexander has reached the zenith of his fortunes, and can advance no farther. The thought in Seneca and Velleius Paterculus goes still further. Whatever has reached its acme is near its decline and fall. The rhetorician of course must not say this to Alexander. Cf. Sen. phil. *Ad Marciam*, 23, 2, "quidquid ad summum pervenit, ad exitum prope est"; *ib.* 23, 3, "nam ubi incremento locus non est, vicinus occasus est, et ita est indicium imminentis exitii maturitas et appetit finis, ubi incrementa consumpta sunt"; Vell. Pat. I, 17, 6, "naturaque quod summo studio petitum est, ascendit in summum difficilisque in perfecto mora est, naturaliter quod procedere non potest, recedit".

**17. orbem...relinquo.** In Curtius (IX, 6, 20) Alexander himself says "iamque haud procul absum fine mundi, quem egressus aliam naturam, alium orbem aperire mihi statui". Cf. also this suas. (1, 24), "quod noveram, vici; nunc concupisco quod nescio".

**20. ista...infusa caligo.** An expansion of the thought in "vicimus qua lucet" (1, 17). We have conquered wherever there was light: this darkness on the sea forbids a view of it, still more the exploration of it.

**22. terribilis ille...conventus.** According to Q. Curtius (IX, 2, 19) Alexander's army was impressed by the size of the animals in India, and the swarms of men: "utrumne vos magnitudo beluarum an multitudo hostium terret?"

26. **rudis et inperfecta natura.** Cf. note on *natura*, 1, 2. *natura* is here equal to 'the creations of nature'. *rudis* means 'shapeless'. Nature's force has so far failed that it has not produced perfect shapes, only monstrosities.

28. **sacrum.** Cf. the passage from Horace quoted in note on *intemptatum*, 1, 29.

29. **circumfudit.** For use of *circumfundo*, cf. Cicero, *Scipio's Dream*, 6, 13: "omnis enim terra...circumfusa illo mari", and for the idea Catullus, 64, 30: "oceanusque, mari totum qui amplectitur orbem"; Ovid, *Met.* 1, 30:

"circumfluus humor
ultima possedit, solidumque coercuit orbem";

*ib.* 37:    "tum freta diffundi, rabidisque tumescere ventis
iussit, et ambitae circumdare litora terrae".

**illi.** These are the *mathematici* or *physici*, the physical philosophers.

**collegerunt meatus:** 'who have computed or calculated the movements or paths of the stars'. *sidus* is generally a constellation as opposed to a single star (*stella*). It can also stand for either sun or moon. The meaning is clear: the astronomers or astrologers know all about the movements of the stars, they have fixed the length of the year, in fact they know all about the *mundus*, the ordered universe, but they dispute about the constitution of the Ocean. It is interesting to note however that they knew there was a connection between the moon and the tides. Cf. Sen. *De Prov.* 1, 4: "cum illae [*sc.* aquae]...ad horam ac diem subeant, ampliores minoresque, prout illas Lunare sidus elicuit, ad cuius arbitrium Oceanus exundat".

31. **de Oceano...dubitant.** The view seems to be that the world is a circle of lands (*orbis terrarum*) surrounded by the stream of Ocean, or that the Ocean is a huge sphere by itself, the *orbis terrarum* merely being a small island in it. The navigable bays or gulfs, *sinus* (the Red Sea, the Persian Gulf, the Caspian, the Adriatic, possibly the Mediterranean also is included), are as it were the vents through which the Ocean breathes. The ebb and flow of the waters in these gulfs are due to the Ocean's breathing. Pliny the elder in Book II, 68, talks of the Ocean as "fundens recipiensque aquas et quicquid exit in nubes, ac sidera ipsa tot et tantae magnitudinis pascens". In II, 6, he says there are four elements, fire, air, earth, water, the earth being supported in the midst along with the fourth element of water by the force of the air. From the former passage we get the key to *augmentum*. The ocean has the element of fire behind it, and it feeds this by its exhalations. So in Plutarch, *Placita Philosophorum*, 1, 3, Dox. 276 (quoted in Ritter and Preller, p. 10) we have αὐτὸ τὸ πῦρ τὸ τοῦ ἡλίου καὶ τὸ τῶν ἄστρων ταῖς τῶν ὑδάτων ἀναθυμιάσεσι τρέφεται, καὶ αὐτὸς ὁ κόσμος. Poseidonius

put the element of air immediately behind the ocean, then fire. (Cf. περὶ κόσμου, § 3.) This is referred to in *an spiritum*. For the belief that there were air-passages into the earth, cf. Lucan, x, 247:

> "sunt qui spiramina terris
>     esse putent".

Sen. phil. *Nat. Quaest.* VI, 23, 4: "spiritus intrat terram per occulta foramina, quemadmodum ubique, ita et sub mari". It is curious to note that the words beginning with *quasi* down to *suae* would be a trochaic tetrameter catalectic, but for the fact that the first syllable of *quasi* is short.

**3, 2. hoc genus suasoriarum**: 'in this class which consists of suasoriae', not 'in this kind of suasoriae'. In *controversiae* the scene is always a law court and the general rules of declamation hold good: but in suasoriae it may be a king's council, or a senate, or an assembly of the people, and the manner of presenting the arguments will vary accordingly. Even in a king's council the tone will vary according to the character of the king. (See note on the text A, p. 99.)

**6. facile**: here equal to *manifesto*, see Forcellini.

**7. quos superbissimos.** Aelian, *Varia Historia*, IX, 3, describes the oriental splendour of Alexander's court thus: ἐν μέσῃ δὲ τῇ σκηνῇ χρυσοῦς ἐτίθετο δίφρος, καὶ ἐπ᾽ αὐτῷ καθημένος Ἀλέξανδρος ἐχρημάτιζε, περιεστώτων αὐτῷ πανταχόθεν τῶν σωματοφυλάκων. περιῄει δὲ τὴν σκηνὴν περίβολος, ἔνθα ἦσαν Μακεδόνες χίλιοι, καὶ Πέρσαι μύριοι, καὶ οὐδεὶς ἐτόλμα ῥᾳδίως προσελθεῖν αὐτῷ· πολὺ γὰρ ἦν τὸ ἐξ αὐτοῦ δέος, ἀρθέντος ὑπὸ φρονήματος καὶ τύχης εἰς τυραννίδα.

**supra mortalis animi modum inflatos**. Sen. phil. has similar expressions, *De Ben.* I, 13, 1, "Alexandro Macedoni quum victor Orientis animos supra humana tolleret", and again a similar idea, (2) "tamquam coelum, quod mente vanissima complectebatur, teneret, quod Herculi aequabatur".

**9. orbis illum suus non capit**: 'his own world has not enough room for him, does not satisfy him'. Cf. Greek use of χωρεῖ. This use of *capio* is interesting and can easily be paralleled: Q. Curtius, VII, 8, 12, "si dii habitum corporis tui aviditati animi parem esse voluissent, orbis te non caperet"; Sen. *Herc. Fur.* 960,

> "non capit terra Herculem,
>     tandemque superis reddit";

Lucan, I, 109,

> "populique potentis
> quae mare, quae terras, quae totum possidet orbem,
> non cepit fortuna duos";

x, 455, an example of *sufficio* in a similar sense:

> "hic, cui Romani spatium non sufficit orbis";

Juv. x, 148,

"hic est, quem non capit Africa" (of Hannibal);

x, 168, another example of *sufficio*,

"unus Pellaeo iuveni non sufficit orbis" (of Alexander).

Mayor (Juvenal) (note on x, 148) quotes a number of others. Cic.
*Pro. Imp. Cn. Pomp.* 66, "quae civitas est...quae unius tribuni militum
...spiritus capere possit?" *Pro Milone*, 87, "capere eius amentiam
civitas, Italia, provinciae, regna non poterant"; Stat. *Achill.* I, 151,

"nunc illum non Ossa capit, non Pelion ingens,
    Thessaliaeve nives";

Ovid, *Tristia*, III, 4, 29,

"nec natum in flamma vidisset, in arbore natas,
    cepisset genitor si Phaethonta Merops";

Livy, XXXIX, 16, 3, "crescit et serpit quotidie malum. iam maius est,
quam ut capere id privata fortuna possit"; Florus, II, 13, 14, "pro
nefas! sic de principatu laborabant, tamquam duos tanti imperii
fortuna non caperet"; Claudianus, *In Ruf.* II, 156,

"regit Italiam, Libyenque coercet,
Hispanis Gallisque iubet: non orbita solis,
non illum natura capit";

Q. Curtius, IX, 3, 7, "quicquid mortalitas capere poterat, implevimus".

11. **praeceptori eius.** This refers to Callisthenes, Aristotle's
cousin (*amitino*), being the son of the sister of Aristotle's father.
He had been educated along with Alexander, whose tutor was
Aristotle himself. Seneca can hardly have been ignorant of this latter
fact, nor can he well have confused it. Callisthenes accompanied
Alexander on his Asiatic expeditions and offended the king by his
frank opposition to the king's adoption of Asiatic customs and regal
splendour. He was later put to death by Alexander for alleged partici-
pation in a conspiracy against him (Q. Curtius, VIII, 8, 21). Curtius
says (VIII, 5, 13), "gravitas viri et prompta libertas invisa erat regi".
Arrian (IV, 12, 7) uses words very similar to Seneca's, οὔκουν ἀπεικότως δι'
ἀπεχθείας γενέσθαι Ἀλεξάνδρῳ Καλλισθένην τίθεμαι ἐπὶ τῇ ἀκαίρῳ τε
παρρησίᾳ καὶ ὑπερόγκῳ ἀβελτερίᾳ. Callisthenes wrote a famous history
of Alexander's expeditions, which seems to have been the source of
the fabulous accounts of Alexander current in the Middle Ages. He
certainly acted the part of mentor to Alexander, and hence Seneca
loosely calls him teacher (*praeceptor*). It was Clitus however whom
Alexander slew in a drunken brawl with a blow of a pike (σάρισσα).
(Q. Curtius, VIII, 1, 38–52; Arrian, IV, 8, 9; Plutarch, *Alexander*,
50, etc.) We cannot expect historical accuracy from Seneca. He is only
telling an anecdote to illustrate a rhetorical point to his boys.

15. ἰχώρ. The quotation is from Homer, *Iliad*, v, 340. Sen. phil.

attributes this remark to Alexander himself (*Ep.* 59, 12). So do Plutarch (*Alex.* 28) and Dion Chrysostom (*Or.* 64, 21). (Müller and Bornecque assign the quotation in Dion (wrongly) to Antipater.) Diogenes Laertius (IX, 10, 60) attributes it to Anaxarchus, adding that Plutarch gives it to Alexander himself. In spite of his remarkable verbal memory Seneca is not accurate in his historical allusions.

17. **multum iocatur.** The letter referred to is Cic. *Ad Fam.* xv, 19. Cassius says, "peream, nisi sollicitus sum ac malo veterem et clementem dominum habere quam novum et crudelem experiri. scis Gnaeus quam sit fatuus: scis quomodo crudelitatem virtutem putet: scis quam se semper a nobis derisum putet. vereor ne nos rustice gladio velit ἀντιμυκτηρίσαι". Seneca's memory again is not quite accurate. He remembers vaguely the suggestion that Pompey had been ridiculed by Cicero and Cassius, and the pointed statement at the end. There is nothing explicit to justify *multum iocatur.*

21. **ἀντιμυκτηρίσῃ**: μυκτηρίζω, 'to jeer' or 'sneer'. ἀντιμυκτηρίζειν, 'to sneer back at', from μυκτήρ, 'the nose' or 'nostril'. The Latin use of *nasus* is similar. Cf. Hor. *Sat.* ii, 8, 64, "Balatro suspendens omnia naso", and I, 6, 5, "naso suspendis adunco". Forcellini says the use is derived from the sagacity of dogs, who track hidden things by smell. Inquisitive people are usually malicious. Cf. use of *nasus* below (3, 32), where it means 'wit', but the sense of ridicule is not far away.

28. **Liberum.** This sojourn in Athens took place in the winter of 39–38 B.C. after Antony's plundering of Asia Minor and subsequent marriage to Octavia, and after his meeting with Cleopatra in Cilicia. Plutarch (*Ant.* 23, 2) says he behaved with moderation to the Greeks, amused himself with their philosophers and games, and loved to be called a lover of Greece, and still more a lover of Athens, to which city he gave many gifts. He mentions that Antony claimed to be descended from Hercules and imitated Bacchus in his way of living, and was called the Young Bacchus. Dio Cassius (XLVIII, 39, 2) says that he desired to be called the "Young Dionysus", and has this story of his being asked to marry Athene, but he gives the exaction as 1,000,000 drachmae—4,000,000 sesterces. Seneca's 1000 talents makes six times this sum. Plutarch (*Ant.* 26, 2) says when Cleopatra came to visit Antony first in Cilicia, καί τις λόγος ἐχώρει διὰ πάντων, ὡς ἡ Ἀφροδίτη κωμάζοι παρὰ τὸν Διόνυσον ἐπ᾽ ἀγαθῷ τῆς Ἀσίας.

38. **contumeliosi libelli**: 'lampoons, satirical epigrams'. So in the sixteenth century pasquils or pasquinades (so called after a citizen famous for his lampoons) used to be attached to the Pasquino (the mutilated relic of an antique group of Menelaus with the body of Patroclus) in Rome. Replies to these were attached to the Marforio (statue of a river god). See Baedeker's *Italy* (1909), 2nd edition, pp. 233 and 238.

4, 4. **res tuas tibi habe.** The formula of divorce, used by the husband to the wife, apparently also can be used by the wife to the husband. The verb is usually *habeto*, the legal imperative.

5. **Dellius**: probably the Q. Dellius to whom Horace addresses *Odes*, II, 3. He is mentioned by Vell. Pater. II, 84, 2. The latter passage is defective and has been restored by Ruhnken evidently from the statement here. He is also mentioned in Plutarch, *Ant.* 59, 2, as one of the friends of Antony driven away by the insolence of Cleopatra's flatterers. He was the envoy sent by Antony to summon Cleopatra to his presence, and it was by his advice that she went boldly to Antony in Cilicia. He took part in Antony's disastrous Parthian campaign, of which he wrote a history (Strabo, II, 13, 3, p. 523 c). (For a good sketch of his character, his lack of principle, his love of pleasure, his wit see Cucheval, *Histoire de l'Éloquence Romaine*, I, vi, pp. 176–177.)

**desultorem.** In addition to the chariot races in the circus there were horse races in which each rider had two horses, and jumped from the one to the other while going at full gallop. It is difficult to render the word in English: 'jockey' is hardly sufficient. Changing the figure 'trimmer' or 'turn-coat' might do. Ovid uses the expression, *Amores*, I, 3, 15, "desultor amoris", of a fickle lover.

9. This sentence is supposed by Kiessling to be an interpolation. The existence of these *lascivae epistolae* is perhaps the ground for saying that Dellius was one of Cleopatra's lovers. They are otherwise unknown.

12. **at tamen dicito.** This is the *bellissimam rem* above. The point of the story is a little difficult to make out. In case of divorce the dowry had to be restored to the divorced wife. This might entail hardship on the husband if exacted to the full at once. Accordingly he might pay it in three annual instalments, "annua, bienni, trienni die." If Antony had received the dowry—the exaction levied on Athens—and had divorced Minerva, he might be held liable to pay it back in three instalments. The jest consists in Dellius's amusing perversion of the legal point. "The Athenians say Minerva has divorced you; take an analogy then from the law of divorce, and grant them the time they ask by permitting them to pay the sum exacted in three annual instalments." The statement of Dellius is of course preposterous. It is unnecessary to make the retort exactly in harmony with the law. If one did so all the point would be lost. It is just because the legal analogy is farcical that there is a jest at all.

19. **de matre.** Several of the rhetoricians make reference to Alexander's regard for his mother, Olympias (Fabianus, **4**, 39; Damas, **5**, 36). Koinos refers to her too in trying to persuade Alexander to return, Arrian, *Anab.* v, 27, 7, τὴν μητέρα τὴν σαυτοῦ ἰδών.

25. **quae arbitrio suo constitit**: 'which has stopped of its own free will', i.e. has not been constrained by agencies outside itself. Here is evidently a thought inspired by the αὐτάρκεια of the Stoics. The wise man tries to be self-sufficient, limits his desires to what is within his own power, is not too much bound up in externals. Hence he is free from anxiety and fear. Cf. Cic. *Tusc. Disp.* v, 12, 36, "semper in se ipse omnem spem reponet sui"; Sen. *De Ben.* VII, 2, 5, where he

says the "sapiens nihil sperat, aut cupit, nec se mittit in dubium, suo contentus". Cf. also Sen. *Ep.* 119, 6 and 7: "he who restricts himself to the elementary necessities of nature is not only beyond the sense but beyond the fear of poverty".

26. **locum**, i.e. *communem*, a passage of general application which might fit into any speech.

27. **nihil esse stabile, omnia fluitare**, etc.: suggests πάντα ῥεῖ καὶ οὐδὲν μένει.

28. **absorberi terras et maria siccari**. This idea can be illustrated from Pliny, *Nat. Hist.* II, 89, "rursus abstulit insulas mari iunxitque terris, Antissam Lesbo" etc., and 90, "in totum abstulit terras, primum omnium, ubi Atlanticum mare est, si Platoni credimus, immenso spatio; mox interno, quae videmus hodie, mersam Acarnaniam Ambracio sinu, Achaiam Corinthio, Europam Asiamque Propontide et ponto". So also Seneca speaks of the sea encroaching on the land in *Nat. Quaest.* VI, 7, 6, "nam apud nos quoque multa, quae procul a mari fuerant, subito eius accessu vapulavere; et villas in conspectu collocatas, fluctus qui longe audiebatur, invasit".

29. **exempla regum**. Croesus and Darius and many others.

40. **trepidavit**: the direct form, then Seneca irregularly quotes the subord. clause in the indirect form, as if *quomodo illam trepidavisse* had preceded. C. F. W. Müller to remove the irregularity puts "etiam quom Granicum transiturus esses".

5, 1. **Glycon**: a Greek rhetorician, frequently mentioned by Seneca.

3. **Plution**: mentioned by St Jerome who dates him 33 B.C.

5. **Artemon**: a Greek rhetorician, quoted several times by Seneca.

7. **ἄμπωσιν**: the ebb, which would give a current of considerable use for the voyage out to sea. In the ocean, of course, this tide is imperceptible; near the shore it is noticed and can be used to advantage. Here is an added difficulty in attempting to sail the ocean—no light, sluggish waters resisting the oars, no favouring tides or currents, treacherous shoals etc.

8. **οὐδὲ 'Ινδός.** Alexander had had considerable difficulties in sailing down the Indus, from the rapids at the junctions with its tributaries, the whirlpools, and the tidal bore; see Arrian, *Anab.* VI, 5 and 19.

9. **πρεσβύτατον στοιχεῖον**: 'the oldest or original element', so considered by some of the ancient philosophers. Homer considers the Ocean the beginning of all things, and from him and his wife Tethys spring the gods. Hence the expression, γένεσις θεῶν.

11. **ἐκ μιᾶς φορᾶς**. Schg. says *uno impetu*. The meaning seems to be that, as the Ocean is a stream flowing all round the world, if you submit yourself to it, you are bound to go from east to west.

13. **corruptus**: a term opposed to *sanus* in 6, 36, "nec separando a corruptis sana". Quintilian says (VIII, 3, 57), "corrupta oratio in

verbis maxime impropriis, redundantibus, comprehensione obscura, compositione fracta, vocum similium aut ambiguarum puerili captatione consistit", i.e. the faults of style are impropriety in the use of words, tautology or pleonasm, ambiguity, jerky style, childish play on words. So in II, 5, 11, he tells us that the true and natural style seems to have nothing clever about it ("nihil habere ex ingenio videtur"). *corruptus* then denotes the style that is vicious through excess or defect: the style sound in expression and taste is *sanus*.

14. **insanire**: the verb to express the idea in *corruptus*. The writer loses sanity of judgment and writes *corrupte*. Seneca and those who agree with him feel that there is something unhealthy about the new qualities sought after in this decline of eloquence, as they consider it.

15. **Dorion**: a Greek rhetorician, mentioned several times by Seneca not always with disapproval. He seems to have written a paraphrase of Homer in Greek hexameters. There is no other evidence, however, of the existence of this paraphrase, and it is possible that he merely paraphrased a line of Homer in a declamation. Gertz restored the quotation from the Greek phrases which follow in Maecenas's criticism. Schott emended the Latin to "tunc excaecatus Cyclops saxum in mare iecit". This is an hexameter, but there is nothing *corruptum* about it. It is curious that this and the Greek which follows make an hexameter so easily. Paraphrases of Homer seem to have been common in antiquity. Schott mentions several. If we accept Gertz's restoration the passage becomes clear and consistent. "A mountain is torn off, and an island suited to his hand is thrown" is certainly in the highest degree extravagant in idea. It is an example of κακοζηλία. See note on *cacozelos* (12, 28). On how to avoid it see Hermogenes, Spengel, II, 257 and below. U. de Wilamowitz-Moellendorf (*Hermes*, XIV, p. 172) discusses this passage also, and thinks the quotation from the lost *Cyclops* of Philoxenus.

18. **et magna et tamen sana**: 'grand without extravagance'.

19. **Vergilium**. Vergil and Cicero are always treated with great respect by the rhetoricians.

**tumidum** and **inflatum** are synonyms here, expressing the same idea by a different metaphor, *tumidum*, any kind of swelling, *inflatum*, distention by air.

28. **excusatur antequam dicitur**: Seneca's way of expressing what the Greek rhetoricians call the figure of προδιόρθωσις or προθεραπεία.

29. **Menestratus**: mentioned here only by Seneca, otherwise unknown. The *corruptior sententia* is lost.

34. **Charybdis**. In the *De Oratore*, III, 41, Cicero calls the employment of *Charybdis*, in the phrase "Charybdin bonorum", far-fetched and prefers to say *voraginem*. Here there is a further straining after effect, and the next is still more violent.

36. **ethicos**: Greek ἠθικῶς, 'expressing character'. ἠθος is the

quality in a speech when it fits the speaker. The old man must speak like an old man, the young man like a young man etc. It therefore indicates dramatic propriety. It is also the quality in a speech when the speaker adapts himself to his audience, speaking differently to young and to old, to princes and to fellow-citizens etc. Here the adverb means that he aimed at a dramatic representation of a mother's feelings.

40. **Latro sedens.** Seneca says in the preface to the first controversia (§ 21) that Latro dictated the heads (*quaestiones*) of his controversiae, *sedens*, i.e. before he began to declaim. Then apparently he stood to deliver the formal declamation. Here the quotation seems to belong to the declamation proper. Hence *sedens* is not appropriate. Bornecque emends to *sequens*, 'imitating or developing this sententia'.

6, 6. **viguerunt.** *vigeo* = Greek ἀκμάζω, *spiritus* = πνεῦμα. The Latin declaimers do not 'rise high enough'.

7. **curiose.** As Schott says, they describe κατὰ λεπτολογίαν τεχνικήν (with too much scientific detail), "more mathematicorum aut physicorum". *curiose* means *cum cura et diligentia*, 'curiously' in the sense of 'minutely careful'. Cf. Cic. *De Fin.* II, 9, "reperiam multos, vel innumerabiles potius, non tam curiosos, nec tam molestos, quam vos estis,quibus quidquid velim,facile persuadeam". The previous descriptions of the Ocean have certainly more philosophy than poetry in them.

8. **[Albinovanus] Pedo.** This is probably the *praefectus equitum* of Tac. *Ann.* I, 60. At any rate he was a great friend of Ovid (see *Ex Ponto*, IV, 10). He wrote a *Theseis*, and Quintilian mentions him as a writer of epics (*Inst. Or.* X, 1, 90, "Rabirius et Pedo non indigni cognitione si vacet"). He seems to have written another epic on a subject of Roman history, of which these lines which follow are an extract. He must have been a brilliant and versatile person, could tell a good story (Sen. phil. calls him "fabulator elegantissimus",and gives a specimen), was a wit, and literary critic and writer of epigrams. Martial mentions him, and Quintilian (*Inst. Or.* VI, 3, 61) quotes one of his witty sayings. See Controversiae, II, 2, 12 for the story he told about the emendation of Ovid's verses.

**Germanicus.** Almost certainly Nero Claudius Drusus, son of Livia (wife of Augustus), and younger brother of Tiberius. We know that he made the first Roman expedition in the North Sea, and posthumously was honoured with the title of Germanicus by the Senate. It was also to be borne by his descendants (see Suet. *Claudius*, § 1, "senatus...decrevit Germanici cognomen ipsi posterisque eius"). Cf. also Tac. *Germ.* XXXIV, where the historian mentions this expedition of Drusus Germanicus and says nothing of that of Germanicus the younger. Naturally the first attempt would be most striking to contemporaries, and the verses read like those on a first attempt. Besides the expedition of the younger Germanicus was marked by disaster, of which there is no evidence here. See Bergk, *Mon. Ancyr.* p. 97. Cf.

for the expedition of the younger Germanicus Tac. *Ann.* II, 23. The former expedition took place in 12 B.C., and the latter in A.D. 16.

9. **iamque vident.** See note B, p. 100.

11. **audaces ire**: same thought and construction as in Hor. *Odes,* I, 3, 25, "audax omnia perpeti" etc.

12. **metas**: the limits of the race-course, hence 'the limits of the world'.

13. **nunc**, vivid; referring back to "iamque vident" (6, 9), 'already they *see*', *nunc*, 'now they are *on* the fabled Ocean'. Or perhaps putting a period at *mundi*, and comma at *prensis* and *metus*, take all the infinitives from *consurgere* onwards, dependent on *credunt*, reading "accumulat...metus" in parenthesis. These all denote their fears. They think the Ocean is rising to attack, the ships settling on shoals etc. See note B on text, p. 100.

**pigris.** See note on *pigra moles*, 1, 10, and on *natura*, 1, 2.

**immania.** See note on *figurae*, 1, 11, and cf. Hor. *Odes*, III, 27, 26, "scatentem beluis pontum", and Cato, *Dirae*, I, 55, "pigro multa mari dicunt portenta natare". Cf. also Tac. *Ann.* II, 24, espec. subsection 6.

14. **pristis**: connected with the Greek πρίζειν, 'to saw', evidently the sword-fish.

15. **aequoreosque canes** = *canes marinos.* Pliny describes them, IX, 46, and their ferocity in attacking men. Cf. also Verg. *Ecl.* VI, 77, "timidos nautas canibus lacerasse marinis" (of Scylla).

**consurgere.** Schg. points out this indicates the action of those who wage offensive war, and quotes Florus, I, 33, 3, "Hispaniae numquam animus fuit adversum nos universae consurgere", II, 6, 5, "cum omne Latium atque Picenum...postremo Italia contra matrem suam ac parentem urbem consurgeret". Cf. also Verg. *Aen.* VII, 529:

"paulatim sese tollit mare et altius undas
erigit, inde imo consurgit ad aethera fundo".

**prensis.** Cf. Hor. *Odes*, II, 16, 2,

"otium divos rogat in patenti
prensus Aegaeo...."

16. **accumulat...**: an effective parenthesis.

**sidere**: depending on *credunt*, two lines below.

**limo**: 'mud'. Cf. Tac. *Ann.* I, 70, "quo levior classis vadoso mari innaret vel reciproco sideret". Cf. also Ovid, *Fasti*, IV, 300,

"sedit limoso pressa carina vado".

18. **per inertia fata.** Wernsdorf says it means, "ignavo mortis genere quale est fame et maris fluctibus perire", i.e. they think they are to die a coward's death, torn in pieces by sea monsters. Better to take it, 'they are abandoned by the careless fates', i.e. even the fates

have forgotten them. The order supports this. M. Haupt quotes Ovid, *Metam.* vii, 544, "gemit leto moriturus inerti"; Val. Flac. i, 633,

"haec iterant segni flentes occumbere leto",

which rather support the first interpretation.

19. **laniandos.** Schg. points out that this verb can refer to the fleet, and quotes Ovid, *Her.* vii, 175,

"laniataque classis
postulat exiguas semirefecta moras".

He quotes also Suas. vi, **24**, 14, "proscribente Antonio et rempublicam laniante", remarking that *respublica* is often compared to a ship.

20. **caecum.** Cf. Suas. vi, **28**, 15, "caeco volvente fluctu"; *caecum*, not that which cannot see, but that which cannot be seen, or through which one cannot see. Haupt compares Verg. *Aen.* iii, 203,

"tris adeo incertos caeca caligine soles
erramus pelago".

21. **pugnaci visu**: a bold phrase, 'with fighting', i.e. 'struggling or straining vision'. Wernsdorf does not understand this; he wants *nisu*, explaining, "quando quis corpore manibusque iactatis crassam caliginem rumpere et discutere conabatur", an amusing picture.

22. **mundo** = *coelo*. Wernsdorf compares Lucilius, *Aetna*, 54, "removet caligine mundum" and Verg. *Aen.* i, 88,

"eripiunt subito nubes coelumque diemque
Teucrorum ex oculis".

23. **obstructa**: 'stifled'. He feels himself enclosed by darkness and terror.

26. **cardine**: by synecdoche—a region of the sky; cf. use of *axis* also.

27. **flabris intactum**: untouched by storm-blasts, 'a world where never creeps a cloud or moves a wind' (cf. Tennyson's *Lucretius*).

28. **di revocant.** Cf. Tac. *Germ.* xxxiv, "nec defuit audentia Druso Germanico, sed obstitit Oceanus in se simul atque in Herculem inquiri. mox nemo tentavit, sanctiusque ac reverentius visum de actis deorum credere quam scire". Cf. note on **1**, 29 and **1**, 9.

30. **divumque quietas**.... Wernsdorf notes that according to the opinion of the ancients it was sin for man to behold what the gods had set apart for themselves. What is beyond the limits of the world is the abode of the gods. Cf. Tac. *Germ.* xlv, "sonum insuper emergentis solis audiri, formasque deorum et radios capitis adspici, persuasio adicit". The last line is an echo of Lucret. iii, 19, in all probability, like Tennyson's lines in *Lucretius*.

34. **magnifice.** *magnifice* and *corrupte* must be transposed (as Thomas did); or else, as Prof. Phillimore suggested to me, we must emend *sed non* to *si non* or to *nisi*.

40. **iudici sui**: locative gen., like *anxius animi*, ' some critics are doubtful of the taste of the *sententia* which follows'. Seneca pronounces against it. No doubt he thinks it bombastic.

### NOTE A.

#### (Page 3, line 2 *et seq.*)

This is a very corrupt passage. The MSS. appear to give the following: "Aiebat Cestius hoc genus suasoriarum aliter declamandum esset quam suadendum. non eodem modo in libera civitate dicendam sententiam, quo apud reges, quibus etiam quae prosunt ita tamen ut delectent suadenda sunt. et inter reges ipsos esse discrimen: quosdam minus aut magis usveritatem facti. Alexandrum exisse quos" etc. Müller after Novák, inserted *alibi* before *aliter*, changed *esset* to *esse*, and deleted *quam suadendum*. Gertz proposed to read, *alias aliter declamandum esse: suadenti enim* etc. Schott changed *usveritatem* to *osos veritatem*. Kiessling emended *facti* to *facile*. Haase changed *exisse* to *ex iis esse*. Novák changed *aut* to *alios*. So the reading of Müller's text was arrived at.

F. Leo (*Hermes*, XL, p. 608), pointing out that the distinction Cestius is making here rests on the character of the king, wishes to emend thus: "aliter declamandum esse prout persona alia apud quam suadendum". Further, in consideration of the fact that *f* is often put for *p* in the MSS. of Seneca, he reads *pati* for *facti*. He deletes the *us* before *veritatem* as a mere repetition of the last syllable of *magis*, rejecting the emendation *osos* on the ground that Seneca does not employ this form. Thus he gets, "quosdam minus aut magis veritatem pati. Alexandrum exisse quos superbissimos" etc.

This is very attractive. It explains the presence of *quam suadendum*, and gets rid of the difficulty about the meaning of *facile*.

*quosdam* followed by *alios* can be paralleled in Seneca. See C. x, 4, 8, "quosdam ambitio gloriae provocavit, alios odia et simultates protraxerunt". Thomas emended "quosdam minus contumaces usos veritate facili", 'certain less stubborn have availed themselves of the truth frankly spoken'. This is not convincing, and loses the distinction which seems wanted between kings who liked frankness and those who did not.

*exisse* with the accusative is another difficulty. I think we must have *ex iis esse*. Seneca's diction is nearer that of the Ciceronian period, and there seems no parallel to this use of *exire* in his writing. Eussner wished to read *exisse quo*, quoting Tac. *Agr.* 42, "obsequium ac modestiam...eo laudis excedere", and Livy, VIII, 33, 9, "quo ultra iram violentiamque eius excessurum fuisse".

I should on the whole prefer to read this vexed passage thus: "Aiebat Cestius hoc genus suasoriarum aliter declamandum esse prout persona alia apud quam suadendum. non eodem modo in libera civitate dicendam sententiam quo apud reges, quibus etiam quae prosunt, ita tamen, ut delectent, suadenda sunt. et inter reges ipsos esse discrimen: quosdam minus, alios magis veritatem pati. Alexandrum ex iis esse quos" etc.

## NOTE B.

### Page 6, line 9 *et seq.*

The first line in the MSS. begins with *iam pridem*; for the second *iam pridem* A reads *iam quidam*, B V *iam quidem*, D *iam pridem*. Gertz emended to *iamque vident*. The *iam . . . iamque* then denotes their anxious fear: but the words ought to be close together. Cf. Verg. *Aen.* VI, 602, "quo super atra silex iam iam lapsura". If the MS. reading *iam pridem* is retained we have two lines beginning with *iam pridem*, not impossible. If emphatic they make good sense; but then *relictum* must be emended to *relincunt*, as Haupt did. Then we are left with nothing to govern *illum . . . Oceanum consurgere* etc. They are rather far from *credunt* with the parenthesis between.

With Gertz's conjecture the only difficulty is *iam . . . iamque. audaces ire* in both is parallel to "audax omnia perpeti" of Horace. The *vident* is understood to be repeated with the vivid *nunc*, and *illum . . . Oceanum . . . consurgere* depends upon it.

I prefer to put *iamque vident* in place of the first *iam pridem*, and to retain the second. 'They first of all leave the well-known limits of the world, then voyage into darkness, and leave day and sun far behind (a much farther step), then they see the Ocean all round them, and their ships in its power'. (*accumulat* etc. is a parenthesis.) *sidere limo, desertam classem, relinqui* all depend upon *credunt*, as Schott pointed out. 'Their ships settle on a shoal. (Well, the wind will blow them off.) No! the wind falls: alas, they are abandoned to the perils of the sea'. These are the thoughts passing through their minds, as implied by *credunt*. The passage then is a wonderful representation of their terrors.

Bornecque seems to take the various infinitives as historic, but this is impossible as the subjects are in the accusative case. However, he may merely be translating freely.

If *iamque vident* is put at the beginning of the second line, then I should read Haupt's *relincunt* in the first and put a period after it. The *iam* suspended and then caught up by the vivid *nunc* seems to me to produce a particularly fine effect.

# SUASORIA II

The scene is Thermopylae. The three hundred Spartans have been left alone. It is assumed that there are three hundred from each of the other Greek states. All these have retreated. The Spartans are now holding a council of war to decide whether they too should go or stay. The rhetor in each case speaks as one of the Spartans.

**7, 1. Trecenti...treceni.** It must not be forgotten that the suasoria is an imaginary speech. The rhetores do not need to be accurate in their history: this was a recognised convention. Compare what Atticus says in the *Brutus* of Cicero, 11, (42), "quoniam quidem concessum est rhetoribus ementiri in historiis, ut aliquid dicere possint argutius". When in the extracts the Spartans are spoken of we always have in the MSS. *trecenti*. When the others are referred to the reading wavers between *trecenti* and *treceni*. Cf. §§ 2, 3, 4, 7, 8. One MS. D and the corrector of the Codex Toletanus have *Troezeni* instead of *treceni*. Possibly some scholiast knowing that *treceni* was historically wrong, and that the Athenians had sent their wives and children to *Troezen*, altered *treceni* to *Troezena*, which subsequently was changed to *Troezeni*. Not much point seems to be gained by the declaimers in assuming *treceni* in the theme.

**6. insuetaque arma....** Schott pointed out that this passage could easily be altered into verse, and thought it a reminiscence of an old poet:

> "armaque non passura manus hebetataque ferri
> corpora vulneribus".

Schultingh thought this quotation an example of Fuscus's "explicatio splendida quidem sed operosa et implicita". It is certainly *fracta compositio*, 'broken in rhythm', and has plenty of vigour.

**7. an Lacedaemoniorum electos.** I have adopted the emendation of Gertz. BV give *an Lacedaemonios? an Eleos?*; D *aelaeos*; A omits. Bursian, quoting "electi sumus non relicti" (**8**, 32), emended to *an electos*. Müller and Bornecque follow Bursian. If we choose to follow A and omit, we may explain the corruption by supposing that *electos* was a marginal note on *potissimos*, and being felt to be weak when put in the text was then changed to *Eleos*. *Eleos* gives no good contrast, *electos* is feeble.

**10. sine moenibus.** This is Bursian's emendation (adopted by Müller) of the MSS., which are very corrupt here. They give *siremianibus, siremanibus, si remanemus, si remeabimus*. Bornecque accepts Gertz's correction, *his de manubiis*. Bursian's gives the best sense and is in harmony with what the rhetores say elsewhere. Cf. Triarius (**8**, 10), "ne sit Sparta lapidibus circumdata: ibi muros habet, ubi viros",

Cestius Pius (9, 16), "adhuc non sum ex ulla parte Atheniensium similis, non muris nec educatione". The rhetores are fond of referring to the fact that Sparta is not a walled city. Nothing exasperated the Greeks more than these attacks on their temples, and it is quite in keeping with history for the declaimers to refer to this in order to inspire the Greeks to resistance.

12. **ite adversus barbaros.** The MSS. have *et*, which is quite intelligible. 'L. (is it so you feel) even in the presence of barbarians?' or emend with Gertz the following to "non refert opera vestra animus". 'L. even when front to front with barbarians does your mind not recall' etc. Bornecque suggests and adopts, "o L. ita adversus barbaros!"

13. **refero.** The MSS. have *revero, revera, reveremini*. This is Madvig's emendation adopted by Müller and Bornecque.

**avos.** All the MSS. but one give *animus*.

15. **en, loco tuti sumus.** ABV give *filico*, D and T *vel loco*. The text, which is O. Jahn's vigorous emendation, is Müller's: who suggested in his notes *hoc loco*, adopted by Bornecque. As Müller points out, the speaker goes on as if the Greeks were gathered at Salamis; but the rhetoricians are no more bound by geography than by history. It must never be forgotten that a declamation is fiction.

16. **metuentibus explicet inutilem navium numerum.** The MSS. give "metuentibus explicet inutilem numerum". Bornecque retains *intuentibus* from Müller but reverts to the *inutilem* of the MSS. and keeps the insertion of *navium*. I should prefer to keep the MSS reading with insertion of *navium*: 'Let him deploy before your fearful gaze his useless host'. The first adjective is a gibe, the second shows that the fear is groundless. The statement is scornful.

17. **quod tantum ex vasto patet.** Müller and Bornecque, following Gertz, read *ex vasto* before *urguetur*. All the MSS. have "quod tantum ex vasto patet". There is no need to change the position of *ex vasto*: 'This sea, which coming from the great Ocean extends so widely, (here) contracts into very small compass (*in minimum*)'.

19. **vixque minimo aditus navigio est.** The smallest vessel can hardly enter, and such a vessel cannot cross the stormy expanse outside: only large vessels can cross, and they cannot enter. The passage therefore cannot be forced.

24. **nudus:** probably 'without the shield'. Cf. Philostratus, *Lives of the Sophists*, I, 24, ἀνὴρ Λακεδαιμόνιος μέχρι γήρως φυλάξας τὴν ἀσπίδα ἡδέως μὲν ἂν τοὺς γυμνοὺς τούτους ἀπέκτεινα. The reference is to the prisoners from Sphacteria; cf. also C. IX, 6, 2, "gladiator quem armatus fugerat nudus insequitur". Here again 'without the shield'. Cic. *De Oratore*, III, 136 (of orators who enter on political life without knowledge), "nudi veniunt atque inermes", metaphorically 'naked and unarmed', the one referring to the shield, the other to sword and spear. The Spartan says he will fight till he is *nudus*, without

his shield, and probably with his weapons broken, and then he will fall on the spoils of the Persians—the shields and spears of the men he has slain.

28. **erratis si metuendam creditis mortem.** Seneca in *Ep.* 82, 20, as Bornecque remarks, shows that this passage as an incitement to bold action is futile. Dialectic is of no use here: you must appeal to the feelings.

29. **statque** (one of Fuscus's Vergilian echoes). Cf. Verg. *Aen.* x, 467,

> "stat sua cuique dies; breve et inreparabile tempus omnibus est vitae".

30. **orsus est.** *ordior,* 'make at the beginning', opposed to *continuare* and *pergere.*

31. **sub eodem pueritia fato est,** i.e. of being liable to sudden death. Bornecque refers us to Sen. phil. *de Prov.* 5, 5, "fata nos ducunt, et quantum cuique restet, prima nascentium hora disposuit...accepimus peritura perituri": and to *Ad Marciam*, 22, 2, "nihil est tam fallax, quam vita humana, nihil tam insidiosum".

33. **adeo**: 'so much is it', 'to such a point is it a retreat'.

**8, 1. proximeque deos sic cadentes colunt.** The MSS. here are very corrupt. This is Dräger's emendation adopted by Bornecque. Müller's text gives "proximique deos sic †ageses agunt", the reading of AB. VD have *sic agessa satagunt.* A large number of corrections have been suggested, none convincing. The passage still awaits the master hand. Schultingh compared Cic. *Pro Milone*, 97, "hanc (gloriam) denique esse cuius gradibus etiam in caelum homines viderentur ascendere", which leads me to suggest "proximeque deos sic agentes scandunt"[1].

2. **feminis quoque frequens** etc. Cf. C. II, 2, 1, where Fuscus has a similar thought: "quaedam ardentibus rogis se maritorum immiserunt, quaedam vicaria maritorum salutem anima redemerunt. quam magna gloria brevi sollicitudine pensata est!" C. x, 3, 2, Clodius Turrinus pater says "aliqua spiritum viri redemit suo, aliqua se super ardentis rogum misit", and C. II, 5, 8 (Triarius), "alia desiderio viri attonita in ardentem rogum se misisse". In mythology compare the stories of Evadne and of Alcestis. See Prop. III, 13, 15, for 'suttee' in the East.

3. **Lycurgum.** Schott remarks that Plutarch tells us how Lycurgus, the Spartan lawgiver, that his laws might be eternal, made his countrymen swear to observe them till he returned, then left his country, and starved himself to death.

5. **Othryadem.** Herodotus, I, 82, merely says that after the battle fought between three hundred champions of Sparta and three hundred of Argos, Othryades remained on the field of battle and spoiled the

---

[1] Prof. Phillimore suggested to me, "sic aggressi fata sunt." This is very attractive.

dead, while the two Argives who survived went home and claimed the victory. The other story to which the rhetores make such extravagant allusions (see later § 16) was that Othryades was severely wounded and left for dead. He came to, however, and finding himself the sole survivor on the field wrote with his blood on his shield, "I have conquered" and then died. Val. Max. refers to the story, III, 2, ext. 4, "Othryades, qui sanguine suo scriptis litteris direptam hostibus victoriam tantum non post fata sua in sinum patriae cruento tropaei titulo retulit"; and Flor. I, 18, 14 (Halm) of an incident in the first Punic war, "ac sic pulcherrimo exitu Thermopylarum et Leonidae famam adaequavit, hoc inlustrior noster, quod expeditioni tantae superfuit, licet nihil inscripserit sanguine".

**adnumerare**: 'though I summon Othryades only from the dead, yet, as he is equal to three hundred, I have an example to assign to each of the three hundred before me'. Schultingh illustrated the sense of *adnumerare* from Quint. *Decl.* XII, 14: "non ignis defunctos cremavit, non ferae laceraverunt, non aves attigerunt; et tamen cadavera mortuis (mortibus) adnumerare non possumus", i.e. 'we have no dead body for each of the men we have lost' (because during a famine they have been reduced to cannibalism), and also Quint. *Decl.* 369, "detracta arma dicis? nego. mentior? eamus in rem praesentem: adnumerare volo: si quidquam defuerit, damnari volo". It might also be taken 'though I name O. alone, in our annals for everyone of the three hundred I have an exemplar'.

7. **ne pugna quidem.** Cf. Cestius (9, 13), "ita ne bello quidem, sed nuntio vincimur", and Latro (8, 23), "rumori terga vertitis".

8. **magnum est...Laconem.** Bornecque reads "magnum alimentum virtutis est nasci Laconem". The MSS. are corrupt here and, while the sense is clear, many emendations have been suggested. From the MSS. we get "magnum est [es], alimentum [alienum] [alumnum], virtutis est nasci Laconem". AB have *es*, ABV *alienum*, D *alumnum*. *alimentum* is the reading of the corrector of the Codex Toletanus: the second *est* is omitted by VD. Bursian read, "magnum aes alienum virtutis est nasci Laconem", 'it is a great debt to valour to be born a Spartan'. Schultingh read, "magnum est alumnum virtutis nasci et Laconem". Gr. suggested *adiumentum*, Gertz *columen*, Madvig *alimonium*.

10. **ibi muros habet ubi viros.** Bornecque compares Plut. *Apoph. Lac.* 210, E, 29, ἄλλου δ᾿ ἐπιζητοῦντος, διὰ τί ἀτείχιστος ἡ Σπάρτη, ἐπιδείξας τοὺς πολίτας ἐξωπλισμένους· 'Ταῦτά ἐστιν, εἶπε, τὰ Λακεδαιμονίων τείχη.' ἄλλου δὲ τὸ αὐτὸ ἐπιζητοῦντος· 'οὐ λίθοις δεῖ καὶ ξύλοις τετειχίσθαι τὰς πόλεις,' ἔφη, 'ταῖς δὲ τῶν ἐνοικούντων ἀρεταῖς.' (Agesilaus speaks.)

12. **montes perforat, maria contegit.** The first refers to the making of the canal through Mt Athos peninsula, the second to the bridging of the Hellespont by Xerxes. Lucian (*Rhet. Praec.* 18) ironically recommends that allusions to these topics should be intro-

duced in all declamations—καὶ ἀεὶ ὁ ᾿Αθως πλείσθω καὶ ὁ Ἑλλήσποντος πεζευέσθω καὶ ὁ ἥλιος ἀπὸ τῶν Μηδικῶν βελῶν σκεπέσθω καὶ Ξέρξης φευγέτω· καὶ ὁ Λεωνίδας θαυμαζέσθω, καὶ τὰ ᾿Οθρυάδου γράμματα ἀναγιγνωσκέσθω, καὶ ἡ Σαλαμὶς καὶ τὸ ᾿Αρτεμίσιον καὶ αἱ Πλαταιαί, πολλὰ ταῦτα καὶ πυκνά, κ.τ.λ.—and this just means that Lucian knew these were the commonplaces of declamation. Juvenal shows the rhetorical training in mentioning these and similar topics in x, 173 et seq. Cf. Grandio, quoted by Seneca later (13, 4), "qui terras circumscripsit, dilatavit profundum".

13. **solido.** Note the absence of the preposition, poetical usage. Schott calls this an elegans γνώμη and compares Verg. Aen. xi, 425:

"multa dies variique labor mortalibus aevi
rettulit in melius: multos alterna revisens
lusit, et in solido rursum fortuna locavit".

A similar thought beautifully expressed by Latro occurs in C. ii, 1, 1, "fragilis et caduca felicitas est et omnis blandientis fortunae speciosus cum periculo nitor".

15. **quae ad invidiam perducta sunt.** The old Greek idea—that human prosperity rouses the jealousy of the gods (φθόνος).

18. **posset.** Xerxes' thought, after the death of the three hundred, is thrown into the final clause form, 'Let us die, that Xerxes may say to himself, "Here first I found what I could not change"'.

19. **cur non potius in turba fugimus?** Schultingh says 'to be less conspicuous' and compares 8, 37 (Marullus), "in hoc restitimus, ne in turba fugientium lateremus", and 9, 30 (Hispanus), "non latebit in turba Laco; quocunque Xerxes aspexerit, Spartanos videbit".

21. **cogeremus.** The words after cogeremus down to tardissimi have been transposed to this place by Gertz from 9, 20 where in all the MSS. they follow after recipiunt. They have no connection there, and fit in excellently here. C. F. W. Müller and Linde placed them after fugam (9, 18).

30. **ceteri quidem fugerunt.** quidem has been doubted, because quidem is used again three words later. If we were sure that Latro spoke the words as they stand the criticism would have point. We must not forget, however, that Seneca is quoting selections. Bornecque gets over the difficulty by indicating that the quotation stops at fugerunt, and an entirely new one, perhaps from a much later passage, then begins.

32. **patrocinium:** the function of a patronus, one who speaks on behalf of another, an advocate, hence 'I shall speak as advocate both for ourselves and for Greece'.

**electi sumus, non relicti.** A play upon words, hard to render in English.

34. **de fuga:** inserted by Gertz (before the verb, however), not in the MSS., retained by Müller and Bornecque. To my mind it is not at all

necessary to insert it. It can quite easily be understood. Its insertion is supported by "quod deliberassent de fuga" (12, 17). It is interesting to note how the rhetores emphasise the military pride of the Spartans.

9, 6. **Thebae sacris**: referring to its great legendary importance; the myths of Cadmus, Oedipus and the Seven centre in it, and it was famous as being the birthplace of Dionysus and Hercules and native city of the great seer Tiresias.

**ideo**: 'for this reason' i.e. that Sparta might be famous for arms. Gronovius and Schultingh read the four clauses beginning with *ideo* as rhetorical questions. 'Sparta is famous for arms, and is it for this' etc., then instead of saying "ut Lacones se numerent non aestiment", the rhetor breaks off with "o grave maiorum dedecus!"—a spirited reading but possibly not the most natural way of taking the words. However I prefer and have adopted it.

8. **Taygeti**: the words *enitimur in* were inserted by Müller before *Taygeti* and retained by Bornecque. The sentence is intelligible without them.

10. **ideo muri nostri**. Cf. note on **8**, 10.

13. **nuntio vincimur**. Cf. note on *ne pugna quidem* (**8**, 7).

14. **hercules**, expletive, not the subject. The insertion of *is* after Hercules is almost necessary. The person referred to is of course Xerxes.

17. **muris**. Again a reference to the unwalled condition of Sparta. Cf. note on **8**, 10.

20. **Thermopylae paucos recipiunt**. For the idea and for this sense of *recipio* cf. Sen. phil. *De Ben.* VI, 31, 6, "verum est quod dicitur, maiorem belli apparatum esse, quam qui recipi ab his regionibus possit, quas oppugnare constituis . . . ob hoc ipsum te Graecia vincet, quia non capit" ('has no room for you').

23. **ceperit**: 'shall have room for'. Cf. note on *capit*, "orbis illum suus non capit" (**3**, 9). To the passages quoted there may be added Cic. *De Oratore*, II, 334, "contio capit omnem vim orationis"; Sen. *C.* II, 1, 32; II, 1, 13; II, 6, 2, and Verg. *Aen.* IX, 644, "nec te Troia capit".

33. **praecepta matrum**. Schott, after pointing out that the bodies of soldiers were carried to burial on their shields, quotes Plutarch, *Apoph. Lac.* 241, §§ 16, 17, ἄλλη προσαναδιδοῦσα τῷ παιδὶ τὴν ἀσπίδα καὶ παρακελευομένη, τέκνον, ἔφη, ἢ ταύταν ἢ ἐπὶ ταύτας. ἄλλη προιόντι τῷ υἱῷ ἐπὶ πόλεμον ἀναδιδοῦσα τὴν ἀσπίδα, ταύταν, ἔφη, ὁ πατήρ σοι ἀεὶ ἔσωζε καὶ σὺ οὖν ταύταν σώζε, ἢ μὴ ἔσο.

34. **inermem reverti**. Blandus means that to retreat with your shield (without fighting) is a greater dishonour than to retreat without it, i.e. after having fought and having been defeated.

36. **non servio**: 'I cannot be a slave'. Bornecque refers us to Sen. phil. *Ep.* 77, 12, "Lacon ille memoriae traditur, impubes adhuc, qui captus clamabat, 'non serviam' sua illa Dorica lingua; et verbis fidem

imposuit. ut primum iussus est fungi servili et contumelioso ministerio (afferre enim vas obscoenum iubebatur) illisum parieti caput rupit". Schott illustrates the haughty spirit of the Spartans from Plutarch, *Apoph. Lac.* 233, B, 21, Λάκων αἰχμαλωτισθεὶς καὶ πιπρασκόμενος, τοῦ κήρυκος λέγοντος, 'Λάκωνα πωλῶ,' ἐπεστόμισεν εἰπὼν 'αἰχμάλωτον κήρυσσε.' 234, D, 40, Ἄλλος αἰχμάλωτος πιπρασκόμενος, τοῦ κήρυκος ἐπιλέγοντος ἀνδράποδον πωλεῖν, "κατάρατε," εἶπεν, "οὐκ ἐρεῖς αἰχμάλωτον;" 235, B, 53 (Philip), ὅτε δὲ ἐνέβαλεν εἰς τὴν Λακωνικὴν καὶ ἐδόκουν ἅπαντες ἀπολεῖσθαι, εἶπε δὲ πρός τινα τῶν Σπαρτιατῶν "τί νῦν ποιήσετε, ὦ Λάκωνες;" "τί γάρ," ἔφη, "ἄλλο ἢ ἀνδρείως ἀποθανούμεθα; μόνοι γὰρ ἡμεῖς Ἑλλήνων ἐλεύθεροι εἶναι καὶ μὴ ὑπακούειν ἄλλοις ἐμάθομεν." Of this nature also was the austere reply of Astycratides that the Spartans would prefer death to slavery (*ib.* 219, B, 9).

36. **potuit non capi**: Bornecque. *non potuit capi*, Müller. Müller's is hardly the required sense, which is not 'he could not have been captured', but 'he could have avoided capture'.

**10, 1. videat trecentos Xerses**. Bornecque compares Sen. phil. *De Ben.* VI, 31, 5, " tot ista gentium milia trecenti morabuntur", and 6, "aestimabis futura damna, cum computaveris quanti Thermopylarum angusta constiterint".

2. **revertamur**...**novissimi**: the point being that the latest news is best (as most reliable).

4. **descriptio Thermopylarum**. Schott was troubled because there was no description, but as Gronovius rightly explained, these are not complete speeches, but only quotations. Seneca mentions that here came a description of Thermopylae, to show the setting of the next sententia. Cf. also "describe tempestatem", S. III, 2; "descriptio pugnantis viri fortis", C. I, 4, 2, inserted with like purpose to the passage under discussion, for it is followed by "Dii boni, et has manus aliquis derisit?" See also C. I, 3, 7; C. IX, 2, 10.

15. **non vincent nos, sed obruent**: echoed in Sen. phil. *De Ben.* VI, 31, 2, "nihil esse dubii quin illa mole non vinci solum Graecia sed obrui posset".

16. **rerum natura**: the reference to Athos and the Hellespont again.

18. **subtilitas**: a very common word, along with the adjective *subtilis*, both in our author and in Cicero's rhetorical works. The metaphor is, like so many in Latin applied to style, from weaving. *subtilis* means 'fine spun'. Here it applies to the ingenuity that the subject might or might not stimulate. Obviously there was not the same field for this in the topic under discussion as there was in most of the controversiae. *subtilitas* denotes acute analysis, fineness or subtlety of argument, or of style, just the quality that declamation, especially the controversiae, tended to emphasise. It is the distinctive quality of the *Attic* style (Lysias), 'close-textured', 'full of detail' (hence, realistic), also subtle in seeing possible arguments and forestalling objections.

20. **ipse sententiam non feram**: but he has already given his judgment very lucidly in C. II, Praef., "erat explicatio Fusci Arelli splendida quidem, sed operosa et implicita, cultus nimis adquisitus, compositio verborum mollior, quam ut illum tam sanctis fortibusque praeceptis praeparans se animus pati posset; summa inaequalitas orationis, quae modo exilis erat, modo nimia licentia vaga et effusa: principia, argumenta, narrationes aride dicebantur, in descriptionibus extra legem omnibus verbis, dum modo niterent, permissa libertas; nihil acre, nihil solidum, nihil horridum, splendida oratio et magis lasciva quam laeta". Fuscus's manner of developing his subject (the metaphor is from unrolling cloth), that is, of viewing it and all that it contained from every point of view, and illustrating it, was brilliant or gorgeous (*splendida*), but laborious and involved (here the pattern of the cloth is confused). The ornaments were far-fetched. The manner of putting the words together, or rhythmical structure, was too soft or luxurious for a philosophic style (*illum* refers to Fabianus, the philosopher, in his youth a pupil of Fuscus). The style was uneven (*inaequalitas*). It was now plain (*exilis*) or dry (*aride*), now diffuse, with an excessive freedom. In description he allowed any word provided only it was brilliant or striking (*niterent*). To sum up, the style was brilliant, and exuberant or luxuriant rather than rich. Here the sons of Seneca are asked to say whether they think the style of Fuscus brilliant (*nitide*) or excessively free (*licenter*). They are asked to say whether his development of his subject is vigorous or riotous. At the end of this suasoria Seneca says the style of Fuscus is jerky (*fracta compositio*). This refers to the short staccato sentences. *compositio* refers to the manner of combining the words into phrases, and the phrases into clauses and sentences. Quintilian says it is in prose the counterpart of versification in poetry, i.e. it is a matter of rhythm (Quin. IX, 4, 116). Prose should be rhythmical but not metrical (*ib.* 56). Seneca has already said that Fuscus's *compositio* is *mollior* (too soft for a philosopher). There is no contradiction. Much of the phrasing in the passage quoted in this suasoria is smooth and flowing; and the jerky style is also illustrated. The animation of the style is quite obvious to the modern reader. There is also a strong flavour of poetry about it: we probably see his freedom in the use of words in *hebetata, senio, excidia, Orientem, internata, aspera scopulorum* etc., as also his *cultus nimis adquisitus*.

22. **suadere, sed ludere**. Pollio said it was literary pastime, not grave deliberation. Declamation had a seriousness of its own. The illusion of reality had to be kept up.

25. **inclinatio...modulatio**. *inclinatio* refers to the pitch, *modulatio* to rhythm or measure. The Romans had a very musical language and were very sensitive to rhythm. It is obvious that the pitch of the voice in singing is something different from that in poetry, and this again different from what is permissible in prose. These three things must be carefully distinguished. If in reading poetry you emphasise

the music of the words too much, you cease to read and begin to sing or chant. Note Augustus' criticism of a person's delivery, "si cantas, male cantas, si legis, cantas" (Quin. 1, 8, 2). If the pitch of the voice is badly regulated in speaking prose, taste is offended. The Roman stage seems to have tended to emphasise this defect, as a Roman play (except in the Senarii) was chanted by the actors rather than declaimed. The rhythm of the three types had also to be carefully distinguished. For the rhythm of prose, a rhythm of quantity, the Roman had a very sensitive ear. Apparently the youth of Seneca's day were fond of delivering rolling passages from Fuscus, one choosing one tone and rhythm, one another. Quintilian criticises the use, because of their attractive sound, of senseless illustrations, VIII, 3, 76, "nam et falsis utuntur" (similes) "nec illa iis quibus similia videri volunt, applicant. quorum utrumque in his est, quae me iuvene ubique cantari solebant: 'magnorum fluminum navigabiles fontes sunt' et 'generosioris arboris statim planta cum fructu est'". He criticises the tendency to chant in delivery in the following passage: XI, 3, 57, "sed quodcunque ex his vitium magis tulerim quam, quo nunc maxime laboratur, in causis omnibus scholisque, cantandi, quod inutilius sit an foedius nescio. quid enim minus oratori convenit quam modulatio scenica et non-nunquam ebriorum aut comissantium licentiae similis?" Tac. Dial. de Orat. 26, 3, criticises the same fashion, "quodque vix auditu fas esse debeat, laudis et gloriae et ingenii loco plerique iactant cantari saltarique commentarios suos".

27. **etiamsi nihil**...: even although the passages he remembers have been admired only in the schools, i.e. are purely of academic interest.

36. **sociorum fuga**.... The MSS. have only *socior paucitas*. Kiessling inserted *fuga*, Gertz added *vestra ipsorum*. Linde (adopted by Bornecque) read *hostium copia, vestrorum paucitas*, nearer the MSS.

**11, 1. apud Herodotum.** The Greek quotation is not found in Herodotus. Diodorus, XI, 9, 4, has Λεωνίδης δὲ τὴν ἑτοιμότητα τῶν στρατιωτῶν ἀποδεξάμενος, τούτοις παρήγγειλε ταχέως ἀριστοποιεῖσθαι, ὡς ἐν ᾅδου δειπνησομένους. Plutarch, *Apoph. Lac.* 225 D, 13, (Leonidas) τοῖς δὲ στρατιώταις παρήγγειλεν ἀριστοποιεῖσθαι, ὡς ἐν ᾍδου δειπνοποιησομένους. Val. Max. III, 2, Ext. 3, renders it in Latin, "ideoque tam alacri animo suos ad id proelium, quo perituri erant, cohortatus est, ut diceret: sic prandete, commilitones, tanquam apud inferos coenaturi". Seneca has a similar error in quotation in C. IX, 1, 13, where he attributes to Thucydides a passage which is not found in our texts of the historian, the nearest approximation to it being in Demosthenes. The error, Bornecque points out, is possibly due to the fact that he is comparing with it a passage of Sallust, who was regarded as being an imitator of Thucydides. Dorion's eloquent remark has been lost.

2. **Sabinus Asilius**: an irrepressible jester. Several of his witticisms are given in C. IX, 4, 17 *et seq.*

7. **subtilissimus**. For the various uses of *subtilis* see Wilkins, *De Oratore*, p. 91, I, 17, where he gives the following meanings: (1) (originally) finely woven, (2) fine, thin, delicate, (3) precise, accurate, (4) plain (τὸ ἰσχνὸν γένος of oratory), unadorned. Here it seems to mean most refined, or most acute in thought. See note on **10**, 18. The quotation from Attalus is lost.

10. **Cornelius Severus**: a friend of Ovid, wrote an epic on the *bellum Siculum* waged with Sextus Pompeius 38 B.C. Ovid refers to him at least twice, *Pont.* IV, 16, 9,

> "quique dedit Latio carmen regale Severus";

and IV, 2, 1,

> "quod legis, o vates magnorum maxime regum,
> venit ab intonsis usque, Severe, Getis".

Quin. X, 1, 89, criticises him thus: "Cornelius autem Severus, etiamsi versificator quam poeta melior, si tamen, ut est dictum, ad exemplar primi libri, bellum Siculum perscripsisset, vindicaret sibi iure secundum locum" (among epic poets, Vergil being first). The fine lines on Cicero in S. VI, 26 and this quotation here are probably from this epic.

13. **stratique per herbam**: possibly imitated from Vergil, *Aen.* IX, 164, "fusique per herbam".

14. **hic meus est...dies.** So Seneca's *Medea* (1017) says,

> "perfruere lento scelere; ne propera, dolor.
> meus dies est: tempore accepto utimur".

15. **elegantissime**: 'with good taste, in the choicest manner'.

17. **magnitudo.** Here Seneca's admiration for Rome comes out.

19. **Porcellus grammaticus.** The grammaticus precedes the rhetor in Roman education. First the boy learns to read and write, then he goes to the *grammaticus*, who teaches him *ratio loquendi* (principles of grammar) and *enarratio auctorum* (which corresponds to our lessons in literature) and gives him his first lessons in simple composition. (See Quin. I, 9.) These latter consisted of oral narratives of Aesop's fables, paraphrases from the poets, *sententiae, chriae,* and *ethologiae*; the exact meaning of the latter two is rather obscure. The Roman *grammatici* in Quintilian's day went further and initiated the boys in declamation, at any rate in the simpler forms, e.g. suasoriae, which Quin. would have given to the rhetor (see *Inst. Or.* II, 1, 2), "sed ad prosopopoeïas usque ac suasorias, in quibus onus dicendi vel maximum est, irrumpunt. hinc ergo accidit ut, quae alterius artis prima erant opera, facta sint alterius novissima", 'what ought to be the first task of the rhetor has become the last of the grammarian'. We have had a similar charge in our day that the top classes in our schools were doing the work of the Universities and *vice versa*.

20. **soloecismum.** Quin. explains the term in I, 5 *et seq.* He has previously defined a barbarism as an error in a single word: he proceeds to show that a solecism arises from wrong combination of words. Each word may be right in itself, but is wrong in relation to others. It may be the adjective in the wrong gender, the verb in the wrong number, i.e. it is an error in concord. In § 36 he quotes as a solecism, "si unum quis ad se vocans dicat, 'venite,' aut si plures a se dimittens ita loquatur 'abi' aut 'discede'". This is just the point in Seneca's passage, but Seneca does not agree, hence "quasi".

26. **grammaticorum,** sarcastic, just like "in choro manu ducente grammatico" (referring to the simultaneous reading of the schools, the teacher setting the pattern).

27. **habere locum**: a common phrase in Cicero, *De Oratore*; cf. II, 64, "locum suum in his artibus quae traditae sunt, habent nullum"; II, 219, "in hoc altero dicacitatis quid habet ars loci?" II, 274, "sed habet non nunquam aliquid etiam apud nos loci". It means, 'to have a place', or 'not to be out of place'.

33. **ποῖ φεύξεσθε, ὁπλῖται, τείχη;** Cf. 8, 10 "ibi muros habet, ubi viros"; 9, 10, "ideo muri nostri arma sunt".

37. **per sepulchra nostra iurabitur.** Cestius was a Greek. The famous oath of Demosthenes (*De Corona*, § 208) must have been well known to the rhetoricians, especially to the Greeks. It is remarked upon, among the minor Greek rhetores, by Aristides, Hermogenes, and Longinus. The first of these points out that this oath introduces examples by means of a figure: ἐσχημάτισε (ὁ Δημοσθένης) πρός τε τὸ λαμπρὸν ἅμα καὶ τὸ ἀξιόπιστον εἰς ὅρκον φαντασίαν, 'to carry conviction and produce the quality of splendour in the style, D. throws his idea into the form of an oath'. Quin. refers to this famous oath several times, IX, 2, 62, 98; XI, 3, 168; XII, 10, 24.

38. **phantasiam movit.** *phantasiam movere*[1] is 'to start a visual idea', 'raise a mental picture'. Note *motus animi* is not an emotion, but any movement of the mind. According to Sander *phantasia* is one of the Greek terms first introduced into Latin by Seneca. The Latin term is *imago*. Cf. C. I, 6, 12, "Q. Haterius a parte patris pulcherrimam imaginem movit". What Nicetes said is lost, as it would, of course, be in Greek. There is a lacuna in the MSS. after "adiecit". After Demosthenes the MSS. give CIPTOY *cui dicere.* Müller did not attempt to emend. Bornecque after Gertz reads as given. Gertz had cleverly suggested that the passage ran thus after *adiecit*: "(οὐχ ἁμαρτησόμεθα, ὦ ἄνδρες Λακεδαιμόνιοι, τὸν ὑπὲρ τῆς ἁπάντων σωτηρίας κίνδυνον ἀράμενοι, μὰ τοὺς ἀλλαχοῦ προκινδυνεύσαντας τῶν προγόνων καὶ τοὺς ἐν τοῖς δημοσίοις μνήμασι κειμένους ἀγαθοὺς ἄνδρας, οὓς ἡ πόλις τῆς καλλίστης ἀξιώσασα τιμῆς ἔθαψεν, nitide) nisi antiquior Xerxes fuisset, quam ut Demosthenis ὅρκον hic dicere (liceret)". At any rate the general meaning is clear. It was a clever *phantasia* were it not that

[1] See *Cic. Letters*, Tyrrell and Purser, 531 and note.

to mention Demosthenes, when the time is that of Xerxes, is ana-
chronistic. It is interesting to note that the rhetoricians recognise
and condemn anachronisms. Cf. below **14**, 12, *veni, vidi, vici.*

**12, 2. hanc suam dixit sententiam.** After *hostibus* Bursian
suspected a lacuna, the original sentiment of Nicetes being here too
lost, but we should rather suspect the lacuna before *hanc.* If the
quotation came at the end of the sentence we should have *illam*
instead of *hanc.*

5. **Potamon**: a famous Greek rhetorician of Mitylene, born 65 B.C.
died A.D. 25 (probably); contemporary and rival of Lesbocles, came on
embassies to Rome in 45 and 25 B.C.; taught rhetoric at Rome, and
engaged there in rhetorical discussions; left works on rhetoric and on
history.

6. **Lesbocles**: a rhetorician of Mitylene. In the preface to C. IV
Seneca tells how Asinius Pollio on the death of his son Herius made
no change in his usual manner of life. Later, on the death of C. Caesar
in Syria, Augustus wrote a friendly letter of complaint to Pollio, be-
cause he had dined in full company while the mourning for this loss
was still going on. To this Pollio replied, "I dined on the day on which
I lost my son Herius". With this is contrasted the feeble spirit of
Haterius, as shown by the way in which he bore the death of his son.
Seneca passes no such comment on Pollio as he does here on Potamon.
Is this the anti-Greek prejudice again? He is more indulgent to the
Roman: "o magnos viros, qui fortunae succumbere nesciunt et
adversas res suae virtutis experimenta faciunt" (C. Praef. IV, 6).

18. **insanierunt**: the word used for extravagance in thought or
language: 'they lost all sanity, all sense of proportion'.

20. See note on **8**, 5.

27. **Catius Crispus**, called in C. VII, 4, 9, "anticus rhetor". The
MSS. have only the word *municipalis.* Müller inserted *orator*, and
Bornecque retains this, translating "orateur de petite ville". Why not
*municipalis rhetor*?

28. **cacozelos**, adverb. The noun is *cacozelia*, a Greek technical
term found first in Seneca, see C. IX, 1, 15, and IX, 2, 28. Hermogenes
(Spengel, *Rhetores Graeci Minores*, II, 257) discusses this vice and shows
how Homer uses hyperbole without falling into the error. Quintilian
uses the term both in its Greek and Latin dress. See *Instit. Or.* VIII, 3,
56: "Κακόζηλον, id est mala affectatio, per omne dicendi genus peccat.
nam et tumida et pusilla et praedulcia, et abundantia et arcessita et
exultantia sub idem nomen cadunt. denique κακόζηλον vocatur,
quidquid est ultra virtutem, quotiens ingenium iudicio caret et specie
boni fallitur, omnium in eloquentia vitiorum pessimum. nam cetera
parum vitantur, hoc petitur. est autem totum in elocutione. nam
rerum vitia sunt stultum, commune, contrarium, supervacuum; corrupta oratio in verbis maxime impropriis, redundantibus, comprehensione obscura, compositione fracta, vocum similium aut ambiguarum

puerili captatione consistit. est autem omne κακόζηλον utique falsum, etiamsi non omne falsum κακόζηλον; κακόζηλον vero est, quod dicitur aliter quam se natura habet et quam oportet et quam sat est". The term then denotes affectation or excessive striving after effect. The style is false or untrue to the matter. This vice produces bombast, and its opposite, feebleness, verbosity, what is far-fetched, and what is extravagant. It shows that the mind lacks judgment, and is misled by the specious. All unnatural, unbecoming, extravagant expressions are examples of κακοζηλία. The *pueriles sententiae*, just given, are good examples of the extravagances to which the rhetores at their worst descended. They are all in a way ingenious, even clever, and all have some point, and illustrate some rhetorical form (at any rate in its abuse). This *cacozelia* becomes a disease with the next rhetor mentioned— Seneca Grandio. (Abraham Cowley knew his Seneca. He has a humorous translation of this Seneca story in his essay "Of Greatness".)

36. **esset**: from *edere*.

**mariscas**: a large and insipid variety of fig.

38. **cognomen, cognomentum**. The latter is the more ornate word.

**ut Messala ait**. Sen. C. II, 4, 8, says, "fuit autem Messala exactissimi ingenii quidem, in omni studiorum parte, sed Latini utique sermonis observator diligentissimus: itaque cum audisset Latronem declamantem dixit: 'sua lingua disertus est'", i.e. Latro (to Messala) was a good speaker, but his Latin was not pure Latin. This is M. Valerius Messala Corvinus, great statesman and orator, first a supporter of Caesar, then of Antony, lastly of Augustus. For his reputation as an orator cf. Cic. *Ep. ad Brutum*, I, 15, 1: *Brutus*, § 246: Tac. *Dial. de Or.* 18: Quin. x, 1, 113. He is mentioned in the Suasoriae in the following passages: I, 7; II, 20; III, 6; VI, 27.

39. **aliquando iuvene me**: emendation by F. Jonas, adopted by Müller and Bornecque. ABV have *aliquando invenire*, D *inveniret*.

40. **contradictio**: rhetorical term for an objection of the opponent.

**13, 6. ponat contra caelum castra**: the rhetoricians are fond of representing Xerxes' war as impious. Cf. S. v, 2–4.

9. **decentissimi generis**. The rhetorical form, repetition of conjunction, Seneca approves of; the idea he thinks foolish.

13. **sed viri** etc. For the form cf. Sen. phil. *De Const. Sap.* 13, 5, "habes sub te Parthos, Medos et Bactrianos, sed quos metu contines, sed propter quos remittere arcum tibi non contigit, sed postremos, sed venales, sed novum aucupantes dominium".

18. **belli mora**: a phrase neat, terse and full of meaning, of which Seneca implies Latro was the original author. Vergil, however, has it in *Aen.* x, 428,

                "primus Abantem
oppositum interimit, pugnae nodumque moramque".

Arbronius Silo adopted it and the phrase became famous. It took the fancy and was copied again and again. Cf. Ovid, *Met.* XII, 20,

> "gaudete Pelasgi,
> Troia cadet; sed erit nostri mora longa laboris";

Sen. *Troades*, 124,

> "columen patriae, mora fatorum,
> tu (Hector) praesidium Phrygibus fessis,
> tu murus eras";

Sen. *Agam.* 211,

> "non sola Danais Hector et bello mora";

Lucan, *Phar.* I, 100,

> "nam sola futuri
> Crassus erat belli medius mora".

The phrase is easy to paraphrase, but difficult to translate, 'we shall at least delay the conclusion of the war, we shall gain time at least'. Changing the figure, 'we shall be a stumbling-block in the war'. It is difficult to see how Vergil's rendering of the idea is prettier (*decentius*).

19. **pantomimis.** The *pantomimus* is a kind of ballet—dancing with dumb show. Under Augustus, Pylades founded tragic pantomime, Bathyllus (the favourite of Maecenas) comic pantomime. 'An actor appearing in different parts and costumes, as the story (*fabula*) required, represented in a succession of solos the chief incidents of a plot, while a choir sang the words during and between the dances'. This connecting text was very subordinate, and it was apparently undignified for a great writer to descend to the writing of such (from Teuffel and Schwabe, *History of Rom. Lit.* vol. I, p. 11).

20. **polluit**: because such representations were very licentious.

22. **magnum paeana canentes.** Cf. *Iliad*, XXII, 391 and Verg. *Aen.* VI, 657.

24. **maligni**: 'jealous, grudging, critical'. Seneca criticises the effeminate youth of this time for their laziness in C. I, Praef. 10, "sententias a disertissimis viris iactas facile in tanta hominum desidia pro suis dicunt", and gives this as one reason for his book's existence. Seneca is not given to exaggeration, and the ignorance must have been great if the Verrines were not well known. Cicero was, of course, now not fashionable, at any rate with the school of Pollio and the younger generation. The passage from Vergil is in *Aen.* XI, 288 *et seq.* Cf. with Messala's criticism, Ovid's in C. VII, 1, 27, of Varro's verses:

> "'desierant latrare canes urbesque silebant;
> omnia noctis erant placida composta quiete'.

solebat Ovidius de his versibus dicere, potuisse fieri longe meliores, si secundi versus ultima pars abscideretur et sic desineret:

> 'omnia noctis erant'.

Varro quem voluit sensum optime explicuit, Ovidius in illius versu suum sensum invenit; aliud enim intercisus versus significaturus est, aliud totus significat". (A good instance of Seneca's sober sense.) Note that Maecenas and Messala are leaders of rival literary circles.

37. **Corvus.** Bornecque remarks that it might be thought that Seneca was referring to the fable of Phaedrus (I, 13, 12),

"tunc demum ingemuit corvi deceptus stupor",

but, he adds, this, according to M. Havet, had not yet been published.

38. **suo mari**: *suo*, emphatic, 'on the sea he has made his own'.

**14, 1. Sosius.** Cf. Tac. *Hist.* v, 9. After the provinces had submitted to M. Antonius, Pacorus, King of the Parthians, took possession of Judaea, but was slain by P. Ventidius, and the Parthians were driven back beyond the Euphrates ("Judaeos C. Sosius subegit"). C. Sosius was consul in 39 B.C., proconsul of Syria 38 B.C., triumphed over the Jews 34 B.C., consul again 32 B.C. (Bornecque). We have frequent allusions to these declamations before great personages throughout Seneca, before Augustus, Agrippa, Maecenas (C. II, 4, 12 and 13), Lamia (VII, 6, 22), among others.

2. **controversiam.** This controversia is not one of those found in Seneca's book, which is not therefore exhaustive of the subjects treated in the schools. In C. II, 4, 8, he mentions a suasoria on Theodotus, which Latro declaimed for three days, and says he will state what Latro said when he comes to the Suasoriae. As he does not do so in the book we have, we infer that there was at least one more book of Suasoriae. From the extract here quoted we infer that the rhetor was evidently trying to give a picture of luxurious society women. It is certainly ridiculous, but we should understand it better if we had the setting.

6. **mitrata.** All the MSS. have *mirata*. Schott says a friend of his suggested *mitrata*; he does not name him. Gron. suggested *myrrhata*. For *mitrata* Schott compares Lucr. IV, 1125,

"et bene parta patrum fiunt anademata mitrae";

Verg. *Aen.* IV, 216,

"et nunc ille Paris, cum semiviro comitatu,
Maeonia mentum mitra crinemque madentem
subnixus, rapto potitur";

*ib.* IX, 616,

"et tunicae manicas et habent redimicula mitrae".

Schott adds, "mitratus etiam Attis inducitur a scriptoribus Cybelis". The *mitra*, an oriental head-dress just like a turban, is a mark clearly of effeminacy in men and of luxury in women. Cf. also Verg. *Copa*, 1, "Copa Syrisca, caput Graia redimita mitella" (dim. of *mitra*).

7. **Tuscus**. We have the account of the death of Mamercus Scaurus in Tac. *Ann.* VI, 29. His accusers (*ib.* 30) are called Servilius and Cornelius. Probably the latter is the person meant here. This trial and death of Scaurus took place in A.D. 34. This part of the book of Suasoriae, if not in fact the whole book, must have been written then after A.D. 34. Scaurus was capable but dissolute.

12. **veni, vidi, vici**. See Suet. *Caesar*, 37. For the objection to anachronism see note on **11**, 38.

17. **nimius cultus**. See note on style of Arellius Fuscus (**10**, 20).

# SUASORIA III

The preceding suasoria is drawn from Greek history, this from Greek legend. The speaker is evidently Agamemnon, and naturally the argument is adverse to the course proposed by Calchas. There are no political, no strategic, no sentimental arguments. These apparently are too obvious. To sacrifice Iphigenia is homicide, nay parricide. Iphigenia is worth far more than Helen. Most important of all the rhetores are interested in the philosophical question whether any trust is to be put in augury. Of course we have only quotations, and no means of knowing what formed the rest of the speech, but the *divisio* seems to show that the main outline hinged on the above questions. Seneca in accordance with his promise of S. 11, 10 and 23, begins by quoting a long description by Arellius Fuscus.

**15, 4. condicionem.** Cf. C. v, 1, "tu putabas te ea condicione accepisse ne perderes?" See note below on **15, 6.**

**omnis ex voto iret dies.** Schott compares Cic. *Ep. ad Att.* xiv, 15, "incipit res melius ire quam putaram".

**votum**: either the thing vowed, or the thing desired, or the prayer itself. Here it is the last. The argument is that the changes of weather, whether on sea or land, are controlled by the influence of the stars, the moon or the winds, or at any rate by something that cannot be changed by human prayers or vows.

**6. sub eadem condicione.** Cf. 7, 32, "sub eodem pueritia fato est". *condicio* expresses the law of their being, the terms on which they exist. The development of Triarius in C. 11, 5, 8, should be compared. "non ex formula natura respondet nec ad praescriptum casus obsequitur; semper expectari fortuna mavult quam regi. aliubi offenditur improvisa segetum maturitas, aliubi sera magno fenore moram redemit. licet lex dies finiat, natura non recipit". This is just the opposite of the modern view of science.

**alias negatis imbribus.** The influence of these exercises of the rhetorical schools is traced in the following passage from Seneca's *Oedipus*, 41–50:

> "deseruit amnes humor, atque herbas color,
> aretque Dirce. tenuis Ismenos fluit,
> et tingit inopi nuda vix unda vada.
> obscura caelo labitur Phoebi soror;
> tristisque mundus nubilo pallet novo.
> nullum serenis noctibus sidus micat:
> sed gravis et ater incubat terris vapor.
> obtexit arces coelitum ac summas domos
> inferna facies. denegat fructum Ceres‘
> adulta; et altis flava cum spicis tremat,
> arente culmo sterilis emoritur seges".

7. **lugent**: Haase; MSS. "legunt".

**et haec interdum anno lex est**: reads like a marginal note inserted in the text.

8. **serena**: sc. *sidera*, the stars of cloudless weather (?) or better the cloudless parts of the sky are hidden. "serena (caeli)": cf. "aspera scopulorum" (**7**, 21).

9. **subsidit solum.** The idea is quite clear to anyone who has seen his seeds washed out of the garden by heavy rain after sowing. The soil seems to subside and leave the seeds exposed.

11. **variantur tempora**: *tempora*—'the weather'.

12. **quidquid asperatum aestu** etc.: a good example of the fondness of Arellius for saying simple things in a very strange way. "nimius cultus" (**14**, 17), I suppose.

14. **luna cursu gerit**: *regit*, the conjecture of an anonymous scholar, quoted by Schott, may be right. Here we have a fresh hypothesis—if it is not the stars that govern the weather, possibly it is the moon—and then comes, of course, another opportunity for a brilliant description, inspired by a passage from Vergil's *Georgics*, which he proceeds to give. For the ancient belief regarding the moon's influence on the weather compare the following passage from Pliny the elder, *Nat. Hist.* XVIII, 347: "proxuma sint iure lunae praesagia. quartam eam maxume observat Aegyptus; si splendens exorta puro nitore fulsit, serenitatem, si rubicunda ventos, si nigra, pluvias portendere creditur. in quinta cornua eius optunsa pluviam, erecta et infesta ventos semper significant" etc. He also quotes Varro (later): "si quarto die luna erit directa, magnam tempestatem in mari praesagiet, nisi si coronam circa se habebit et eam sinceram, quoniam illo modo non ante plenam lunam hiematurum ostendit".

15. **sive plena lucis suae.** Hyginus, *Astron.* 4, 14, discusses the question of the source of the light of the moon, and incidentally gives a correct explanation of eclipses: "si enim suo lumine uteretur, illud quoque sequebatur, eam semper aequalem esse oportere, nec die tricesimo tam exilem aut omnino nullam videri, cum totum transegerit cursum.... praeterea, si suo lumine uteretur, huius nunquam eclipsin fieri oportebat".

**splendensque pariter adsurgit in cornua**: brilliant and striking phrase to picture the steady and equal waxing of each horn of the crescent.

16. **occurrente.** In **16**, 29, where we find the passage quoted again, the word in the MSS. is *occupata*, which Gronovius emended to *occurrente*. Here the MSS. which give *occurret de* or *occurrit de* point rather to the reading of the text, which is the emendation of Gertz and Novák.

17. **finit**: sc. *imbres*. The new moon, if bright, foretells dry weather: if misty, it foretells rain, which will not cease till it becomes bright again (*lucem reddit*).

**lucem reddit.** Cf. Latro, C. II, 2, 8, "non vides ut immota fax torpeat, ut exagitata reddat ignes?"

19. **quidquid horum est.** This connects the digression to the main subject, and the connection is very loose: 'It was no order of a god that made the sea safe for an adulterer, since the weather depends upon the stars, or the moon or the winds etc., and not upon human wishes'.

20. **at non potero.** Gertz adds *aliter*, Bornecque deletes. The force of the word *aliter* is implied in *at*, and the emendation is unnecessary. If the last lines of Fuscus's speech may be taken as connected, and not isolated sentences, we should have an example of his *fracta compositio*, the broken rhythm of his style.

21. **ne...timerem persequebar.** Idiomatic imperfect: referring to the time when the expedition was conceived. We should use present.

27. **describe nunc tempestatem.** See note on **10**, 4, "descriptio Thermopylarum".

**parricidium:** strictly the slaying of a father or of a mother, then of any near relation; cf. Cic. "civem Romanum necare prope parricidium" (*In Verrem*, II, 5, 66 (170)).

28. **deae templo:** Bornecque compares Ovid. *Met.* IV, 798 and XII, 28.

IV, 798,

> "hanc pelagi rector templo vitiasse Minervae
> dicitur";

XII, 28,

> "nec enim nescitve tacetve
> sanguine virgineo placandam virginis iram
> esse deae....
> victa dea est, nubemque oculis obiecit, et inter
> officium turbamque sacri" etc.

32. **infestae sunt tempestates** etc.: variation on Cestius' sententia above.

34. **adulteris clauderentur.** Cf. above, Fuscus, "extra iussum dei tutum fuit adultero mare" (**15**, 19).

**16**, 4. **malum familiae nostrae fatale.** The violation of Aerope cost Thyestes his children's lives: now for a second time an adulterous wife Helen costs the life of her brother-in-law's child.

7. **Divisio.** Seneca now gives a brief summary of the main divisions of Fuscus's argument. The quotation in § 1 obviously comes from the part that dealt with "illam moram naturae maris et ventorum esse".

16. **diligenter divisit.** Cestius developed more fully the argument that 'the will of the gods is not known to men'.

21. **auguriis negavit credendum.** Schott quotes the saying of Cato the Censor, from Cic. *De Divin.* 2, "mirari se si augur auguri,

aruspex aruspici occurrens non rideat", so that the scepticism is fairly old.
We see it in Euripides, *Iphig. in Aulis*, 879, where the old man says in
reply to Clytemnestra, θέσφαθ', ὥς γέ φησι Κάλχας, ἵνα πορεύηται
στρατός. Cf. Achilles also, line 955 *et seq*.,

πικροὺς δὲ προχύτας χέρνιβάς τ' ἐνάρξεται
Κάλχας ὁ μάντις. τίς δὲ μάντις ἐστ' ἀνήρ;
ὃς ὀλίγ' ἀληθῆ, πολλὰ δὲ ψευδῆ λέγει
τυχών· ὅταν δὲ μὴ τύχῃ διοίχεται.

There were various methods of foretelling the future in antiquity, and
opinion on their reliability varied. Hence the orator had to learn the
various methods of confirming or rebutting evidence alleged from
these. Note Quin. *Inst. Or.* v, 7, 36, "aliter enim oraculorum, aliter
aruspicum, augurum, coniectorum, mathematicorum fides confirmari
aut refelli potest". Similarly, in III, 11, 6, he says that if Orestes
defends himself by saying that he was impelled by an oracle to slay
his mother, the question arises "an responsis parere debuerit?" The
*oraculum* is as Seneca says the "voluntas divina hominis ore enuntiata"
(C. 1, Praef. 9); the *aruspex* tells the future from an examination of the
entrails of animals, the *augur* from the flight of birds, the *coniector* from
dreams, the *mathematicus* from the stars. This evidence is admissible
in the courts, but not only have the facts to be established, but the
general question whether such are to be believed at all may have to
be debated. Here Silo says that even if some forms of divination are
possible augury at any rate is not one. Livy's remarks in bk. XLIII, 13,
are interesting: "non sum nescius, ab eadem neglegentia qua nihil
deos portendere vulgo nunc credant, neque nuntiari admodum nulla
prodigia in publicum neque in annales referri. ceterum et mihi,
vetustas res scribenti, nescio quo pacto antiquus fit animus; et quaedam
religio tenet, quae illi prudentissimi viri publice suscipienda cen-
suerint, ea pro indignis habere, quae in meos annales referam". The
belief then was dying out in Livy's day; but Seneca the younger, while
still believing in portents, thinks the art of divination should take
account of all events, and that it is imperfect yet (*Nat. Quaest.* II, 32, 3).
The next suasoria opens with an attack on the *mathematici* by Fuscus.

26. **Fuscus Arellius Vergilii versus voluit imitari**: see next
paragraph, and also S. IV, 4 and 5. Here he is imitating Verg. *Georgics*,
I, 427 *et seq*.

31. **occupata**: Gronovius emended to *occurrente* to agree with § 1.

35. **si nigrum obscuro comprenderit aera cornu**: not 'if her
dim crescent clasp dark air', as Sidgwick, but 'if on dim crescent she
has caught dark mist', i.e. 'if her crescent is dim and surrounded with
mist'. Vergil knew quite well that the unlit body of the moon was
between the horns. Vegetius, *De Re Militari*, v, 11, also imitates this
passage: "multis quoque signis et de tranquillo procellae et de tempestatibus serena produntur, quae velut in speculo Lunae orbis
ostendit. rubicundus enim color ventos, caeruleus indicat pluvias.

ex utroque commixtus, nimbos et furentes procellas. laetus orbis ac lucidus serenitatem navigiis repromittit, quam gestat in vultu; praecipue si quarto ortu, neque obtusis cornibus, rutila; neque infuso fuerit humore fuscata". Sen. *Oed.* 505 may also be compared: "lunaque dimissos dum plena recolliget ignes".

38. **ortu quarto**: 'on the fourth day after new moon'.

**17, 2. imputaret**: (Schott) *expensum ferret*, 'put it down to Maecenas's account with him, take credit for it'. He compares also VI, 20, (Popillius) "victoribus id ipsum imputaturus, occupat facinus". The word is found frequently in the Controversiae. See C. II, 5, 7; II, 5, 13 and 14; II, 6, 2; III, 6; IV, 5; IV, 7; VI, 7; IX, 1, 11; IX, 2, 15.

**totiens enim pro beneficio** etc.: 'he so often used to tell as a service (*pro beneficio*) (rendered to Maecenas) how he had pleased Maecenas or (absolutely) had pleased the audience (i.e. had been successful) in some Vergilian description.'

**totiens**: used absolutely. The sentence corroborates the preceding statement.

4. All the MSS. have "cur iste inter eius ministerium placuit" (*sc. deo*). Linde suggests "inter eius modi ministerium". Madvig emended "cur iste interpres et eius". Gertz, "iste vates et eius ministerium" which Bornecque adopts. Thomas, "iste in interius ministerium". Müller reads Fr. Leo's emendation, "cur iste in interpretis ministerium". Thomas's is nearest the MSS., and gives good sense, 'for his more intimate service'. Bornecque's note assumes *interpres* in the text however, and refers us to Verg. *Aen.* III, 359, for the use, "Troiugena, interpres divum"; Sen. *Troades*, 351, "potius interpres deum | Calchas vocetur", and 938,

> "utinam iuberet me quoque interpres deum
> abrumpere ense lucis invisae moras".

7. **plena deo.** The phrase is not found in our text of Vergil. We at once think it must be in *Aen.* VI, 40–80: and it may have been there in the first version, or in a version current in Seneca's day. It is curious that line 51 can be easily altered to take it,

> "plena deo, 'iam tu cessas in vota precesque,
> Tros' ait 'Aeneas?'"

or line 77,        "plena deo nondum patiens".

In any case the phrase took the fancy and was frequently imitated by later poets, as well as by Ovid, quoted later **17, 27**. Cf. Lucan, IX, 564,

> "ille deo plenus tacita quem mente gerebat";

Stat. *Theb.* X, 164,

> "impatiensque dei, fragili quem mente receptum
> non capit";

Sil. Ital. III, 673, "tum loca plena deo"; v, 80, "plenus et ipse deum"; Val. Flacc. I, 230, "plenus fatis Phoeboque quieto"; Ovid, *Fasti*, I, 474,
"ore dabat vero carmina plena dei".

**aptissime ponere**: 'to quote aptly, to the point'.

9. **impetu**: *impetus* applied to oratory means 'strong feeling, rush, energy, "go", in the style'.

12. **caldus**: 'hot, fiery, impassioned', apparently the form preferred to *calidum* in Augustus' day, as Quintilian tells us in I, 6, 19, "Augustus quoque in epistolis ad C. Caesarem scriptis emendat, quod is calidum dicere quam *caldum* malit, non quia id non sit Latinum sed quia sit odiosum et, ut ipse Graeco verbo significat, περίεργον".

12. **scholastici**: purely schoolmen, who took no part in the practical oratory of the forum; those who practised as lawyers were called *pragmatici*.

If the phrase *plena deo* really came from the description of the Sibyl in *Aen.* VI, it must have vividly recalled the picture of lines 47-50 to those who knew their Vergil:

"subito non vultus non color unus,
non comptae mansere comae: sed pectus anhelum,
et rabie fera corda tument, maiorque videri
nec mortale sonans, adflata est numine quando
iam propiore dei".

It appeared to hit off the exaggeration of the style very pointedly. A declaimer should not rave like an inspired sibyl.

When Gallio applied it to Haterius of course Tiberius was puzzled. The grammar seemed wrong, and he asked for an explanation. In C. IV, Praef. 7, Seneca gives a description of the style of Haterius and quotes a witticism of Augustus on it: "tanta erat illi velocitas orationis ut vitium fieret. itaque divus Augustus optime dixit: 'Haterius noster sufflaminandus est'. adeo non currere sed decurrere videbatur". (See the whole passage.)

21. **Theodoreus**. The declaimers divided themselves into two schools, Asiatic and Attic, and in addition into followers of Apollodorus and of Theodorus. Apollodorus was probably rather Attic in style, Theodorus was Asiatic or rather Rhodian. The former was the tutor of Augustus, the latter of Tiberius. Nicetes by style seems to lean to the Theodorei. Then "Tiberius ipse Theodoreus" must mean Tiberius although he was a follower of Theodorus (and hence should have liked Nicetes) disliked him, and was pleased with Gallio's story. Bornecque thinks that *ipse Theodoreus* must mean 'because he was a follower of Theodorus and hence opposed to Apollodorus and his school, disliked Nicetes'. This interpretation makes Nicetes a follower of Apollodorus. Apollodorus belongs to the generation preceding Theodorus, and Nicetes (according to St Jerome) was a contemporary of Theodorus, but this would not prevent him from being a follower

of the latter. The difference between the two schools cannot now be made out very clearly. See Bornecque, *Les Déclamations et les Déclamateurs d'après Sénèque le père*, pp. 140 *et seq.*

23. **Gallio Nasoni suo.** Cf. for this intimacy, Ovid, *Pont.* IV, II, where Ovid in a letter of consolation to Gallio on the death of his wife strangely ends with the suggestion that he may still have the happiness to find another. Gallio was also a great friend of Seneca, and adopted the latter's eldest son, Annaeus Novatus.

25. **palam mutuandi.** Seneca means that Ovid was not strictly plagiarising, but borrowing to give pleasure to his readers by echoing their favourite poet. We may instance the Vergilian echoes in Tennyson and the Shakespearian in Thackeray.

27. **feror huc illuc**: appears to be a quotation from Ovid's tragedy, *Medea*, mentioned twice by Quin. VIII, 5, 6; X, 1, 98; and by Tacitus in the *Dial. de Oratoribus* (12, 6), by both with admiration.

29. **verisimilitudinis.** Schultingh's emendation of the reading of all the MSS. *similitudinis.* Bornecque adopts Müller's suggestion, *simili huic tractatione* which seems better, 'in a development similar to this one'. Aul. Gell., XIV, 1, gives a long rendering of the main arguments used by a Greek philosopher Favorinus against the belief in astrology.

The subject of this suasoria is taken from the history of Alexander the Great. Seneca quotes only Fuscus on this topic, and merely an extract from his handling of it, consisting of an attack upon the *mathematici*—those who foretold the future from the stars. In fact this is just a *locus communis* "in omnes qui hanc adfectarent scientiam " (cf. S. III, 4). Seneca says (Divisio, § 4) that these were the only questions that Fuscus discussed in his treatment of this subject. Fuscus speaks, not as Alexander, but as one of his councillors.

**18, 6. canat**: because oracles were usually given in verse.

**eodem contentus utero**: i.e. he must claim supernatural birth.

**contentus**: with the full force of its meaning here, ' confining oneself within the limits of a thing and so content with it'.

7. **inprudentes**: with emphasis on its original meaning (*in* + *pro* + *video*), 'we who unlike the prophets cannot foresee the future', prophets being (as Schultingh says) above all *prudentes*, if they are true prophets.

10. **habitum**: generally, 'state, condition', here almost approaching the meaning of *modus* in Horace, "modus agri non ita magnus", 'measure or limit'. Cf. also Livy, I, 42, "ex quo (censu) belli pacisque munia, non viritim, ut ante, sed pro habitu pecuniarum fierent". The argument here is in accordance with the advice of Cestius in S. 1, 5, that the declaimer must suit his language to his company. This is flattery of Alexander. We have here a good example of *explicatio*, the development of the theme that the true prophet must be more than man, and really a god. Fuscus really implies, of course, that the prophet is false, being mere man, and no god.

12. **non eodem vitae fine**: the MSS. give after this, *aetate magna*, which Bornecque emends to *non aetate maligna* (after Gertz). Both will be loose ablatives of description. I do not believe either phrase is correct as it stands. They both look like a gloss on the next sentence.

**extra omnem fatorum necessitatem**: *fatorum* is Schultingh's emendation of *futurorum*, which is given by all the MSS. Schg. points out that the phrase means *calamitates et mortem*, the fates being often put for what they bring.

16. **qua licet**: 'by the path by which it is permitted', i.e. by astrology.

**visimus**: MSS. *visuimus* or *visumus*. Hence F. Walter (*Berliner Philologische Wochenschrift*, 1918 (10)) suggests *visu subimus*, comparing Verg. *Aen.* x, 447, "obit...omnia visu".

17. **inutili**: 'useless', as compared with this knowledge of the future.

18. **attero**: 'to wear out by rubbing'.

**pignore**: a *pignus* is something upon which we rely as a guarantee for another person's conduct. Thus accomplishments are a guarantee or security against misfortune. Here the thing on which we rely for the development of intellect is "futuri scientia".

19. **ingenia surrexerint**. Fuscus evidently liked this phrase. Cf. "ab infantia surgit ingenium" (7, 14). *surrexerint* is potential in force.

20. **fatorum pignora**: i.e. horoscopes: a true horoscope is a guarantee of what is going to happen, a pledge, something on which we may rely, that it will happen.

**natales**: *sc. dies*, i.e. horoscopes.

22. **contrane durus steterit**: to use the language of astronomy, 'whether the sun was in opposition or conjunction'.

23. **plenam lucem an initia surgentis (lucis) acceperit (Luna)**: 'whether it was at the full or just beginning to wax'. Here we have good examples of *nimius cultus* and *fracta compositio*. The whole thing is vivid and beautiful in its way. The poetical flavour is strong, but there is no flow in the style. It is not a case of art concealing art. Note the first five clauses refer to moon and sun only, no prediction being associated with them: then there are five clauses in each of which a planet is associated with what it portends.

25. **Saturnus**: as God of husbandry. Born under his star you will be a farmer; under *Mars*, a soldier; under *Mercurius*, a merchant; under *Venus*, you will be fortunate in love (hence "blanda adnuerit"). *Jupiter* gives dominion or power.

28. **tot circa unum caput tumultuantis deos**: ironical as also the next clause, "futura nuntiant". Messengers when credible announce the *past*. Next he gives three examples of false prognostications, and draws the conclusion—'There is no true science of augury, and we live uncertain of our fate'. The last two clauses are isolated *sententiae*. We need not take them as having followed in that connection in the speech of Fuscus. His style can scarcely have been so jerky as that.

29. **diu**: inserted by Gertz.

30. **dies**. Linde unnecessarily wanted to emend this to *deus*. *dies* stands for *dies fatalis* or *dies suprema*, 'one day overwhelmed them', or 'the day of doom overwhelmed them'.

33. **incertae sortis**: predicative genitive.

34. **eruuntur**: inserted by Gertz, not absolutely necessary: the sense of *finguntur* is repeated with a sort of zeugma: in the first phrase it means 'fabricated', in the second the idea of falsity disappears and it means merely 'moulded'.

**19, 2. Babylon ei cluditur.** According to Arrian it was on Alexander's return to Babylon, after his expedition down the Indus, that he was warned not to enter Babylon, or at least not to enter except from the west. Alexander is represented as inclined to fall in with the advice, while suspecting that the prediction is caused by self-interest. The ancients did believe in astrology; hence Arellius's argument is not historically probable. The ancients doubted which predictions were true, which false. Alexander would not have doubted that there *was* a science of the stars from which omens could be drawn. On this general question of the credibility of astrology it is worth comparing Sen. phil. *Ep.* 88, 12. Here Seneca argues that this knowledge gained from the stars is useless. It can only trouble the soul. Fate controls everything, and the knowledge of its action benefits in no way. If the stars give sure predictions there is no gain in knowing beforehand what one cannot escape. The best thing is to hope for the best, and to be prepared to meet the worst. Compare also Lucan, *Phars.* I, 641 *et seq.*, and Manilius, *Astron.* IV, who shows in this book the influence each constellation has at birth, and the relative importance of each. Tacitus (*Ann.* VI, 22) doubts whether chance or fate or merely natural laws rule the world, and seems to believe that in spite of the errors and trickery of some exponents of the science still there is a science of astrology, as examples from ancient days and from his own time show. The discourse of Favorinus summarised by Aulus Gellius (XIV, I) is also worth noting in this connection. He gives many clever and sometimes amusing arguments to show that such a science is unworthy of belief. The *Divisio* merely tells us that Fuscus discussed nothing in this suasoria but these questions relating to astrology, and is mainly taken up with an anecdote which amused Seneca and his contemporaries.

7. **controversiam de illa**... etc. The subject of this controversia, which apparently was a well-known theme in the schools (although it is not one of those quoted by Seneca) is thus stated by Faber: "A woman had had three children still-born. She dreamed that, if next time she had a baby, she went to a grove to bring it to birth, it would be a living child. She obeyed the dream, bore a living child in secret, and asked the grandfather to recognise it. He refused and the cause came to court".

10. **vos scire**: the MSS. read "quam ego intellego me dicere... Fuscus" etc. Some words have dropped out. Seneca apparently said that he would insult his sons' intelligence, if he quoted the whole controversy with which he is well aware they are acquainted. This would imply something like "si totam controversiam, quam ego intellego vos scire, fusius exposuero", which I read. Schultingh took *contumeliosus* as meaning that the story is unfit for the ears of the young ("maxima debetur puero reverentia"), and emended thus, "si totam controversiam quam ego intellego me scire, dixero".

Gertz emended thus, "...quam ego intellego me scire, fusius

exposuero. hanc ergo cum Fuscus" etc. To both of these there is the same objection, that there seems no point in the *ego* and *me*.

12. **locum**, i.e. *locum communem*.

15. **Vergili versum**: Verg. *Aen.* IV, 379. (The second from *Aen.* II, 553.)

18. **cuius pudori parco**: by not naming him.

25. **abdidit ensem**: imitated five times in Seneca's tragedies. (Bornecque) *Troades*, 48,

"alto nefandum vulneri ferrum abdidit";

*ib.* 1155,  "ut dextra ferrum penitus exacta abdidit";

*Thyestes*, 722,

"ast illi ferus
in vulnere ensem abscondit";

*Octavia*, 370,

"rogat infelix, utero dirum
condat ut ensem";

*ib.* 733,  "ensemque iugulo condidit saevum Nero".

26. **molestus**: denotes 'importunity'. Cf. C. x, Praef. 1, "quod ultra mihi molesti sitis, non est".

27. **cultius**: reverting to the question raised in 10, 20, where see note. Note that Fuscus liked suasoriae and preferred them in Greek. His pupil Fabianus is said to have been "suasoriis aptior" (C. II, Praef. 3). Ovid (C. II, 2, 12) is said also to have preferred suasoriae, "libentius dicebat suasorias; molesta illi erat omnis argumentatio". Suasoriae gave more scope to the poetic imagination.

30. **οἷον...ὀχύρωμα**. This implies that Hybreas assumes that Alexander was warned before entering Babylon for the first time (see note on **19**, 2). One can hardly believe that Seneca wrote these words in this connection.

## SUASORIA V

The subject again is connected with the Persian Wars: but is more purely fictitious. There is no evidence that Xerxes ever sent such a message. In the other four the setting is genuine history (except in S. 1, the assumption of three hundred from each Greek state).

**20, 3. tollerentur.** The sequence is curious but is that usually employed in the titles. Cf. S. vii, title, "deliberat Cicero an scripta sua conburat promittente Antonio incolumitatem si fecisset"; and S. iv, title, "cum denuntiatum esset"; S. ii, "fugissent"; and C. vii, 7, 19, "ut in illa suasoria in qua deliberat Alexander, an Oceanum naviget, cum exaudita vox esset: 'quousque invicte?'". Evidently the present is felt as historic present. In the titles of the Controversiae the circumstances are stated first historically, and the question that is being tried is put in the present tense. C. vii, 2, title, is typical: "Popillium parricidii reum Cicero defendit: absolutus est. proscriptum Ciceronem ab Antonio missus occidit Popillius et caput eius ad Antonium rettulit. accusatur de moribus". We might turn this into the suasoria form thus: "accusatur de moribus Popillius, cum Ciceronem occidisset". Conversely the suasoria title could be expressed thus: "Xerses minabatur rediturum se nisi tropaea tollerentur. deliberant Athenienses". There appears to be no doubt that the secondary tense is the correct reading here and in S. vii.

**6. tot caesa milia**: the preceding sentence is really the result of this one—'So many thousands have been slain that I am ashamed if' etc. Arellius is fond of this form. Cf. S. iv, 1, "tantum enim regem" etc. The avoidance of subordination produces the staccato style.

**11. pignus.** Arellius is fond of this word. He uses it twice within a few lines in S. iv, 1 and 2 (where see note **18**, 18 and 20).

**13. in gaudio.** This is O. Jahn's emendation of the reading of all the MSS. *in gaudia*. Müller compares **20**, 33, "in melioris eventus fiduciam surgere". If this is of any value it shows the emendation to be unnecessary.

**ex praesenti metitur.** The statement is not general. It has definite reference to Xerxes. When he looks at the power around him he exults, when he thinks of his past disasters he is depressed.

**16. haeret circa damna sua**: his mind cannot get away from his losses.

**17. suis ira ardet ignibus.** Schg. emended to *saevis*, unnecessarily. *suis* is emphatic, 'with no borrowed fire'.

**21. arma indenuntiata.** Historically not true; he sent to all the Greek states except Athens and Sparta to demand earth and water, the tokens of submission; to Athens and Sparta none were sent, because of their treatment of the heralds sent by Darius (Herod. vii, 132 and 133).

23. **in deos arma tulerat.** Cf. 13, 6, "ponat sane contra caelum castra: commilitones habebo deos"—a commonplace of the rhetoricians.

**tot ante Xersen milia**: in the first invasion launched by Darius, which ended at Marathon.

25. **Salamina.** Cf. Cic. *Tusc.* I, 46, 110, "ante enim Salamina ipsam Neptunus obruet quam Salaminii tropaei memoriam", *et seq.* **Cynaegiron.** Cf. Plut. *Paral.* 305 B: Δᾶτις ὁ Περσῶν σατράπης μετὰ τριάκοντα μυριάδων εἰς Μαραθῶνα παραγενόμενος, πεδίον τῆς Ἀττικῆς, καὶ στρατοπεδευσάμενος πόλεμον τοῖς ἐγχωρίοις κατήγγειλεν· Ἀθηναῖοι δὲ τοῦ βαρβαρικοῦ πλήθους καταφρονήσαντες ἐνακισχιλίους ἔπεμψαν, στρατηγοὺς ποιήσαντες Κυνέγειρον, Πολύζηλον, Καλλίμαχον, Μιλτιάδην. συμβληθείσης δὲ τῆς παρατάξεως, Πολύζηλος μὲν ὑπεράνθρωπον φαντασίαν θεασάμενος τὴν ὅρασιν ἀπέβαλε καὶ τυφλὸς ἐγένετο· Καλλίμαχος δὲ πολλοῖς περιπεπαρμένος δόρασι καὶ νεκρὸς ἐστάθη· Κυνέγειρος δὲ Περσικὴν ἀναγομένην ναῦν κατασχὼν ἐχειροκοπήθη. See also Val. Max. III, 2, 22.

21, 2. **aestumat quam vos**: 'Xerxes sets more value on the trophies than he sets upon you.' He is willing to give up the conquest of Greece, if he can have the trophies destroyed. Otherwise *vos* may be nominative case. He sets a higher value on the trophies than you do. He is more eager to destroy them than you to preserve them. The former has more point.

7. **hoc non est diu colligendum**: 'needs no long argument to establish it'.

15. **illorum bellum fuit.** See note on *in deos arma tulerat* (20, 23).

17. **hic omnia...pertinentia.** Another example of these parenthetic remarks of Seneca; cf. *descriptio Thermopylarum* (10, 4); *enumeratio bellorum* (21, 20); and *hic dixit et seq.* (22, 9).

19. **numquam magna imperia otiosa.** Cf. Livy, xxx, 44, 9, "nulla magna civitas diu quiescere potest".

23. **reliquias victoriae.** Cf. Verg. *Aen.* I, 30, "reliquias Danaum atque immitis Achilli". "victoriae", subjective genitive.

29. **exceptum est**: *sc. clamoribus*, 'was received with applause': or merely, 'was picked out, considered exceptionally good'. Cf. 25, 38, "illam sententiam quae valde excepta est".

30. **locum movit**: 'started a topic'.

35. **repleat ipse Atho**: see note on 8, 12.

22, 16. **dignam**: not in the MSS., added by Müller, and adopted by Bornecque. Without it we could translate "ponatur" (potential), 'which could be put'.

17. **diutius illi perire**.... Cf. Tac. *Germ.* xxxvii, 2, "tam diu Germania vincitur".

This is quite the most interesting of all the suasoriae, and more interesting than any controversia. Pars. 1–14 give the usual selections from the speeches of famous declaimers on this theme; 14–21 give quotations from various historians, describing in detail Cicero's death; 22–26 give similar quotations describing and criticising his character. Then follows a magnificent appreciation in verse by Cornelius Severus: and the suasoria closes with an anecdote throwing an interesting light on the character of Pollio.

The selections from the declamations are as eloquent as any—grand echoes at least of the old oratory. The descriptions of Cicero's death we would not willingly surrender, and the quotations on his character are of absorbing interest. The schools, in extolling the memory of Cicero and in revering Vergil, must have reflected an opinion that was fashionable and that does credit to Roman society however decadent.

The speaker assumes that he is one of Cicero's friends, giving the old statesman advice in a council held to consider whether he should stoop to beg Antony for life or not. The known facts of Cicero's death are found either here, or in Appian, Dio Cassius and Plutarch. Here we get the accounts of Livy, Aufidius Bassus, Cremutius Cordus, and Bruttedius Niger, in whole or in part.

There was a fiction current in the schools that Cicero had successfully defended a certain Popillius when accused of parricide, and that during the proscription Popillius by order of Antony had slain his benefactor. This, of course, as subject of a controversia, in which Popillius should be accused of ingratitude, gave great scope for *sententiae* and other products of ingenuity. C. VII, 2, is on this theme. There appears to be no foundation in fact for the story. Of all the authorities named above or quoted from Seneca only Plutarch, Appian and Bruttedius Niger mention Popillius. The last names Popillius as the executioner, and also states that he had been defended by Cicero, but does not mention the charge. Plutarch says that Popillius (whom Cicero had defended on a charge of parricide) came with Herennius in search of the orator, but states that Herennius did the deed. Seneca himself declares, in C. VII, 2, 8, that few of the historians name Popillius as Cicero's executioner, and even these do not say that Cicero had defended Popillius for parricide, but in a private suit (see also Val. Max. V, 3, 4).

**23, 5. verba deficient**: the quotations from the rhetoricians in this suasoria are, as we should expect, full of allusions to Cicero's writings. Here there is an echo of Cic. *Ad Fam.* II, 11, 1, "putaresne unquam accidere posse ut mihi verba deessent", and XIII, 63, 1, "non putavi fieri posse ut mihi verba deessent".

9. **exhaustum crudeliter, repletum turpiter**: 'cruelly drained of its best blood in the civil wars, and now in the proscription (al-

though the speaker somewhat anticipates), and then dishonoured by the additions made to it'. Cf. C. vii, 3, 9. Caesar had introduced Gauls; Antony his creatures. Later Augustus purified the senate.

10. **Cn. Pompeium**: the great Pompey, slain at Alexandria after Pharsalia.

11. **M. Catonem**: who committed suicide after Utica.

**Lucullos**: the conqueror of Mithridates, and his brother, both claimed as supporters by Cicero in *Phil.* ii, 5 (12). The one died in 56, the other in 49 B.C.

12. **Hortensium.** Quintus, the famous orator, died in 50 B.C.

**Lentulum.** P. Cornelius Lentulus Spinther, consul in 57 B.C., proposed Cicero's recall from exile. Cicero speaks of him in *Phil.* xiii, 14 (29) as dead.

**Marcellum**: M. Marcellus, a bitter opponent of Caesar, who pardoned him and permitted him to return to Rome after Pharsalia. Marcellus was assassinated in 46 B.C. as he was coming back. Cicero delivered the *Pro Marcello* thanking Caesar for his clemency in the case.

13. **tuos consules Hirtium ac Pansam**: the consuls of the next year after Caesar's death. *tuos* emphatic, because Cicero had taken such a large part in the business of the state during their consulate, and because they had been his intimate friends. Both perished in the war against Antony round Mutina. Cicero called them (Suet. *De Rhet.* 1, 25) "discipulos et grandes praetextatos", as they had practised declamation with him. See what Seneca says, C. 1, Praef. 2, "alioqui in illo atriolo, in quo duos grandes praetextatos ait secum declamasse, potui adesse" (but for the civil wars which kept him in Spain). Cf. Cic. *Ad Fam.* ix, 16, 7, "Hirtium et Dolabellam dicendi discipulos habeo", and vii, 33; cf. also *Ad Attic.* xiv, 12, 2, "haud amo vel hos designatos, qui etiam declamare me coegerunt".

14. **iam nostra peracta sunt**: an echo of Cic. *Ad Brutum*, i, 2 a, 2 (Oxford text), "sed de hoc tu videris; de me possum idem quod Plautinus pater in Trinummo:

'mihi quidem aetas acta ferme est; tua istuc refert maxime'".

**M. Cato.** Cato had pitched his camp near Utica and awaited the issue of the battle. On receiving the news of Caesar's victory he made arrangements for the safety of his friends and said farewell to them. Then he retired and after reading for some time Plato's *Phaedo* he slept for a little. Waking he stabbed himself with his sword. The doctors summoned bound up the wounds, but after they left he tore these open with his own hands and so died. This death impressed the later writers strongly. They hold up Cato as the pattern of high moral tone, stern adherence to principle, and champion of the old liberty. He is their counterpart of Aristides the Just. Whether he was so or not, their imaginations idealise him as the true embodiment of all the virtues most dear to the Roman heart. The fact that he shed no Roman blood is emphasised. (Hence, here, "puras a civili sanguine manus".)

Cato and M. Marcellus had strenuously resisted the massacre of Caesar's partisans in Thessaly. Cato was not personally present either at Pharsalia or at Thapsus. In the former case he was at Corcyra, holding it for Pompey, in the latter he was at Utica; Scipio commanded in the battle. In C. x, 3, 5, Labienus says, "M. Cato, quo viro nihil speciosius civilis tempestas abstulit, potuit beneficio Caesaris vivere si ullius voluisset". (Cf. also Sen. phil. *De Const.* II, 2.) From other writers, compare Vergil, *Aen.* VIII, 670, "his dantem iura Catonem"; Val. Max. III, 2, 14; Vell. Pat. II, 35, 2, "homo Virtuti simillimus et per omnia ingenio diis quam hominibus propior". Paterculus calls him also "omnibus humanis vitiis immunis". With *puras a civili sanguine manus*, compare Sen. phil. *De Prov.* II, 6 and 7, "ferrum istud etiam civili bello purum et innoxium", and Sen. *Ep.* XXIV, 7, "stricto gladio quem usque in illum diem ab omni caede purum servaverat"; with "pectus sacerrimum" cf. also *De Prov.* II, 8, "sacrum pectus" and "illam sanctissimam animam".

18. **Scipio.** This is Quintus Metellus Scipio, father-in-law of Pompey. After the death of Pompey, when the senatorial party rallied in Africa he was elected commander-in-chief (*imperator*). He did not maintain the military renown of the Scipios. He was and had been an inefficient commander. The story of his death is told by Livy, Epitome, 114; Val. Max. III, 2, 13; Sen. phil. *Ep.* XXIV, 9; Florus, II, 13, 68; Quin. *Declam.* p. 420, 18 (Teubner, Ritter).

After his defeat at Thapsus, Scipio escaped by sea, but when he saw that his ship was about to be taken he stabbed himself. When the pursuers boarded his vessel and enquired for the imperator he said, "imperator bene se habet", the natural reply if he had been victorious ("victus vocem victoris emisit"). Obviously the phrase denoted triumph over death. So Seneca phil. takes it. Val. Max. says, "tantumque eloqui voluit, quantum ad testandum animi fortitudinem aeternae laudi satis erat". Seneca the elder says (S. VII, 8) that this gives him a title to be ranked with his ancestors. Compare what Burrus says in Tac. *Ann.* XIV, 51, and what Cicero represents Socrates as saying in the *Tusc. Disp.* I, 41 (97), "magna me spes tenet, iudices, bene mihi evenire quod mittar ad mortem".

21. **vetat me Milo rogare iudices**: this has caused difficulty, because the exact words are not found in Cic. *Pro Mil.*, but the sense is found. See § 92, "quid restat nisi ut orem obtesterque vos, iudices, ut eam misericordiam tribuatis fortissimo viro, quam ipse non implorat", and § 105, "hic se lacrimis defendi vetat".

**i nunc et**: a phrase quite frequent in the Controversiae. Cf. Hor. *Ep.* II, 2, 76,

"i nunc et versus tecum meditare canoros";

and I, 6, 17,

"i nunc, argentum et marmor vetus aeraque et artes suspice".

Wilkins's note on the phrase is: "an ironical imperative to do something which under the circumstances is impossible, or at least not to be expected, usually followed by *et*".

26. **Sullana sitis**: referring to the massacres and the proscription—the first one—authorised by Sulla.
**ad triumviralem hastam**. The *hasta* is the sign of an auction. The goods of those slain in the proscription were confiscated and sold by auction. The right to levy the taxes was sold to companies of *publicani* by auction (*locare vectigalia*). Here the rhetor makes out that what is put up to auction and let is what can be got out of the deaths or murders of Roman citizens. The buyers of the goods would cut them up into lots and resell them and hope to make a profit. Compare Cicero's play on the word *sector* in the *Pro Roscio Amerino*, 29, 80, "nescimus per ista tempora eosdem fere sectores fuisse collorum et bonorum?" and in *Phil.* II, 15 (39), "et eius viri nomine me insectari audes, cuius me amicum, te sectorem esse fateare?" (where see King's note, Clarendon Press edition of Cicero's *Philippic Orations*). Further, in another sense the *mortes* are put up to auction, as the goods would be seized and sold as soon as the name was put on the list of the proscribed. The buyer then would be interested more than anyone in seeing that the proscribed owner was duly killed, to avoid troublesome claims in the future. Hence the highest bidder would besides getting the property have bid as it were a price to entitle him to kill the owner.

27. **unius tabellae albo**: i.e. the list of the proscribed put up on a white tablet (*unius tabellae*, Gron.'s ingenious and certain emendation of the MSS. which give "iniusta bella"). Cf. Dio Cass. XLVII, 3, 2: τά τε ἄλλα, ὅσα ἐπὶ τοῦ Σύλλου πρότερον ἐπέπρακτο, καὶ τότε συνεφέρετο, πλὴν ὅτι δύο μόνα λευκώματα, χωρὶς μὲν τῶν βουλευτῶν, χωρὶς δὲ τῶν ἄλλων ἐξετέθη. There appear to have been two lists, but the rhetoricians speak generally of only one. Cf. 25, 7, "tota tabula tuae morti proluditur", and 33, 20, "pendet nefariae proscriptionis tabula".

29. **consularia capita auro rependuntur.** Latro mainly has in mind the story that Popillius received one million sesterces from Antony for the head of Cicero, or perhaps figuratively refers to the reward given to the slayers of the proscribed whose heads as they were brought were fixed on the rostra. Cf. C. II, 1, 1. Val. Max. (IX, 4) relates how Opimius the consul said he would buy back with its weight in gold the head of C. Gracchus and how L. Septimuleius filled the head of Gracchus with lead to make it heavier.

30. **o tempora, o mores!** quoted from Cic. *In Cat.* I, 2; *In Verrem*, IV, 56. Bornecque points out that this expression became almost proverbial, and refers to Quin. IX, 2, 26, who gives this phrase as an example of one of the figures of thought—*simulatio*. Cf. Martial, IX, 71, 1 and 5,

"dixerat, o mores! o tempora! Tullius olim,
    sacrilegum strueret cum Catilina nefas".

32. **illas fauces.** It is worth while comparing this with the relative passage in Cic. *Phil.* II, 25, 63, which evidently inspired it: "tu istis faucibus, istis lateribus, ista gladiatoria totius corporis firmitate tantum vini...exhauseras, ut tibi necesse esset in populi Romani conspectu vomere postridie", and later, "magister equitum cui ructare turpe esset, is vomens...totum tribunal implevit". Quintilian analyses this passage from Cicero's *Philippic* with great approval. Cf. *De Inst. Or.* VIII, 4, 8 and 16; 6, 68; IX, 4, 23 and 29. Antony was *magister equitum* in 48 B.C., when Caesar was dictator.

**per quas bona Cn. Pompei.** How Antony bought the property of Pompey at the auction instituted by Caesar's orders and quickly dissipated it all is told in Cic. *Phil.* II, 64 *et seq.* Latro refers to this auction of Pompey's goods in C. II, I, I: "vidi ab ambitiosa turba clientium limina deserta sub domino sectore venalia", and Pompeius Silo in S. VII, § 5.

**24, 3. Verres.** Müller says Seneca represents Latro as in error, if we are to believe Lactantius who in *Inst. Div.* II, 4, 34 says Verres died after Cicero, though in the same proscription; but this really, as we have seen before, is of no consequence to a rhetor who to make a point can handle history as he chooses.

**5. Cato tuus.** For the literature of the "Catos" see Tyrrell and Purser, *Correspondence of Cicero*, Vol. VI, pp. cii–civ. Brutus and Cicero wrote "Catos" and Caesar and Hirtius "Anticatos". Cicero in his work praised Cato and the old republic.

**8. Cesti Pii.** The quotation from Cestius is inspired by two passages from Cicero: *Pro Marcello*, VIII, 25 (addressing Caesar) "itaque illam tuam praeclarissimam et sapientissimam vocem invitus audivi: 'satis diu vel naturae vixi vel gloriae'. satis, si ita vis, fortasse naturae, addam etiam, si placet, gloriae: at, quod maximum est, patriae certe parum". *Phil.* I, 15, 38, "mihi fere satis est, quod vixi, vel ad aetatem vel ad gloriam; huc si quid accesserit, non tam mihi quam vobis reique publicae accesserit".

15. **ne gemitus quidem tuus liber erit:** an echo of *Phil.* II, 26, 64, "una in illa re (the sale of Pompey's goods) servitutis oblita civitas ingemuit, servientibusque animis, cum omnia metu tenerentur, gemitus tamen populi Romani liber fuit".

18. **quae Charybdis:** quoted almost verbatim from *Phil.* II, 27, 67, "quae Charybdis tam vorax? Charybdin dico? quae si fuit, animal unum fuit: Oceanus me dius fidius, vix videtur tot res tam dissipatas, tam distantibus in locis positas tam cito absorbere potuisse".

22. **Arelli Fusci patris.** The next passage is full of fire and eloquence. The flavour of Vergil, as usual, is strong. Cf. *Aen.* II, 668,

"arma, viri, ferte arma, vocat lux ultima victos";

and I, 89,          "ponto nox incubat atra".

The passage, "animus vero divina origine" etc. reminds us of *Aen.* VI,

723 *et seq.* Note the poetical words or phrases: "ab armis ad arma discurritur", "incubat", "tumulus abscondet", "animus...haustus", "cognata sidera", "ad sedes suas", "observatum viris fortibus", "furentia toto orbe civilia arma", "hausit Aegyptus".

25. **ut non vivat.** All the MSS. omit *non*, which Müller inserted. Thomas suggested "vivere desinat". Cf. **25**, 12, "iam intelleges Ciceronem in mortem cogi posse, in preces non posse", and C. VII, 2, 10, "miraris, si eo tempore necesse fuit Popillio occidere quo Ciceronem mori". The plain sense is of course that Cicero is compelled not to live. Taking the MSS. reading this sense can be made, but it is a strained one. This is in the rhetorician's manner. Cicero is compelled to live, i.e. 'lives under compulsion', 'would die if he were a free agent'. It is doubtful if the Latin could mean this to an attentive hearer. Bornecque's translation agrees with this rendering, and he retains the MSS. reading: 'qui peut croire que Cicéron consente à vivre, à moins d'y être forcé?' V. der Vliet reads, "quis [non] hoc populi Romani statu Ciceronem ut vivat cogi ⟨posse⟩ putat?" This is clear and attractive, but it is difficult to see how the corruption arose.

28. **immortalis humanorum operum.** Bornecque compares with the passage that follows Cic. *De Sen.* XXI, 77, and XXIII, 82; Vell. Pater. II, 66, 4; and Mart. X, 2, 8 and 12.

32. **animus vero divina origine** etc. The best commentary on this is found in the *Somnium Scipionis*, III, "homines enim sunt hac lege generati, qui tuerentur illum globum, quem in hoc templo medium vides, quae terra dicitur: hisque animus datus est ex illis sempiternis ignibus, quae sidera et stellas vocatis: quae globosae et rotundae divinis animatae mentibus, circulos suos orbesque conficiunt celeritate mirabili". Compare with this *De Sen.* XXI, 78, "audiebam Pythagoram ...nunquam dubitavisse quin ex universa mente divina delibatos animos haberemus", and in *Tusc. Disp.* I, 19 (43), "quam regionem cum superavit animus naturamque sui similem contigit et adgnovit, iunctis ex anima tenui et ex ardore solis temperato ignibus insistit et finem altius se ecferendi facit. cum enim sui similem et levitatem et calorem adeptus est, tanquam paribus examinatus ponderibus nullam in partem movetur, eaque ei demum naturalis est sedes, cum ad sui simile penetravit; in quo nulla re egens aletur et sustentabitur iisdem rebus, quibus astra sustentantur et aluntur". Cicero's view, derived of course from Greek philosophy, is that the earth, with its circumambient oceans, is the centre of the universe (*mundus*) and is surrounded by thick air (*aer*) and its own exhalations. Beyond and above this we come to the region of the pure essence of air and fire, in which he finds that which is nearest the nature of the soul. This is the region of the gods, and the stars composed of eternal fire are alive and exist there (*divinis animatae mentibus*). The soul at death will mount to that region, its natural home, and mingle with the stars which are of like nature with itself (*cognata sidera*) and live and be nourished there by the same things as nourish the stars.

36. **sexaginta supergressus es.** Cicero was born on Jan. 3,
106 B.C. and slain on Dec. 7, 43 B.C. Had he lived till the following
January he would have been sixty-four. Cf. § 22 and Arellius Fuscus
in S. VII, 9.

37. **vidimus.** Both Vergil and Horace have passages similar in
tone; see Verg. *Georg.* I, 491,

> "nec fuit indignum superis bis sanguine nostro
> Emathiam et latos Haemi pinguescere campos";

and Horace, *Odes*, II, 1, 29,

> "quis non Latino sanguine pinguior
> campus sepulcris impia proelia
> testatur auditumque Medis
> Hesperiae sonitum ruinae?
> qui gurges aut quae flumina lugubris
> ignara belli? quod mare Dauniae
> non decoloravere caedes?
> quae caret ora cruore nostro?"

We must keep in mind that we have only striking passages from the
speech of Arellius, not the whole speech. He appears now to have
been stating the disasters that Cicero would not have known by an
earlier death. This is an idea frequently worked out after Cicero's
time. Cicero himself has an eloquent passage in the *De Oratore*, III, 8,
in which he shows what Crassus did actually avoid by his death:
"non vidit flagrantem bello Italiam, non ardentem invidia senatum,
non sceleris nefarii principes civitatis reos, non luctum filiae, non
exsilium generi, non acerbissimam C. Mari fugam", etc. Cf. also the
*Brutus* (96 (329)), where Cicero speaks of Hortensius. Similarly Sen.
phil. *Ad Marciam*, XX, 5, shows what Pompey, Cicero and Cato would
have avoided by an earlier death. Of Cicero he says, "non vidisset
strictos in civilia capita mucrones: nec divisa percussoribus occisorum
bona, ut etiam de suo perirent: non hastam consularia spolia venden-
tem: nec caedes, nec locata publice latrocinia, bella, rapinas, tantum
Catilinarum".

25, 2. **quid indignamur.**.... 'If fate permitted an Alexandrian
eunuch to slay Pompey, we cannot complain if a scoundrel like Antony
has the same power over Cicero. (Do not trust Antony,) they fall
disgracefully, like Pompey, who flee for refuge to the unworthy.'
Pompey, in his retreat from Pharsalus, ultimately sought refuge in
Egypt, and was treacherously murdered on the sands at the Casian
promontory by L. Septimius, a former soldier of his, and Achillas,
general of the Egyptian troops.

7. **proscriptus est ille, qui.** Gertz emends *qui* to *quicunque.* The
reference then is general, 'All of your party have been proscribed'. So
Bornecque takes it, although he retains *ille.* Schg. emends to *si quis.*
It may refer definitely to L. Caesar, Antony's uncle, who had supported

Cicero in suppressing the Catilinarian conspiracy, and who generally supported him against Antony. So I have translated.

**tota tabula tuae morti proluditur.** *tabula* (abl.), the first tablet containing the names of proscribed senators, including that of Cicero himself. Facciolati has the following note on *proludere*: "proludere est futurum certamen meditari, et exercendarum virium causa confirmandique animi veluti simulacrum quoddam certaminis inire". Cf. also Sen. phil. *Ep.* 102, 23, "per has mortalis aevi moras illi meliori vitae longiorique proluditur".

8. **alter fratrem proscribi.** Cf. Vell. Pat. ii, 67, 3, "ne quid ulli sanctum relinqueretur ut in dotem invitamentumque sceleris Antonius L. Caesarem avunculum, Lepidus Paulum fratrem proscripserant". Florus, ii, 16, 4, "exitus foedi, truces, miserabiles toto terrarum orbe fugientium. quis pro indignitate ingemiscat, cum Antonius L. Caesarem, avunculum suum, Lepidus L. Paulum fratrem suum, proscripserint?" The story is that the triumvirs could not at first agree on the proscription. Octavius is said long to have stood out for Cicero; finally Lepidus conceded his brother, Antony his uncle, and Octavius Cicero to the desire of the others.

9. **tot parricidia.** *parricidium*, 'parricide', then any heinous crime against a relative, or against one's country, one's *patria*. Here obviously a reference to Cicero's having been called *pater patriae*.

12. **in mortem cogi.** Cf. "ut non vivat cogi", 24, 25, and note.

15. **delicata convivia...popina.** The rhetorician is harping on the well-known theme of Antony's luxury and gluttony. Cf. Cic. *Phil.* ii, 69 (of Antony's abuse of Pompey's house), "huius in sedibus pro cubiculis stabula, pro conclavibus popinae sunt"; and again, iii, 20, "vino atque epulis retentus, si illae epulae potiusquam popinae nominandae sunt".

17. **deficientes oculos.** Cf. C. ix, 2, 7, "languentes oculos", describing the proconsul Flaminius at the banquet where he had a prisoner decapitated to satisfy the curiosity of a courtesan.

18. **hominem nequam.** As Cicero says of Antony in *Phil.* ii, 77.

22. **turpe esse cuilibet Romano.** In S. ii, § 12 (11, 16), despair is considered by Seneca an emotion unworthy of the greatness of the Roman soul.

29. **aut silentium aut vultus.** Cf. Cic. *Ad Fam.* x, 1, 1, where he writes of Antony, "cuius tanta est non insolentia (nam id quidem vulgare vitium est) sed immanitas, non modo ut vocem sed ne vultum quidem liberum possit ferre cuiusquam".

**haud enim placiturus es.** Bornecque reverts to the reading of VD which Kiessling also kept. Müller emended to "aude perire", which has little to recommend it over the MSS. AB have "aut erit". In any case if the text is right the *sententia* does not seem striking.

32. **hic insectatio temporum fuit.** § 3 gives Latro's attack upon the times; §§ 5 and 6, that of Arellius.

35. **temptavit dicere**. The rhetoricians hesitate openly to blame Augustus for the death of Cicero.

37. **gravis es**. Cf. C. I, 1, 6, "non sum hospes gravis", i.e. troublesome, burdensome.

38. **quae valde excepta est**: 'which was emphatically singled out', i.e. admired.

**26, 4. qui servire ne Antonio quidem nondum domino potuit.** Bursian added _ne_ which he thought necessary for the sense. V. der Vliet suggested "qui servire ⟨ne⟩ ⟨Antonii⟩ quidem [nondum] domino, nedum Antonio potuit": but the sense requires "ne domino quidem Antonii". Bornecque reads "qui servire ne Antonii quidem domino potuit, nedum Antonio possit", saying that he has followed V. der Vliet but added _potuit_. It is not _potuit_ that he has added, but _possit_. A rhetorician like Cestius could not have written so clumsy a sentence, and if he had Seneca would not have approved of it. To my mind the simplest correction is to insert _non_ before _potuit_ and read "qui servire, Antonio quidem nondum domino, ⟨non⟩ potuit", who could not be a slave, even though Antony was not yet lord, a reflection upon the great Caesar and therefore _audax_. Cf. C. x, 3, 5, "M. Cato... potuit beneficio Caesaris vivere, si ullius voluisset".

7. **utrum satius sit**. Cestius uses the same turn of expression in 34, 9, "ita dubium est, utrum satius sit cum illis iacere an cum his vivere?"

10. **non simplici modo**. In C. VII, 2, 13, where Varius Geminus represents Popillius as defending himself for slaying Cicero, the following occurs: "cum imperasset mihi Antonius, passus sum, ne aliquis P. Clodi cliens mitteretur, qui contumeliis adficeret antequam occideret, qui vivum laniaret". It was plausible then to a Roman audience to express fear of Antony's torturing Cicero.

23. **Siciliam vindicatam**: by the impeachment of Verres.

25. **Achaiam et Asiam**. Cicero in the _Brutus_ tells us how he studied oratory in Athens, and at the chief centres of Asia Minor, and finally in Rhodes.

**Deiotari regnum**: refers to Cicero's speech _Pro Rege Deiotaro_, a defence of the King of Galatia against the charge of attempting to murder Caesar, 45 B.C.

26. **beneficii memoriam**. Cicero appears to have used his efforts in 58 B.C. to have Ptolemy Auletes restored to his kingdom of Egypt, in the possession of which he had recently been confirmed by the Romans, and from which he had been driven by a popular outbreak. See _Ad Fam._ I, 1, 2, and 4, 5 a, 5 b, 6, and 8. Orelli says, Cic. _Opera_, IV, p. 952, "De Rege Alexandrino, Cn. Cornelio Lentulo, L. Marcio Philippo coss., a.u.c. 698, cum Ptolemaeus Auletes, Aegypti rex, Romam supplex confugisset, Cicero in senatu sententiis ultro citroque dictis orationem habuit de reducendo in regnum rege Alexandrino". This speech of Cicero's is lost.

27. **perfidiae**: refers to the treacherous assassination of Pompey.

30. **vivum consilium dedisse**. The corrector of the Codex Toletanus read "unum" which Schott preferred. For *vivum*, cf. C. III, Praef. 18, "sententiae vivae". V. der Vliet went back to *unum*, and Bornecque follows him. Obviously this advice of Varius is more in touch with reality, than that given by the others; it is more practical, and this *vivum* seems to bring out.

31. **nemo ausus est**. This is clearly contradicted by what follows, and it looks as if *paene* or *fere* had dropped out. Gertz inserts *paene*.

32. **bene...iudicaverunt**. Cicero's reputation is always treated well by the rhetoricians.

36. **mors nec immatura**: quoted also in C. VII, 2, 10, from Cic. *In Cat.* IV, 2, 3, which Cicero quotes himself in *Phil.* II, 119.

37. **idiotam gerit**: 'he is playing the private individual now', i.e. he has come down from his lofty consular pedestal. Note end of § "complura alia dixit scurrilia". This is one of the *scurrilia*. All the MSS. have "perit". Schg. read "idiotam petit" or "petat". 'He is looking for or let him look for someone who does not know much. He cannot hoodwink me' (*non movet me*). F. Walter reads "deceperit", and for the collective singular use of *idiotam* compares 36, 15, "brevem esse vitam homini, multo magis seni", and C. x, 5, 11, "propter hominem Prometheus distortus". Bornecque, reading *gerit*, translates, "cela peut imposer au profane", which translates *deceperit* not *gerit*.

39. **collum tritum habet**: i.e. he has long been used to the yoke. **Pompeius illum et Caesar subegerunt**: notably by his exile.

**27, 5. Ligarium**. Ligarius had taken sides with Pompey. After the Civil War an appeal was made to Caesar for his recall from exile by his brother T. Ligarius. Cicero advocated it in the *Pro Ligario*.

7. **audacter rogaret**. The MSS. are very corrupt here. Bornecque reverts to Schott's reading, "ac laesum rogari".

11. **Vatinio Gabinioque**: Val. Max. IV, 2, 4, "A. namque Gabinium repetundarum reum summo studio defendit (*sc.* Cicero) qui eum in consulatu suo Urbe expulerat. idemque P. Vatinium dignitati suae semper infestum duobus publicis iudiciis tutatus est" etc.; Quin. XI, 1, 73, "dixit Cicero pro Gabinio et P. Vatinio inimicissimis antea sibi hominibus et in quos orationes etiam scripserat".

12. **qui cum tertio esset**: so AB; VD have "tertius". Müller and Bornecque follow AB. It is a strange expression for 'who was associated with other two', or 'who was one of three'. If we are to take Horace, *Ep.* I, 5, 30, as normal, "tu quotus esse velis, rescribe", and that the answer is to be an ordinal numeral, then *tertius* appears capable of meaning 'one of three'. *qui cum tertius esset* then would mean, 'who since he was one of three', and a verb has to be inserted for *qui*. Bursian accordingly added "curaturus esset". Kiessling read "qui, cum tertius esset, reliquis III viris" etc., emending *ne quis* to *reliquis*.

*cum tertio* seems hardly possible. *quicum tertius esset* might be read, *qui* being ablative, but again the expression is strange, and further the connection of the *ne* clause is loose, if it has to be constructed with *exorari*. It seems best to emend as Prof. Phillimore suggested to me, "cui contentio esset ne quis sibi e tribus" etc. 'who was eager that no one of the triumvirs should snatch from him this specious opportunity for clemency', excellent sense and very close to the MSS.

17. **Cassii violentiam.** The traditional qualities of the three are here enumerated. Pompeius can only be S. Pompeius. Cf. **26,** 20 and **28,** 38. Bornecque's note shows a strange lapse. He identifies this Pompey as Pompey the Great, who was dead at this time. The rhetorician confuses the elder with the younger son of Pompey. Sextus, the younger, was a capable leader. Cf. **3,** 17 "multum iocatur de stultitia Cn. Pompeii adulescentis".

23. **Asinio Pollione.** For a discussion of this hostility of Pollio to Cicero see F. A. Aulard, Paris, 1877, *De Caii Asinii Pollionis vita et scriptis.* Pollio's son Asinius Gallus wrote several books comparing his father with Cicero and giving the palm to the former (Pliny, *Ep.* VII, 4). Suetonius mentions a defence written by the Emperor Claudius against these books (Suet. *De vita Caesarum,* V, 41). Gallus's books contained scandalous stories about Cicero, which he may have heard from his father. This attitude to Cicero seemed to Quintilian to contain personal hostility; cf. Quin. XII, 1, 22, "nec Asinio utrique qui vitia orationis eius etiam inimice pluribus locis insequuntur". Pollio was an orator and a jealous one (see the story at the end of this suasoria), and a supporter of Caesar. In style he was Atticist and probably was irritated by the great favour in which Cicero was held. There were therefore both literary and political reasons for this feud between the Pollio family and Cicero.

25. **alterius suasoriae.** This subject, which Pollio is said to have suggested, is the theme of S. VII. Pollio is said to have made this charge against Cicero in the *Pro Lamia,* but Seneca asserts it was not in the speech as delivered but only in the published copy. Seneca's authority for this statement of Pollio is of course good, but one does not like to believe the story against Pollio, still less Pollio's against Cicero.

29. **pro Lamia.** L. Aelius Lamia, a rich Roman knight devoted to the senate, banished by the consuls Piso and Gabinius in 58 B.C. because of his vigorous defence of Cicero; candidate for the praetorship in 43 B.C. (Cic. *Ep. Ad Fam.* XI, 16, 2).

37. **historiis.** Pollio seems to have written a history of the Civil Wars from 60 to 44–42 B.C. Suidas says it comprised seventeen books.

**28,** 3. **accedatis aequiores; hoc...poculi.** This passage is very corrupt in the MSS., and has not been satisfactorily corrected. I prefer to read as given. Müller and Bornecque have "sed, quia hoc propositum...potionem...sumite pocula". The MSS. have "et quia hoc

si tam (tamen D)...sumti (samti) (sumpti) poculi (populi)." Kiessling
reads, "sed quia hoc si iam recta via consequi non potero...absin-
thiati poculi". "summa parte poculi" was suggested by Schg. "a
scholasticis" was inserted by Bursian before *recedatis*. Gertz omitted
*a scholasticis* and changed *recedatis* of the MSS. to *accedatis*. He also
read *solidis* as dative. Reading for *et quia, aequiores*, we get a good
contrast with *contristari*, ' I shall make you come with a more favourable
mind to the reading of the solid truths of history'. There is a distinct
allusion to Lucretius, I, 936 (see also IV, 11),

> "sed veluti pueris absinthia taetra medentes
> cum dare conantur, prius oras pocula circum
> contingunt mellis dulci flavoque liquore".

Seneca is doubtful of making his boys take up the serious study of
history. He merely says, 'Perhaps you are vexed that I introduce
history and abandon my main theme for a moment, but I think you
will be satisfied when you have finished reading my extracts. Of course
I am going to deceive you by giving you the most pleasing portions
first, because if I gave you the serious and solid matter, you would
be repelled'. I do not think Seneca would have attempted to turn the
young men from declamation and oratory. All he would aim at would
be to get them to give more attention to history. Anything more he
must have known to be futile.

5. **T. Livius**: a valuable extract from one of the lost books of Livy,
probably cxx.

7. **ut neget tempus habuisse.** He certainly had no time between
the proscription and the execution.

15. **caeco volvente fluctu.** Forcellini says, "caeci fluctus sunt
quorum non apparet causa, quiescentibus quidem ventis, sed nihilominus aestuante mari et fluctuante": hence 'swell' or 'groundswell'.
A different interpretation, leading, however, to the same translation,
is to be inferred from Suet. p. 244 (Reifferscheid), "Caecus fluctus
tumens necdum tamen canus, de quo Atta in togata sic ait: 'pro populo
fluctus caecos faciunt per discordiam' et Augustus, 'nos venimus
Neapolim fluctu quidem caeco'". Apparently, then, *fluctus caecus* is
'a wave without foam or spray'.

23. **manus quoque** etc. Cf. C. VII, 2, 1 and 9, "abscidit caput,
amputavit manum"; 9, "necesse certe non fuit manum caputque
praecidere mortuo". Cf. Juv. x, 120,

> "ingenio manus est et cervix caesa, nec unquam
> sanguine causidici maduerunt rostra pusilli".

See Mayor's Juvenal and note, where he quotes Val. Max. V, 3, 4;
" (C. Popillius Laenas) caput Romanae eloquentiae et pacis clarissimam
dexteram per summum et securum otium amputavit". He also notes
how in addition to the triumvirs of 43 B.C. Marius, Sulla, Claudius and
Domitian all exposed on the rostra the heads of those whom they had

executed. P. Sulpicius, M. Antonius, C. and L. J. Caesar, and Q. Lutatius Catulus all were so treated. Mayor says Cicero's words on M. Antonius in *De Oratore*, III, 10, might almost seem prophetic of his own fate: "M. Antoni in eis ipsis rostris, in quibus ille rempublicam constantissime consul defenderat...positum caput illud fuit, a quo erant multorum civium capita servata". He compares also Flor. II, 16 (IV, 6, 5), "Romae capita caesorum proponere in rostris iam usitatum erat; verum sic quoque civitas lacrimas tenere non potuit, cum recisum Ciceronis caput in illis suis rostris videret, nec aliter ad videndum eum, quam solebat ad audiendum, concurreretur". Appian, *De Bello Civili*, IV, 20, is also worth quoting: ὁ δὲ Λαίνας, καὶ δίκην τινὰ διὰ τοῦ Κικέρωνός ποτε κατωρθωκώς, ἐκ τοῦ φορείου τὴν κεφαλὴν ἐπισπάσας ἀπέτεμνεν, ἐς τρὶς ἐπιπλήσσων καὶ ἐκδιαπρίζων ὑπὸ ἀπειρίας· ἀπέτεμε δὲ καὶ τὴν χεῖρα, ᾗ τοὺς κατὰ Ἀντωνίου λόγους οἷα τυράννου συγγράφων, ἐς μίμημα τῶν Δημοσθένους, Φιλιππικοὺς ἐπέγριφεν. ἔθεον δὲ οἱ μὲν ἐπὶ ἵππων, οἱ δὲ ἐπὶ νεῶν, αὐτίκα τὸ εὐαγγέλιον Ἀντωνίῳ διαφέροντες· καὶ ὁ Λαίνας ἐν ἀγορᾷ προκαθημένῳ τὴν κεφαλὴν καὶ τὴν χεῖρα μακρόθεν ἀνέσειεν ἐπιδεικνύς· ὁ δὲ ἥσθη μάλιστα καὶ τὸν λοχαγὸν ἐστεφάνωσε καὶ πλέοσι τῶν ἄθλων ἐδωρήσατο πέντε καὶ εἴκοσι μυριάσιν Ἀττικῶν δραχμῶν ὡς μέγιστον δὴ τόνδε πάντων ἐχθρὸν καὶ πολεμιώτατόν οἱ γενόμενον ἀνελόντα. ἡ κεφαλὴ δὲ τοῦ Κικέρωνος καὶ ἡ χεὶρ ἐν ἀγορᾷ τοῦ βήματος ἀπεκρέμαντο ἐπὶ πλεῖστον, ἔνθα πρότερον ὁ Κικέρων ἐδημηγόρει· καὶ πλείους ὀψόμενοι συνέθεον ἢ ἀκροώμενοι, κ.τ.λ.

29. **Bassus Aufidius**...: short sentence by Seneca to pass to the quotation from Aufidius.

36. **quid, si ad me**...: a gibe; 'you are an experienced assassin, yet you tremble; what would you have done had I been your first victim?'

**Cremutius Cordus**...: another short introductory sentence by Seneca.

**29, 2. quibus visis**: i.e. the hand and head of Cicero.

**peractam proscriptionem.** Cf. Vell. Pat. II, 64, 4, "utrique vindicta libertatis morte stetit; sed tribuni (i.e. Cannutius) sanguine commissa proscriptio, Ciceronis ut satiato Antonio paene finita".

**5. quae paulo ante aures praebuerat piis orationibus**: Müller's emendation of the MSS. which read "quae paulo ante coluerat piis contionibus" or "conationibus". The subject of *quae* must be *turba*, *coluerat* then lacks an object. The clause beginning with *quibus* forces us to take *contio* as a speech: but such speeches would not be *contiones* but *orationes*. *piae orationes* would then mean 'dutiful speeches,' speeches in which he showed his devotion to his friends, a use of *pius* which is hard to parallel. Ribbeck suggested *praeclaris*. Bornecque reads, combining the suggestions of Müller and Ribbeck, "quae paulo ante aures praebuerat praeclaris orationibus". It is hard to see why the easy *praebuerat* should have been changed to *coluerat*, and the difficult *piis* substituted for the easy *praeclaris*.

9. **princeps senatus**: not referring to the technical sense, but simply emphasising the leading position Cicero had held during the period that had elapsed since the death of Caesar.

10. **titulus**: probably, as Schott said, daringly put for *decus* or *ornamentum*. Some have thought it corrupt. Gronovius defended it, pointing out that *titulus* means an *honorata inscriptio*, or *elogium*, e.g. on a tombstone, hence it means 'that by which anything is judged or valued or appraised'. We can appraise the Roman people by the merit of Cicero, just as we can appraise the dead lying below by the inscription on the tombstone. The *Romanum nomen* is dead; Cicero sums up its glory. *Titulus* is found in C. IV, 7; VII, 8, II; X, 2, 15, but the meaning in each case seems not unusual.

**pretium interfectoris sui**. Flor. II, 1, 5 is exactly parallel, "misera respublica in exitium sui merces erat", 'the wretched commonwealth was the reward for its own destruction'.

13. **ministra**. The phrase gains vividness when we recall the enormous importance that gesture had in Roman oratory, especially the movement of the hands.

15. **Bruttedius Niger**: orator and historian, accuser of Silanus (Tac. *Ann.* III, 66) and friend of Sejanus, whose fall ruined him also (Juv. X, 83).

18. **Popillium**. See introductory note to this suasoria.

19. **imputaturus**. Cf. S. III, 5, and note (17, 2).

**occupat facinus**. Justin. *Hist.* has the same phrase (I, 9, 9), "quo nuntio accepto, magus ante famam amissi regis occupat facinus, prostratoque Smerde...fratrem suum subjecit". Forcellini explains *occupare scelus* as *facere antequam alter faciat*, the exact sense here.

21. **quod alterutram in partem posset notari**. *notare*, to mark for condemnation. Cicero had been accused of vainglory and timidity, the one a fault of excess, the other of defect. In his death he showed neither, he neither swaggered nor trembled.

28. **sed ipsa narravit**. There was no *oratio funebris* spoken by a near relative of the deceased, recounting to the people his virtues and exploits: but the people with weeping and lamentation recounted to one another Cicero's achievements. Martial has the same thought, V, 69, 7–8, 'It was of no avail to silence Cicero; all speak for him':

> "impius infando miles corrumpitur auro:
> et tantis opibus vox tacet una tibi.
> quid prosunt sacrae pretiosa silentia linguae?
> incipient omnes pro Cicerone loqui".

32. **quotiens magni alicuius viri**.... This does not surprise us, as it has been a custom of all our own historians to give the "character" of a great man, as soon as they have depicted his death. Morawski (*Wiener Studien*, 1882, vol. IV, pp. 166–168) shows how these appreciations became more and more rhetorical, and attributes this, no doubt

rightly, to the influence of the schools of declamation. He also remarks on the frequency with which the rhetoricians describe the evils from which the dead man was saved by his death. The schools however must not be held entirely responsible. As the secondary and university education of a Roman was directed almost entirely to oratory, it was impossible, with or without the schools, that literature should escape both in poetry and in prose an oratorical or rhetorical bias; but the schools of course confirmed it.

38. ἐπιτάφιον. Pericles's speech in the second book of Thucydides over the Athenians who had been killed in the war is the most famous ἐπιτάφιος λόγος. Here Seneca transfers the term to the summing up of a statesman's character, after the narrative of his death. The Latin equivalent of ἐπιτάφιος is *laudatio funebris*, but this, too, is strictly speaking a speech by a near relative at the burial of a distinguished Roman.

vixit tres et sexaginta annos. Fuscus, 36, 3, says sixty-four years; but as Cicero was in his sixty-fourth year, and nearly at the end of it, there is no contradiction between Fuscus and Livy.

30, 1. possit. Strictly one would expect *potuisset*: 'his death would not have seemed untimely, had it not been a violent one'; but Livy feels that a man who has lived for sixty-three years cannot be said to die *inmatura morte*, and the "si vis afuisset" is an afterthought or correction. The full thought seems to be, 'he lived sixty-three years and cannot be said to have died before his time (and we should not have thought so) had he not met a violent end'. The desire for brevity causes the apparent confusion of tenses.

2. magnis interim ictus vulneribus. *interim* seems here to be passing from its classical meaning to its post-classical signification *interdum*. His career was generally speaking long and prosperous, but during it, on certain definite occasions, he was smitten by serious disasters.

5. nihil ut viro dignum erat. Cicero lacked *constantia* in disaster, except in his death. T. Frank (*American Journal of Philology*, vol. XXXIV, No. 135, p. 325) points out that as *indigna* in the next line means 'undeserved', *dignum* must mean 'deserved', and the meaning should be, 'of all his misfortunes, he met with nothing according to his deserts except his death'. He therefore wishes to emend to "quod viro dignum esset" but *viro* must be general and emphatic, and cannot mean Cicero. The text should be retained.

11. candidissimus...aestimator: 'fair-minded critic'.

22. uno ipsius vitio laesa. Aufidius seems to think that Cicero's personal hostility to Antony was a mistake, and *the* mistake that caused the downfall of the republic. It is a pity that we do not know whether Aufidius thought a different handling of Antony by Cicero possible.

24. ut semper aut peteret alterum. Cf. the opening of the second Philippic: "quonam meo fato, patres conscripti, fieri dicam ut

nemo his annis viginti reipublicae fuerit hostis qui non bellum eodem tempore mihi quoque indixerit?" Even Caesar though generally friendly concurred in Cicero's exile.

34. **facies decora.** It is curious that Pollio and apparently the Romans thought it worth noting as a sufficient mark of the kindness of fortune that a great man remained handsome in countenance to the last.

35. **pax diutina**: the years between Sulla and the Civil War of Pompey and Caesar.
**artibus**: the accomplishments of peace: oratory and letters.

37. **noxiorum multitudo.** Cicero's speeches are almost all for the defence.

39. **gerendi magna, munere deum, consilio industriaque.** All the MSS. have "iam felicissima consulatus ei sors petendi et gerendi magna munera deum consilio industriaque", which Kiessling retains. This is not impossible to translate, but *magna munera deum* is awkward for 'great duties laid upon him by the gods', and *deum* would naturally go with what follows. Ribbeck read "iam felicissima magno munere deum consulatus ei sors petendi et gerendi consilio industriaque". Eussner read "magna munera deum" after *industriaque*. Müller reads "magno, munere deum, consilio"; Bornecque "magno munere deum". V. der Vliet suggests "iam felicissima consulatus ei sors ⟨et⟩ petendi et gerendi: magna munera deum consilio industriaque ⟨aequavit⟩ (or ⟨pensavit⟩)". I suggest that the passage originally ran as I have indicated in the text. There were two lucky chances, the first that of gaining the consulate, the second that of getting the opportunity of performing great deeds in it. The latter was a veritable gift of the gods. *magna, munere* would have been almost certain to be corrupted into *magna munera.*

**31, 9. nisi ipse tam miseram mortem putasset.** This is perhaps a bit of Pollio's grudgingness. It is probably a reference to the lamenting of Cicero and his brother Quintus before separating, the latter to go to Rome, to meet his fate there, the former to wait for death in his villa (Plutarch, *Cic.* 47-48).

13. **poenas Ciceroni dabitis.** By reading Pollio's history, even although he is a rather hostile critic, the young men will get a real appreciation of Cicero and so make amends to his memory.

15. **Cornelius Severus.** See note on **11, 10**.

17. **spirantia paene**: 'they had no sooner been killed than the heads were placed on the rostra'.

18. **in rostris suis**: *suis* emphatic, the *rostra* that they had made their own by their fame as orators. So Florus says (II, 16, or IV, 6, 5), "civitas lacrimas tenere non potuit, cum recisum Ciceronis caput in illis suis rostris videret".
**abstulit omnis**: *omnis*, plur. Is it masc. or fem.? Schott took it as

fem. understanding *imagines*, with the sense 'blotted out the sight of the rest, swept them away as it were'. This is hardly possible. Schg. took it as masc. understanding *oculos* and explaining 'drew the care, thought, eyes of all'. This is more natural. Cf. Stat. *Theb.* VI, 669, "et simul omnes abstulit in se oculos".

19. **rapti.** Wernsdorf says *rapti* is used of all who are carried off by a sudden and violent death. Gron. read "carpti" unnecessarily.

21. **iurataeque manus**: refers to the Catilinarian conspiracy.

**foedera noxae.** As Wernsdorf says, this is equivalent to *foedus noxiorum, sceleratorum hominum*, abstract for concrete.

22. **patriciumque nefas**: the Catilinarian conspiracy was one of nobles. Catiline was a patrician.

**extinctum**: Gron.'s emendation for "est tunc", the reading of all the MSS. In support of this Wernsdorf quotes Verg. *Aen.* II, 585,

"exstinxisse nefas tamen et sumpsisse merentis
laudabor poenas".

23. **redit**: *sc. animis*, as above, "redeunt animis".

24. **coetus.** This word has given trouble to some editors. There is no need to emend it. W. rightly says that it refers to "frequentia salutantium officia, deductiones, conciones".

25. **sacris**: W. well explains: "sacrae artes sunt quibus res addiscimus quae sacrae hominibus esse debent, humanitatis studia praesertim philosophia": just the things to which Cicero was devoted all his life.

**exculta.** So Kiessling. The MSS. have "et vita". Schott suggested "exacta", Gertz "devota". Following Thomas, Bornecque adopts "devincta".

26. **aevi decus.** W. compares Verg. *Eclog.* IV, 11, "teque adeo decus hoc aevi"; and Ovid, *Her.* XV, 94,

"o decus, atque aevi gloria magna tui".

27. **conticuit Latiae.** See the anecdote below, § 27, of Sextilius Ena, and cf. Martial, *Ep. in Ant.* V, 69 ;

"quid prosunt sacrae pretiosa silentia linguae?
incipient omnes pro Cicerone loqui".

28. **sollicitis**: *sc. reis*. Cf. Hor. *Odes*, IV, 1, 14,

"et pro sollicitis non tacitus reis";

Mart. V, 16, 6,

"sollicitisque velim vendere verba reis".

29. **egregium...patriae caput.** Cicero was always one of the leading statesmen, and after the death of Caesar, *the* leader; cf. Mart. III, 66,

"illud, laurigeros ageres quum laeta triumphos,
hoc tibi, Roma, caput, quum loquereris, erat"

(the first line refers to Pompey, the second to Cicero).

**ille...vindex** etc. Cicero was the champion of the free republic, as opposed to the despotism of Caesar and his successors—the free republic based on respect for the senate, the law-courts (*fori*), the laws, religion and the ways of peace (*toga*).

31. **publica vox.** The right of free expression of opinion died with Cicero. His might be termed the voice of the old constitution. I prefer to take *togae* with *vindex*, and not as W. with *publica vox*. Cf. Vell. Pat. II, 66, 2, "abscissaque scelere Antoni vox publica est". This refers to Cicero. Lucan, I, 270,

> "vox quondam populi, libertatemque tueri
> ausus".

33. **sacrasque manus**: W. points out that Cremutius Cordus, Plutarch, Dio Cassius and Juvenal speak only of the right hand. Severus follows Livy (see quotation 28, 23); cf. Juv. *Sat.* x, 120, "ingenio manus est et cervix caesa". W. points out that the Romans call anything worthy of exceptional veneration, and more than human, *sacrum*; cf. Martial, III, 66 (referring to Pompey and Cicero),

> "par scelus admisit Phariis Antonius armis;
> abscidit vultus ensis uterque sacros".

**ministras**: as noted before (29, 13) not merely referring to the use of the hand in writing but also to its use in gesture.

35. **nec lubrica fata**: *lubrica*, slippery. Cf. Q. Curtius, VII, 8, 24, "fortunam tuam pressis manibus tene; lubrica est, nec invita teneri potest".

**deosque**: 'thought not of nemesis (Actium)'—of the gods as avengers of crime. Cf. Tibullus, I, 8, 72,

> "nescius ultorem post caput esse deum";

Sen. *Herc. Fur.* 385,

> "sequitur superbos ultor a tergo deus".

37. **Emathio Perse.** Perseus, King of Macedonia, defeated by Aemilius Paulus at Pydna in 168 B.C.: the battle which closed the Third Macedonian war. Perseus died at Alba on the Fucine Lake, a state prisoner. (*Perses*, the Greek form.) *Emathia*, a district of Macedonia, used poetically for Macedonia.

38. **te**: ablative, *in* understood.

**Syphax**, King of the Massaesyli, captured by Scipio towards the end of the Second Carthaginian War, and carried to Rome where he died in captivity (203 B.C.).

**Philippo.** Must refer to Philip the Pretender, who claimed to be the son of Perseus, and was defeated and captured by Q. Caecilius Metellus, 148 B.C. Philip, the father of Perseus, was never captured.

39. **ludibria cuncta.** This phrase has given trouble to the commentators who allege that leading a man in triumph is a *ludibrium*, as no doubt it is; but the context shows that Severus means that the

Romans did not maltreat the dead bodies of the vanquished; all *ludibria* of that kind were wanting. See the last line, "membra tamen" etc.

40. **cadens.** The metaphor is taken from sacrificial victims, which are said to fall to the god. Cf. Verg. *Aen.* 1, 334,

"multa tibi ante aras nostra cadet hostia dextra";

C. x, 3, 16, "non est quod putes illam cecidisse irae patris"; IV, 7, "tyrannum cadere reipublicae volo".

Seneca now characteristically ends this most interesting and varied book with the history of the origin of one of the lines just quoted, and an anecdote concerning Pollio.

32, 4. **ingeniosus magis quam eruditus**: 'gifted rather than learned'.

6. **pingue.** Minerva was goddess of wisdom, also of weaving and spinning. Home-spuns are thick or coarse in texture, hence "crassa" or "pingui Minerva" denotes 'with homely mother-wit', with nothing subtle or fine-spun about it. So here, 'with something homely or rough and foreign in their utterance', not possessing the refinement of the *sermo urbanus*. Sextilius had written a poem on the proscription, and Messala Corvinus had lent him a room in his town house so that he might read the poem to his friends, among whom he had invited Pollio.

19. **umbilicum.** The *umbilicus* is the round piece of wood (cedar or box) or ivory round which the leaves were rolled to make up the *volumen* or roll: hence "ad umbilicum revolvere" is 'to read the book to the end'. Seneca humorously suggests that if he stops at this point his sons, knowing that he had no more *sententiae* after § 16, would just stop there: hence he adds another suasoria to make them unroll the volume to the end. Of course they could not know this unless they had read on.

**similem**: 'on a similar subject'.

For the origin of the theme see S. vi, §§ 14 *et seq.*, and note on **27, 25**. It became a stock theme of the schools. Cf. Quin. iii, 8, 46, "quare et cum Ciceroni dabimus consilium, ut Antonium roget, vel etiam ut Philippicas (ita vitam pollicente eo) exurat, non cupiditatem lucis allegabimus (haec enim si valet in animo eius, tacentibus quoque nobis valet), sed ut reipublicae se servet, hortabimur".

**33, 5. nocere cupientis.** Müller inserted *nocere*. Bornecque accepts this. Schg. suggested, "nihilque superbientes ea magis accendit quam" etc. What we really want is *nocentes*, but it is difficult to see how it could be corrupted into *cupientis*. Gertz suggested "peccantis", or "turpia cupientis". *cupientes* alone is of course very weak. Eussner, "cupidinem nocentis", good sense but difficult again to see how the corruption arose. Kiessling reads "cupidines"; Novák, "saevientes".

**6. difficile est.** "facile est" is used somewhat similarly in C. vii, 1, 16. It seems to mean 'the case is a difficult one, it is hard to know what to do'. Bornecque adopts Gertz's suggestion, "illi se continere difficile est". V. der Vliet suggested, "at mori difficile est", a supposed objection by Cicero: no rhetor would have represented Cicero as making so feeble a remark.

13. **ingenium erat.** Cf. C. x, Praef. 6, where Seneca recounts how the books of Labienus were ordered to be burned and congratulates his country that this new penalty had not been devised in the time of Cicero.

18. **si non civili ense cervicibus illuderetur.** Müller reads with the mss. "luerentur". This might be translated 'if liberty and eloquence were not being wiped out (or atoned for) by our blood with a citizen's sword', i.e. 'if a fellow-countryman's sword were not washing them out (liberty and eloquence) in our blood (*cervicibus*)'. I doubt if Haterius could have expressed himself so harshly and obscurely. Bornecque reads by combining Schott and Schultingh, "si non civili ense civibus luderetur", 'if citizens were not the sport of a citizen's sword'. Prof. Phillimore suggested to me *illuderetur* (previously suggested by Schott), which I have put in the text. Examples of *illudere* with the dative are found in C. i, 2, 8, and ii, 1, 31.

20. **vitam tibi:** the emphasis is on Antonius—'Nothing can be better than death when it is Antony that promises you life'.

23. **nemo est cum quo velis.** S. vi, 1, has the same idea developed by Haterius.

24. **Caesar.** Caesar always showed Cicero the greatest consideration, and made no conditions in receiving him back to Rome after

Pharsalia. It is interesting to note that the schools maintain the position that Caesar destroyed the free commonwealth, but was a good master. Antony is quite another thing. He may be safely reviled and is.

30. **ante te.** Gertz inserted *te*; cf. § 8 (**35**, 29), "poteris perferre, ut quod Cicero optimum habet, ante se efferat?" The MSS. have *in te*.

31. **eloquentiam tuam.** Schg. inserted *tuam*, and read "eloquentiam tuam, Cicero. nam periturum rogo". He suggested also "rem perituram rogo". The reading of the text is not quite satisfactory: 'I make this request of Cicero, who is about to die', i.e. 'It is the last request, Cicero, you will ever grant'. Bornecque takes it, 'I shall ask that Cicero should perish', as if equivalent to "ut C. pereat rogo". Surely this is an impossible rendering.

32. **si te audissent.** Cestius quotes from Cic. *Phil.* II, 24, "meaque illa vox est nota multis: 'Utinam, Pompei, cum Caesare societatem aut numquam coisses aut numquam diremisses'".

**34**, 1. **consulatu honestius**: referring, I suppose, to the honours heaped on Cicero when he returned from exile.

**quid provocatam**: referring to Cicero's speech, *Pro Roscio Amerino*, of 80 B.C., when he openly attacked Chrysogonus, Sulla's favourite, and the great dictator by implication. This was his first speech and made him a marked man.

3. **Antonium avulsum a Catilina.** This is C. Antonius, who was elected consul along with Cicero. The latter won him from Catiline's party by yielding to him the lucrative province of Macedonia.

5. **audiuntur.** Gronovius says 'by Cicero, as he is about to die'. This is weak. Schg. says, 'because if Cicero yields to Antony and destroys his speeches eternal dishonour will blot out the memory of himself and of his deeds'. Is it not, however, a general reflection? 'Whatever happens, now, whether Cicero lives or dies, the days of free speech are over, and perhaps this is the last occasion on which Cicero's great deeds can be extolled'.

6. **Afranium, Petreium.** These were the generals defeated by Caesar in Spain. Later Afranius after Thapsus was slain by Caesar's veterans, Petreius was killed by Juba (see end of this suasoria).

7. **Q. Catulum.** Quintus Lutatius, partisan of Pompey, died 61 B.C. **M. Antonium**: the famous orator, grandfather of the triumvir, slain by Marius. All these are members of the aristocratic party.

8. **Ventidios et Canidios et Saxas.** P. Ventidius Bassus, Canidius and L. Decidius Saxa are all creatures of Antony.

9. **ita dubium est.** Cf. S. VI, 10 (26, 7), "ut aliquis deliberet utrum satius sit vivere cum Antonio an mori cum Catone?"

12. **si hanc tibi p. ferret.** The apodosis is "excepisses".

15. **sacra illa vox.** The quotation is from *Pro Milone*, 101.

18. **crimen**: the Silver Age sense, 'crime'.

25. **loqueretur**. Apart from the fact that the relative clause after "dignus" would have a subjunctive (which would here be present tense) the imperfect denotes that a conditional sense is also implied, the protasis being 'if it were now in existence'.

**care**: Schg.'s emendation of the MSS. "eare". Cf. § 10 (36, 23), "tam care spiritus empti", where unfortunately the MSS. are again corrupt: but in C. I, 7, 6, we find "quam care tyrannicidas vestros emancat!" 'how dearly does he pay for the maiming of your tyrannicides!' "animi sui contemptus" presents another difficulty. How could their self-contempt overwhelm them if they were prepared to purchase life by dishonour? Better to emend, with C. F. W. Müller, *sui* to *pusilli*. The reference is then to gladiators as in the next sentence. Sen. phil. *De Tranq*. II, 3, illustrates the same thought. "gladiatores, ait Cicero, invisos habemus, si omni modo vitam impetrare cupiunt: favemus, si contemptum eius prae se ferunt: idem evenire nobis scias. saepe enim causa moriendi est timide mori". Then follows a disquisition on 'Fortune favours the Brave'.

27. **mori velle**. C. F. W. Müller inserts *velle* perhaps unnecessarily; the rhetorician wishes to be paradoxical. Cf. above Seneca's "timide mori" where we might expect *velle* to be added. 'The cause of life is valiant dying', i.e. being prepared to die valiantly. The present tense *mori* with its implication of *velle* makes the point. The addition of *velle* tends to make the expression normal and flat.

30. **amor**. Instead of this word, which is Müller's emendation, all the MSS. have "quam", which makes no sense. Bornecque agrees with Müller. Schott deleted *quam* and read simply "populus Romanus omnes", which appears to me to be rather better than Müller's. Haase inserted "fama"; C. F. W. Müller, "fortuna"; Ribbeck, "gratia"; Kiessling, "spondet P. R. omnes"; Gertz, "aevum populus Romanus omne".

32. **quale est**. Gertz emends to "grave", which Bornecque adopts, unnecessarily.

35. **faeneratores**: referring to Antony's debts, "pacem" referring to the events immediately following the death of Caesar, and to the arrangement between Antony and the conspirators.

37. **inter scaenicos amores**. Cf. Cic. *Phil*. II, 8, 20, "aliquid enim salis a mima uxore trahere potuisti", and 24, 58, "vehebatur in essedo tribunus plebis, lictores laureati antecedebant, inter quos aperta lectica mima portabatur", etc.

**sanguine civili luxuriantem**. Cic. *Phil*. II, 24, 59, "saturavit se sanguine dissimillimorum sui civium", and 29, 70, "gustaras civilem sanguinem vel potius exsorbueras" etc.; the rhetor referring to Antony's deeds in the Civil War as well as to the proscription.

39. **duorum principum bona**. After the death of Pompey Antony bought his estate for a mere song, and according to Cicero (*Phil*. II, 29, 71) was highly incensed when Caesar demanded the purchase price.

After the death of Caesar he seized the Dictator's property also, and the treasure in the temple of Ops.

**35, 1. tuis verbis.** These words, it appears, are not found in any extant work of Cicero. Müller refers us to Cic. *Phil.* ii, 5, and 60, where Cicero discusses Antony's claim to having done him a favour by not slaying him at Brundisium; but these exact words do not occur in either of these passages, although the general sense agrees.

**7. Iovem obsessum:** referring to the capture of Rome by the Gauls after the Allia.

**10. hostis a re publica iudicatus.** Antony was at last declared a public enemy after the battle of Mutina.

**13. alienae semper dementiae accessio.** Cf. Livy, xlv, 7, "Syphax accessio Punici belli fuerat...Perseus caput belli erat", used of one who joins in a war after another starts it; hence here = 'aider' or 'abettor', in becoming, by nominating him dictator, accessory to Caesar's madness in declaring war on his country, and to Antony's, by joining him after Mutina, and so giving him a fresh lease of life and power. Lepidus was not of high repute as we see from Cicero's letters, and he was only tolerated by the other two triumvirs, till Octavius found it convenient to get rid of him. The rhetor calls him the *mancipium* of each of his colleagues, i.e. with no real power, just ready to do their bidding.

**14. noster dominus est.** This is the last ignominy. Lepidus was left to control Italy, while Antony and Octavius sailed to meet Brutus and Cassius at Philippi.

**16. mentior.** The figure is illustrated in Quin. *Decl.* (Ritter), 405, 16, "potui infitiari quod obicitur. detracta arma dicis? nego. mentior? eamus in rem praesentem".

**22. P. Scipionem.** See S. vi, § 2, and note (23, 18).

**32. Arelli Fusci.** Bornecque thinks this passage must have inspired Vell. Pater. ii, 66, 5, "vivit vivetque per omnem saeculorum memoriam dumque hoc vel forte vel providentia vel utcumque constitutum rerum naturae corpus, quod ille paene solus Romanorum animo vidit, ingenio complexus est, eloquentia inluminavit, manebit incolume, comitem aevi sui laudem Ciceronis trahet omnisque posteritas illius in te scripta mirabitur, tuum in eum factum execrabitur, citiusque e mundo genus hominum quam Ciceronis nomen cedet".

**33. suus...suum:** very emphatic, 'their due reward'.

**36. uno...omnibus:** in the emphatic positions.

**38. ille verus...Cicero:** the Cicero that lives in his speeches.

**36, 3. quattuor et sexaginta.** See S. vi, § 22, and note (29, 38).

**5. per rem publicam:** in the name of the free commonwealth.

**8. neminem scio.** Similarly of the subject of S. vi, he says that *few* declaimed the other side, of this, he says *none*.

10. **cum adeo illa pars non sit mala.** Seneca means that the part of persuading Cicero to burn his books and placate Antony can be defended, and that Cicero would have hesitated had the choice been open to him. Quin. III, 8, 46, gives us an idea of what might be said on this side: "quare et cum Ciceroni dabimus consilium ut Antonium roget, vel etiam ut Philippicas (ita vitam pollicente eo) exurat, non cupiditatem lucis allegabimus (haec enim si valet in animo eius, tacentibus quoque nobis valet) sed ut reipublicae se servet hortabimur".

18. **hic condiciones intolerabiles.** Either "esse" understood, or this is a parenthetic remark of Seneca's own, like "hic insectatio temporum fuit" S. VI, § 9 (25, 32) and others.

21. **insolentis Graeciae.** Cf. C. I, Praef. 6, "quidquid Romana facundia habet quod insolenti Graeciae aut opponat aut praeferat circa Ciceronem effloruit".

23. **tam care spiritus empti.** For *care*, BV have "tangere", D has "degener", the corrector of the Codex Toletanus, "degener" or "degeneris"; *care* is Schott's emendation. Cf. "multos care victuros" and note on **34**, 25.

27. **Silo Pompeius.** After summarising the plausible (*speciosa*) arguments of Cestius, he now gives the more effective ones of Silo.

29. **non esse tam stultum Antonium.** The following considerations are just those which at first sight make the suasoria unreal, but when we remember how often the attempt was made to stamp out books considered pernicious by burning them, we see that the arguments were necessary after all. Tacitus (*Ann.* IV, 35), after narrating the death of Cremutius Cordus, and stating that the senate decreed that his books should be burned by the aediles, remarks on the folly of those who think they can thus destroy the works of genius—"set manserunt libri, occultati et editi. quo magis socordiam eorum inridere libet, qui praesenti potentia credunt extingui posse etiam sequentis aevi memoriam". Bornecque refers us to Seneca, *Ad Marciam*, 1, 3, where he congratulates Marcia, daughter of Cordus, on distributing to the libraries copies of her father's works as soon as it was safe to do so.

35. **de mortis contemptu locutus**: the subject of the first Tusculan.

40. **haec suasoria...insignita.** There is a lacuna in the MSS. here. Gertz suggested "haec suasoria ⟨insania declamatorum⟩ insignita est. dixit enim Senianus", etc. Morgenstern, "insania Seniani".

41. **cacozeliae.** See note on *cacozelos*, **12**, 28. Seneca did not think highly of such plays on words. Macrobius, II, 4, 21, quotes Asinius Pollio as using the same play on words: "Temporibus triumviralibus Pollio cum Fescenninos in eum Augustus scripsisset ait, 'at ego taceo. non est enim facile in eum scribere qui potest proscribere'". There

is some point in Pollio's remark, there is little or none in the one in the text.

**37, 6. dulces sententias**: 'sweetly-sounding' sententiae. "praedulces" indicates that Surdinus pushed this desire for sweet-sounding expressions to excess, until they became "infractae" (having lost all vigorous rhythm), and so effeminate and insipid. Cf. Cic. *Orator*, 170, where, in stating the criticism of those who object to rhythm in forensic oratory, he says, "hoc freti isti et ipsi infracta et amputata locuntur", where *infracta* denotes that the full rounded rhythm of the period is broken. Cf. also 230, "sunt etiam qui illo vitio, quod ab Hegesia maxime fluxit, infringendis concidendisque numeris in quoddam genus abiectum incidant versiculorum simillimum". The well-constructed period, with its rolling music, is vigorous. If in striving after sweetness and beauty of sound and tone you refine this away, you become tame, insipid and effeminate.

7. **iusiurandum**. See note on *a iureiurando*, 37, 33.

9. **nasutissimus**. As Forcellini says, "acutus in deprehendendis aliorum vitiis, irrisor, dicax": he is also called "mordacissimus", C. vii, Praef. 8. In C. i, 3, 10, Seneca recounts another instance of Cestius's criticism: Varus Quintilius, son of the Varus who lost the legions in Germany, had been declaiming in the presence of Cestius. In criticising and condemning a figure which Varus had used Cestius finished by saying: "ista neglegentia pater tuus exercitum perdidit". Seneca's comment is that in scolding the son he reviled the father, "filium obiurgabat, patri maledixit". It is interesting to see that Seneca regards the criticism as unfeeling.

12. **Ciceroni etiam infestus**. In the preface to C. iii Seneca quotes the views of Cassius Severus on the inflated reputation that Cestius enjoyed among certain critics of his time. He says that many prefer Latro and Cestius to Pollio, Messala and Passienus. The young people who crowd the schools would prefer Cestius even to Cicero, did they not fear a stoning. They learn by heart the declamations of Cestius, but not the speeches of Cicero, except those to which Cestius has written a reply. Then Severus tells an amusing story of how he persecuted Cestius to try to get him to admit that he was less eloquent than Cicero, but without avail. In § 13, below, Seneca relates how the son of Cicero took revenge on this rhetorician.

13. **M. Tullius, filius Ciceronis**. This passage is one of the side-lights on young Cicero's character. Seneca marks his wit, his lack of memory and his drunkenness. The story seems to portray a man besotted with drink. Still Augustus had made him proconsul of Asia, so he must have had some capacity. Later Augustus made him *legatus* of Syria. Cicero's son, whom his father attempted to make into an orator and philosopher, seems merely to have been a very ordinary person, fond of physical exercise, a fair soldier, no scholar, and ultimately a devotee of wine and of the table. Pliny tells us that he

took from Antony the palm for being the heaviest drinker of the Roman world, as he could drink a gallon and a half of wine at a sitting! For a detailed account of him see Tyrrell and Purser's note in the *Correspondence of Cicero*, vol. v, pp. lvi–lxiv, probably too sympathetic.

22. **flagra iussit.** As Tyrrell and Purser say, "The chastisement was probably merited; but it represents a strange state of manners to thrash a guest at one's own table for an offence committed at a previous time". Montaigne comments on this story (*Essais*, T. I, LII, 10).

23. **de corio satis fecit.** The same phrase is found in the passive in C. x, Praef. 10, "non ergo debuit de corio eius nobis satis fieri?"

24. **ubi pietas non exigeret.** The subjunctive of actions frequently occurring is used by Livy and later writers, where generally the writers of the Ciceronian age use the indicative. This is an interesting example as *ubi* does not mean 'in every case where', but 'in some cases where'. See Roby, II, 1716. It may be that *ubi* has consecutive or concessive force: 'even on occasions such that piety did not require it' or 'even where *and although* piety did not require it'.

**scordalus**: 'one ready to take offence, a quarrelsome fellow'.

**Hybreae.** An orator of the Asiatic school, who, St Jerome says, flourished in 33 B.C. Val. Max. IX, 14, ext. 2, speaks of him as a native of Mylasa in Caria, and says he was an "orator copiosae atque concitatae facundiae". Seneca quotes him several times, not always with approval.

25. **ἡμεῖς οὖν.** As usual with the Greek quotations the MSS. are corrupt. This is the correction of V. de Wilamowitz. The words in brackets are restored from *Iliad*, IV, 405, which has, however, τοι for οὖν.

27. **postulatione**: *postulatio*, strictly the first step in a trial, when the formal demand is made to the praetor to be allowed to prosecute a definite person on a definite charge. It may here be used generally, 'in a certain case'.

28. Young Cicero is said to have had his father's wit. These do not appear to be particularly witty remarks.

29. **quousque.** The famous opening of Cic. *In Cat.* 1.

30. **Gargonius.** Seneca tells us in C. I, 7, 18, that he was a pupil of a rhetor called Buteo, and succeeded to his school. His voice was hoarse and pugnacious. A certain wit said he had the voice of a hundred hoarse men (*rauci*). Seneca quotes him several times with disapproval.

**fatuorum amabilissimus.** The *fatuus* has no taste: the *stultus* no common sense. *fatuorum* is not in the MSS. Müller inserted it, quoting C. VII, 5, 12, "nihil est autem amabilius quam diligens stultitia"; and X, 5, 25, "non minus stulte Aemilianus quidam Graecus rhetor, quod genus stultorum amabilissimum est, ex arido fatuus dixit" etc. The latter quotation is in the *controversia* in which Parrhasius is being tried for torturing a slave to death in order to enable him to paint

Prometheus on his rock being torn by the vulture. Aemilianus was urging the judges to condemn him, and in the middle of a dull, dry discourse (*ex arido*) he said: "Put him to death lest next time he paints a picture he take one of you as his model".

33. **a iureiurando**: so Surdinus, 37, 7. Seneca remarks that the schoolmen were now becoming fond of this figure. It is one of emphasis. Horace, beginning of *Odes*, I, 3, illustrates it in an elaborate way, 'so may the gods give thee a fair voyage, as you shall bring Virgil safely home'.

34. **dixisset multa**: as we might say colloquially, 'had talked a lot'; contemptuous. Gargonius means to say, 'may Cicero and his works (*totus*) live, or may Cicero die with his works undestroyed, as surely as I shall never destroy what I shall say to-day'. Of course "totus moriatur" is ambiguous, and the last clause is bathos.

38. **Iuba et Petreius**. Mommsen says that King Juba and M. Petreius, fleeing after the battle of Thapsus and being shut out of Zama, retired to one of the king's country houses; and that after a copious banquet the king challenged Petreius to fight him to the death in single combat. Juba killed Petreius, and then caused himself to be stabbed by one of his own slaves. The rhetorician here makes them slay one another. The stupidity of the remark seems to rest in the word *faeneraverunt*; one cannot *lend* death to a man.

The MSS. now say that the second book begins, but this book is lost. There were then at least two books of Suasoriae, perhaps more.

# INDEX

References are to the page and line of this edition of the text in which the word annotated occurs.